When Spider Webs Unite

they can tie up a lion

by

Bruce and Norene Bond

Bruce & Norene Bond

Dedicated to our grandchildren

Ryan
Erika
Laura
Megan
Winsome
Justine
Sophie
Kyle
Jordan
Gareth
Georgia
Harrison

Along with our New Zealand grandchildren we want to thank God for our many Ethiopian children who have adopted us as their "grandparents." You have all brought much joy to us.

Published by Bruce and Norene Bond
26 McLeod Road, RD1, Helensville, Auckland, New Zealand
Telephone (09) 420 2777
Email: bondbn@xtra.co.nz

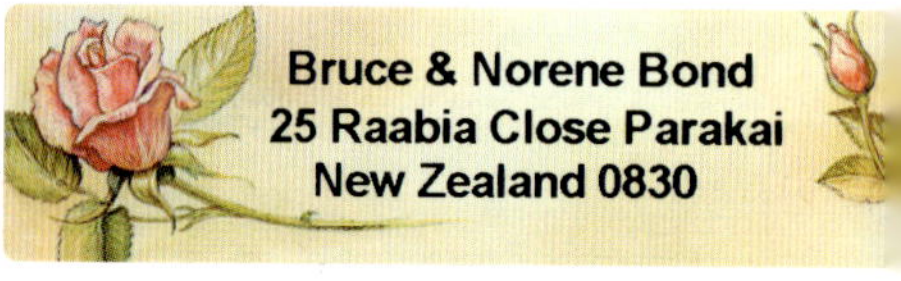

ISBN 0-473-10592-6

Edited by Julie Belding

Art by Lyn Ross. Cover design by Bernard Yeo. Formatting of book, Ashley Tuck

Printed in New Zealand

Contents

Acknowledgements

1. To SIM International, the missionary society which accepted us for service in Ethiopia in 1953. Since that time, until our retirement, we have worked full-time with SIM, being based either in Ethiopia or in New Zealand. *(SIM, now known as Serving In Mission)*

2. To our own dear children and their spouses, who have willingly sacrificed time with us, both when they were young and later when they had children of their own. They have supported us in every way.

3. To our extended families: our parents, brothers, sisters and their spouses who throughout our years in Ethiopia have given us their unreserved support, both financial and practical. This included providing homes for us during our home assignments.

4. To all our supporters who have stood with us both prayerfully and financially. Without you all we could not have remained in Ethiopia all these years. Many kept up a constant correspondence which blessed and encouraged us.

5. To our friends who have encouraged and advised us in the writing of these memoirs: especially Maurice and Jacqueline Betteridge, Chris and Helen Cowie, Hudson and Rosemary Deane, Murray and Pam Dunn, and Gordon and Helen Stanley. Thank you.

6. To Lyn Ross who through the years has used her God-given artistic talent to help us. Her sketches and paintings include the cover design for this book.

Foreword

Lifetime devotion to Christ that scorns the cost is a rare quality among Western Christians today. Many who follow Christ experience limited or little cost. Few put aside their ambitions, leave behind promising careers, and respond without reserve to God's call to lifelong service as missionaries. Some go out for a time and make wonderfully significant contributions to the cause of Christ's kingdom. But rarest of all today are those whose whole lifetimes are devoted to costly service for their Lord.

Bruce and Norene Bond are such people. But they don't think of themselves as special. They see themselves as simply the Lord's servants. His love and grace have motivated them and so they think what they have done is no more than servants should do. They love the Lord deeply and acknowledge it is only because of him that what they've done has been worthwhile. Wanting the glory to be all the Lord's, they shrink from the limelight.

Many of their friends, however, thought their story needed to be told. Bruce and Norene have had some remarkable experiences and been in Ethiopia during a turbulent time in its history. Their gripping story, told with touches of humour, reveals a deep faith in God. On several occasions their lives have hung in the balance as they faced violent people determined to assault them physically or kill them. They also saw remarkable and exciting growth in the church, even when it was forced to go underground. They watched these wonderful Ethiopian believers at close quarters and record how a suffering church remained faithful through persecution, emerging from it strong and vibrant.

This story needed telling not just for their children's and grandchildren's sake. It needed a wider audience. How could they give up so much? How could they bring up a family in such times? How could they keep going in the face of hardships? How did they find strength from God in the midst of perilous times? What was the secret of their trust in God's care and enjoyment of his provision for their personal needs? How did they maintain their spiritual vigour? What was it like for them to obey God and humbly live for him and his people? How could they keep returning again and again to take up every new challenge presented to them?

The reader will be intrigued by the answers to such questions, as well as inspired and encouraged.

Reading their story has certainly given me fresh courage as a Christian. I must admit, these faithful servants of Christ have always been an example to us. For many years my wife Rosemary and I have looked up to them both as we watched them serve in significant roles in SIM (Serving in Mission). I think they challenged all who have known them. My hope and prayer is that through this book many other people will be encouraged to trust Bruce and Norene's Lord more deeply and learn from their example and wisdom.

The last word goes to one of their Ethiopian friends, Shiferaw Wolde/ Michael, a trained lawyer who was chairman of the Ethiopian Word of Life churches (KHC) for some years. He held an important post in the Ethiopian government and is now based in Kenya, in charge of the East Africa section of Compassion, the child sponsorship agency. Here is his tribute to Bruce and Norene:

"How long we live is not as important as how well we live for Christ. I like this statement. But I want to tell you right away that the God you love and serve so faithfully has given you both to us. You are my wonderful examples, models. Your love for God's people is pure and does not have boundaries. You truly are God's people and for you everybody who has been washed in the blood of the Lamb is part of your flesh and bones. I don't think there is anything left in you that the world can take and make use of. All has been exploited for Christ.... I envy you for the way you have been used of God, and my earnest prayer is that my life will be like yours for the people following me."

Hudson Deane
Canterbury, New Zealand

May 2005

Preface

Bruce writes:

Even if spider webs united, what could they possibly do? Our Ethiopian proverb gives us the answer: *They can tie up a lion.* But how can a frail spider web tie up anything, let alone a lion?

During an early safari trip to southern Ethiopia I began to understand the truth of this proverb.

We were passing through the Rift Valley where nothing but the thorny acacia trees grew. To my amazement, stretched between these thorn trees were massive spider webs, some of them several metres across.

If those spider webs are so massive, I thought to myself, what must the spiders be like which made them?

Before long I noticed in the middle of one of these webs a bird which had just been snared and was being subdued by a massive spider. I had the feeling I wouldn't care to trespass in that spider's domain.

Norene and I felt much like spider webs–fragile, weak and unsuitable for the massive task awaiting us in Ethiopia. How could we possibly "tie up a lion"? It was obvious everywhere we travelled in southern Ethiopia that Satan was the strong "lion," feared or worshipped by many. How could two missionaries like us ever learn this complex language and teach these people how to tie up their "lions" as well? It seemed an impossible assignment.

As you travel with us on our journey we trust you will see how God did tie up many lions over the years. Many times we were encouraged by promises from his Word. We certainly proved 1 Peter 5:8 (Living Bible) "Be careful—watch out for attacks from Satan your great enemy. He prowls around like a hungry, roaring lion, looking for some victim to tear apart. Stand firm when he attacks. Trust the Lord."

Several times in our missionary career we saw or heard wild lions, but only once did we come close to one of these kings of the beasts.

It happened in Tanzania in the Ngorongoro crater. While travelling through the game park with our family in the safety of a landrover, we came across a huge black-maned lion ripping apart a newly killed wildebeest. When we tried to drive too close, it threatened to attack us. We watched in awe at its immense power to tear the skin and flesh and gorge itself on the fresh meat.

After a while, hardly able to move, it waddled up the hill and went to sleep.

Our four young children, having eaten their lunch while the lion ate his, were impatient to get going. But our driver wouldn't start the vehicle, and we wondered why. Just then the female members of the pride emerged from the long grass and took their time filling their stomachs. After they were satisfied and moved off, our driver smiled.

"Which of you," he asked, "would have volunteered to get out and crank the engine?"

All kinds of "lions" lurked in Ethiopia in various guises. To face them we needed the protection of knowing we were the children of the living God. Sometimes it was the local witch doctor who exercised tremendous satanic power. Sometimes it was demon-possessed people, sometimes unexplained sickness and even death. Not least it was the strong lion of communism which roared through the land for seventeen terrible years, seeking to destroy the believers.

We want our story to glorify God and not ourselves. Feeble people we were, like flimsy spider webs. But with the strong cord of Jesus intertwined in our lives we were, miraculously, often able to tie up some of those roaring lions.

2 Corinthians 12:9 -10 (LB) says, "I am with you, that is all you need. My power shows up best in weak people. Now I am glad to boast about how weak I am; I am glad to be a living demonstration of Christ's power, instead of showing off my own power and abilities... The less I have the more I depend on him."

Chapter One

Looking Back and Forward

1 Bruce Looks Back

As a family we were privileged to have long summer breaks at the beach where we enjoyed all the activities of an outdoor life. Although my father was a city solicitor we lived in the country, surrounded by our cows, calves, ducks, chickens, guinea pigs, rabbits and who knows what. Together with my older brother Grahame, I roamed the countryside, collecting everything from birds' eggs, blackberries, mushrooms and bones to bottles and wool. The Great Depression left its scars on us all and anything we could collect and sell was valuable.

Living down the road was our friend Mr McIndoe, who would travel the district with his horse and cart.

"Bottles, bones and rags, I buy them all!" he would cry.

With six children, our mother had to be an expert in balancing her meagre budget. Our clothes were carefully preserved and passed down from one member of the family to the next. Dad cared for the family cow which provided all our milk and butter needs. We brothers often joke that we never wore underpants until we were teenagers, and shoes were a luxury for Sunday only. But as children we enjoyed our outdoor activities, and even today, seventy years on, we still get together to celebrate each other's important birthdays.

By the time I was fifteen I was eager to leave school and home to start my chosen career as a farmer. My parents were against such a move. Surely, they reasoned, the son of a lawyer should be able to do better for himself. But I wanted to be a good farmer and enrolled to study agriculture at Massey College in Palmerston North, where I was one of the youngest students. I profited greatly from the studies but needed further practical experience before I could take the next step forward. So I started working on the farm of family friends.

Then the direction of my life changed. One day while bringing in the cows for their afternoon milking, I seemed to hear God speaking to me about missionary service. Not wanting anything to sidetrack me from becoming a farmer, I told no one.

Then it happened again. This time it was at a Sunday evening service in our little Baptist church at Papatoetoe. As a member of the young people's group I enjoyed listening to our pastor, Lloyd Crawford, who wasn't too many years my senior. The passage he spoke from that night was Isaiah 6:1-8, and verse 8 seemed to burn into my soul.

The Lord said, "Who shall I send and who will go for me?"

Isaiah's answer was clear.

"Here am I, send me."

Little did I know God had already chosen me to be his messenger to people living on another continent.

By the time that evening service had concluded I knew my life would never be the same. Somehow God's word had spoken to me, and I had responded. But it wasn't without a struggle. Excuses and arguments poured from my brain.

"What about my four brothers and twin sister?" I told God. "Aren't they far more suitable than I am? Couldn't you possibly call them?"

But the conviction was so strong that I knew I must tell my boss, Trevor Barbour, and follow God's leading.

The following years saw me studying again, first as a night school student, completing School Certificate, and then for two years at the Bible Training Institute (BTI) in Queen Street, Auckland. Again I was the youngest student for that year, graduating just after my 21st birthday.

All the staff made a huge impression on my life, especially the principal, John Deane, who later became a close friend. When I was wondering what to do after Bible College, it was Mr Deane who advised me to pursue further qualifications in agriculture and horticulture before attempting to go overseas.

2 My Elusive Angel

It was during my first year at BTI that two of us were given the "market" assignment. Once a week during the lunch break we had to drive down to the city market to pick up our order of fruit and vegetables and bring them back to the college on Queen Street. In the tree tomato (tamarillo) season we had a regular order of several boxes of this exotic fruit which, we were told, was the answer to any and all health problems. The students would groan when they saw our old 1937 Ford V8 arrive at BTI stacked with boxes of this fruit which had to be consumed within the next few days. In fact it seemed like every day of our two years at Bible College, we were served either stewed apples or stewed tree tomatoes for dessert.

Each Saturday students were free to study or work, and many of us had to work out of sheer necessity. I was grateful that a family on the North Shore, the Wanhills, wanted student help. Early on Saturday mornings I would ride my bike down Queen Street to the ferry building on the waterfront and cross by ferry to the North Shore to do my gardening job.

Most weeks went well, but one wet winter's morning when it was still partially dark, the front wheel of my bicycle became caught in the tram tracks and over I went into the path of the traffic. My front wheel was bent beyond repair, my trousers were torn and my knees were badly grazed. The traffic came to a halt while I picked myself up and hobbled back to the top of Queen Street.

The training at BTI, however, forged habits which have stayed with me for life. I used to watch John Deane, often in obvious pain from a disability, never flinching from his duties as principal. His favourite expression was, "Get out your sweat rag and pull up your socks."

His devotion for God was evident in all his teaching and writing. He established his family home in the Titirangi bush and despite the distance, every Sunday morning at 8am he would be at Queen Street to lead our morning devotions. To me this was one of the most precious times of the whole week. Study was not my forte, but I greatly benefited from those Sunday morning devotional times.

After our worship time, all students had their Sunday assignment. Mine was to help in the newly established Orakei Baptist Church of Christ. This church had started just six years before and already had a thriving Sunday School of 500. On my first Sunday I was feeling a little nervous and, as always, shy.

After Sunday School I entered a full church and found myself sitting near the front. Then the choir walked in. I will never forget looking up and seeing a young lady in the middle of the front row. Something inside me clicked, and instantly I knew this was my "angel."

To convey that to her, however, would be a tortuous journey.

I remember little about the actual service that day. Later, as everyone chatted outside, this same young lady made her way over to me and introduced herself.

Realising I was new, she said, "We live in the same direction as BTI. Could we give you a lift home?"

I was flabbergasted that she even noticed me on that first Sunday, but realised she was just being polite to a newcomer.

On three successive Sundays the family arrived at church in a different car. On one of those days I was invited for a meal in their beautiful home overlooking the Auckland harbour. There I found there wasn't just one daughter but four! I quickly learned, though, that other suitors had already begun to hang their hats at Norene's door. We were miles apart socially, but that couldn't stop a spark of love burning in my heart.

We continued to meet at church and at other functions for the next two and a half years, but never could I progress beyond that polite invitation for a meal or a ride back on Sunday mornings.

3 Norene's Background

Norene:

I had been brought up in the loving Lambourne home with a missionary-minded mother whose sister and brother were long term missionaries in Egypt and China respectively. (Alan Tucker and Nancy Knight.) At eight years old I accepted the Lord as my Saviour, and soon afterwards sensed the strong urge to be an overseas missionary like my other relatives. (Four of my first cousins from the Tucker side of the family also went overseas as long term missionaries.)

I remember some of my cousins joking about my planning to go to "darkest Africa."

"Just remember to take a torch," they would say.

My first years were spent in Mt Albert, Auckland, when the family attended and were very involved in the Baptist Tabernacle in Queen Street. Later we made our home in Parnell and along with other families commenced the Orakei Baptist Church of Christ in a growing and receptive district. Those years, under such caring pastors as Rev Cliff Reay who baptised me, were important in my spiritual development. The Crusader movement was another great blessing during my years at St Cuthbert's College.

Most of my teenage years were overshadowed by my mother's fight with cancer which showed itself when Mother was only about forty. For most of the following seven years she was unwell. The briefness of my mother's life seemed to imprint on my mind that I should be careful to use my time and talents for God. One of my favourite sayings in those years was:

"We have only one life, 'twill soon be past,
Only what's done for Christ will last."

Because of my clear call to missionary service, I decided to train as an elementary school teacher. It was during my first year at Teacher's College that I remember meeting this new BTI student.

Bruce:

At the end of 1949, to my great delight, I discovered Norene was to be one of the team of the CSSM (Children's Special Service Mission) at Browns Bay, Auckland, during the Christmas season. This was a great opportunity for us to get to know each other a little better, although she still had no special interest in me.

In April 1950 Norene and her whole family travelled to England and the USA for seven months on a business trip. At the end of that year, after the family returned, we did another children's beach mission together.

She told me many months later that some of the girls on the team had said to her, "We can't believe how blind you are! Can't you see the way Bruce looks at you?"

Even then she missed it.

Following my graduation from Bible College I enrolled in another study programme, which meant we saw little of each other until we attended the

Ngaruawahia Easter Convention.

At the Sunday afternoon missionary meeting in the huge marquee, an appeal was given for those who felt the Lord was leading them to overseas service to stand. As I stood, I was conscious that on the other side of the marquee Norene was also standing. What joy as I realised we were both heading in the same direction. Perhaps now was the time for action!

In June of that year (1951) I finally plucked up courage to write her a letter expressing my love for her. Would she respond? I was conscious of the other friend she'd had for some time. He'd been like a "thorn in the flesh" for me.

No quick reply came.

One Friday evening as I was tired of study I decided to attend the BTI open-air meeting in Queen Street. As I stood quietly on the outside of the circle, identifying different people, suddenly I saw her. My heart leapt. What a coincidence! Or was it? Could I actually breathe the words of Abraham's servant, when he was commissioned to find a wife for Isaac, and said, "I being in the way the Lord led me?" Could I dare to believe this meeting was of the Lord? Was this the night I would hear her response to my letter?

I had no car in which to offer her a ride. We met up after the meeting and I offered to walk her home. I only hoped she didn't mind the company of my bicycle.

It was about a five kilometre walk – down Queen Street, along the waterfront, up to Parnell and Canterbury Place. Surely the most important walk we have ever made!

Norene explained why she hadn't answered my letter. She wanted to be sure she had the right answer for me. As she often confided in her mother, she had discussed my letter with her also. Her mother urged her to take seriously such a confession of deep love, adding she had never felt Norene's longstanding friendship with the other young man was right for her.

Norene:

For a long time I had realised the other friendship was not from God. But until now I had never given my full attention to Bruce, to hear of his one aim in life to please the Lord. I realised I had lived such a cushy life compared to his. He had undergone his training under great difficulty, having worked his way through all those years of study. The two words "I can't" just didn't seem part of his vocabulary.

I was discovering he had other qualities, too – a liberal amount of determination, displayed during the two and a half years' pursuit for my hand. I was also to learn, as our future unfolded, that for Bruce to accomplish an *impossible* task took just a little longer than a *difficult* one.

That evening it finally dawned on me that my soulmate had been waiting in the shadows for almost three years. I wondered how I had been blind for so long.

On entering the house later, I went straight to my mother to tell her the good news. She was delighted, of course, and said my current boyfriend had been phoning all evening to find out where I was. What to do?

We didn't advertise the fact that we were "going together" so it came as a complete surprise to all our friends and some family when we made our engagement announcement in the New Zealand Herald on 8 December 1951 We were telling the world what had been happening quietly for a long time. I was twenty and Bruce almost twenty-two.

As the saying goes, "Aint love grand!"

4 What Of Our Future?

Bruce:

Normally weddings follow engagements. Not in our case, though. There was the problem of further study for both of us in widely separated locations. I was about to start a two year horticultural course at Massey College, Palmerston North. Norene had one more year of teacher training, with two years of Bible training to follow. We couldn't keep in close physical contact, but we did the next best thing, writing daily to each other and meeting each term holidays. Of course I had to work during each holiday to pay for my studies, but we made the most of every opportunity to be together.

In those days the distance between Papatoetoe and Parnell was significant for someone who didn't own a car. The bus always took a good hour and often I would catch the last bus at night.

During our first two years of engagement we were constantly seeking to know the Lord's will as to where we might serve overseas. As I came to the end of my studies at Massey, the SIM secretary, Lily Davison, sent me a brochure in which was mentioned the need for an agriculturist and school teacher at one of the Bible Colleges in Nigeria to train students living in a rural setting.

Both having Baptist denominational ties we had expected we would end up serving in India, but because of my lack of ordination we were told we were not acceptable. Although this was a disappointment, we knew God would surely have a place where we could serve him. Could this brochure from SIM have any significance, we wondered?

We both knew missionaries working in Africa with the Sudan Interior Mission, but were ignorant about the countries where SIM worked. Hesitatingly we requested further information from the mission. Together we reasoned that if they were happy for Norene to do only one year of Bible training, then we could be married and go overseas together. But it was not to be.

When the BTI principal had word of this possibility, he assured us that although he sympathised with us, it could not be an option. He explained the primary task of missionaries was to teach the Word of God in whatever situation they might find themselves. So Norene needed to complete the two years of formal study.

It was a bitter pill to swallow. We were very much in love and naturally wanted to marry and travel to our destination together. Norene remembers tearfully sharing this news with her mother whose counsel she always valued highly.

"Well, my dear," her mother replied, "because I have had a missionary sister and brother, I can only say this is the first of many trials and disappointments you will experience in your career."

No truer words were ever spoken.

In a poem taken from the SIM publication *In the Potter's Hands*, missionary Elspeth Slater put it like this:

Goals
So what if the things that I treasure and plan
Have so often come to nought?
He's seen the end since before time began
And no one His purpose can thwart.
He knows the vessel He wants me to be
And how it will best be perfected.
His goal is fullness, completeness for me,
His purpose is never deflected.

So, Lord, when I plan, as it's human to do,
Other things I think lead to the goal,
And I'm caught by surprise at what You lead me through,

Forgetting you see the whole,
Help me then not to struggle, resisting your care,
Not to bear it with thin-veiled resentment,
But to learn in each day what you have for me there,
And increase child-like trust and contentment.

Norene's mother died in January 1953. Her older sister Jean was married by then, Norene was twenty-one, Judi eighteen and her youngest sister Robyn only eleven. The two younger ones still at home were a great comfort to their father in his bereavement at forty-seven years of age.

A few weeks later Norene entered BTI for training. Those were traumatic days for her. She was so grateful for the friendship of Ailsa, who was feeling homesick for her family and friends in Invercargill. They were in adjacent rooms and would hear each other shedding tears. (Norene was fortunate to have had several special friends all through her school years, then a dear friend, Jacqueline, during her teacher training course and now Ailsa who met her needs of friendship in BTI.) We were grateful Norene's mother had seen us happily engaged and preparing to go to Africa.

Lily Davison, the SIM secretary, was delighted in our interest, telling us we could submit our application. But before a final decision was made a letter arrived from Mr Glen Cain, the SIM director for East Africa. Having heard of our possible assignment to work in Nigeria, he wrote to the New Zealand office and requested that we be sent to Ethiopia. He pointed out this country was not nearly as far away as Nigeria and moreover there was an urgent need for a teacher and agriculturalist to work in a newly established leprosarium at Shashamane in the south.

As we were just as ignorant about both countries, we accepted this new possibility and worked hard to find out as much as possible about this little-known land of Ethiopia. We had heard how Italy had invaded the country just before the second world war and how thousands of soldiers and civilians had been killed with mustard gas and bombs. Also we knew Mussolini and his army had perpetrated terrible atrocities on men and women before the Italians were finally driven out and King Haile Selassie was restored to his rightful place.

Because my training had been completed and Norene still had another year of Bible College to go, we decided I should go ahead, start my language learning and prepare a home for us to settle into once we were married. Meanwhile Norene would begin her second year of Bible training. Having been voted in as women's prefect, she had added responsibility along with her study and teaching a teenage Bible class. All this would keep her busy during the months of separation.

As for me, I expected to be in Ethiopia within a month.

5 SS Monowai

Signing the will aboard ship. Left to right, Bruce, Grahame and Ian

January 22, 1954, was D Day (Departure Day) as we said our final farewells before the *S.S. Monowai* set sail from Auckland. Thousands of colourful streamers dancing in the wind connected passengers with their loved ones on the wharf below.

The gangway connecting the ship to the wharf was about to be raised when my lawyer brother Grahame rushed on board waving my will and asking me to sign. (Surely a will with so little at stake had never been signed before.) I had given my last hugs to my family and a special kiss for Norene. It would be a long five and a half years before I would see my family and friends again and thirteen months before I would welcome my fiancée.

Three blasts on the ship's horn signalled we were moving and the handful of streamers gradually tightened and broke. Here was I, a country boy of just twenty-four, leaving for the unknown not having met a single soul on board. The coast of New Zealand was blurred with my tears as I stood on the deck. Had it not been for the assurance that God had called me and promised to be with me, I would have had second thoughts about what I was doing and where I was going.

Travelling on the cheapest available fare meant I would be sleeping in the bowels of the ship in a 4-berth cabin which was below the water line with no air conditioning. But despite my initial loneliness and sharing the cabin with three strangers, I enjoyed ship life. I soon began to meet other Christians and we decided to meet daily for a time of Bible study and prayer. In fact some of these passengers became lifelong friends.

When we experienced hot nights in the tropics, I simply bundled up my mattress and slept on deck until disturbed at daybreak by the crew hosing down. The month-long journey was interesting and exciting as I anticipated entering that mystical country of Ethiopia.

I knew the Italians had invaded Ethiopia in 1936. We'd read the heart-rending speech Emperor Haile Selassie had made to the League of Nations, but everybody around seemed woefully ignorant about this ancient country which had resisted all attempts at colonisation except for that brief Italian incursion. In a few days I'd be there and find out for myself all about that land.

Or so I thought.

The announcement over the ship's PA system sent everyone scurrying to port-side as the coast of Africa came into view. I was tingling with excitement as I caught sight of this great continent 250 times the size of New Zealand. Some magical enchantment seemed to be drawing me closer to the land where our lives were to be invested.

After standing with the jostling crowd for a few minutes I began wondering where all those waving coconut palms and idyllic beaches were. All we could see was mile after mile of sand dunes. Not a blade of grass or a leaf of a tree. Was this the country we had been called to work in? Surely God knew how I loved the rolling green fields of New Zealand.

Somehow word had spread that I was heading for Abyssinia, as Ethiopia had previously been called. I was aware of a few caustic remarks, obviously voiced for my ears, which more or less called my sanity into question. Actually what we were seeing was the barren, dry coast of Somalia and not Ethiopia at all.

6 Disappointment

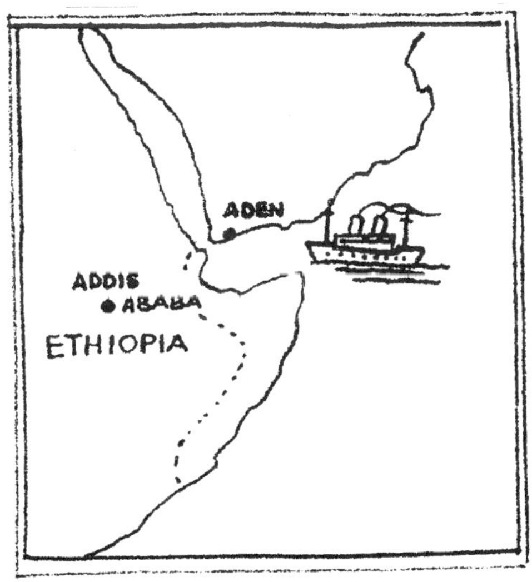

Finally we arrived at the port of Aden, which at that time was a British protectorate. I was the only one of the 1,500 passengers to disembark there. But where was the wharf? There was no such thing. Our giant anchors and chains rattled down into the water and we were immediately surrounded by lighters, or small crafts filled with eager merchants selling their wares. After all, Aden, being the gateway into the Suez Canal, was a duty free port and one of the busiest in the world. I'm sure the eyes of every passenger were on me that day as I headed down the gangway to the immigration lighter.

The temperature was nearing 40 degrees. Surrounding the port were low rocky mountains which glistened in the sun, just adding to the intense heat. By now my fellow passengers *knew* I was crazy and I'm sure some felt I'd be lucky to come out of this place alive.

But I was full of confidence. Aden was just a stepping stone to fulfilling my cherished dream. On shore, outside the immigration shed, I was met by our SIM representative.

"I'm sorry to tell you, Bruce," he said, "but your Ethiopian visa has not been granted and you will have to wait in Aden until it arrives."

"How long might that be?" I asked.

"Perhaps a few months," he muttered.

My anticipation of travelling to Ethiopia the next day evaporated, as did the confidence in my "call" to missionary work. That night, as the majestic liner left the harbour to continue its journey to England, I lay on my bed bathed in sweat with the overhead fan rattling on. How could I alert Norene, my family and church to pray for a breakthrough with the visa situation?

Immediately I wrote to them about my delay, but realised the letter would take the best part of a month to reach them. Faxes and emails didn't exist back then. I reasoned with myself that God already knew about the delay before I did and was working things out accordingly.

Constantly I thought of Norene and prayed that she, too, would not be delayed in Aden when she arrived in a year's time. This would not be a congenial place for a single girl on her own. With time to pray and reassess the situation, I read Psalm 42, and was encouraged by verse 5:

"Why are you downcast O my soul? Why so disturbed within me? Put your hope in God, for I will yet praise him, my Saviour and my God." (NIV)

Finally I began to realise this delay must be part of God's plan. I was all of 24 years old, with lots of energy. There must be something useful I could do despite the heat.

I learned more about Aden, which is situated at the tip of Arabia. The population of 800,000 people consisted of Arabs and Somalis who were all strict Muslims. With rain only about once a year, grass, flowers or trees would not grow unless they were watered every day.

Since Aden was a British protectorate, it was included in Queen Elizabeth's 1954 itinerary and her visit was scheduled for April 27. Apart from the British Air Force personnel, few Commonwealth citizens lived in Aden and so each of us received a personal invitation to attend a garden party in the Queen's honour. A few months earlier the Queen had visited New Zealand and I, like most people, had stood on the roadside waving to her speeding entourage. Now I, a young missionary, was being invited to actually meet her!

We were told to wear suitable formal dress. In the tropics this consisted of a white short-sleeved shirt and white trousers with a cummerbund wrapped around our middle. This country boy felt out of place in such august company but under no other circumstances would I ever meet the Queen of England.

Her Majesty spoke with me for some time, showing great interest in the work I was assigned to do in Ethiopia.

7 Lives Threatened

At the time SIM had a small presence in Aden, with just two couples who carried out three different ministries. First there was the clinic for women, where no male could ever show his face. Secondly there was a literature programme where reading skills were taught, and thirdly a colporteur ministry. I was assigned to the third and did my best to sell portions of Scripture on the street to anyone who was interested. Once a week I was asked to lead a Bible study for British airmen at their airbase.

The depth of hatred for Christians was obvious if one looked at the SIM buildings. All the windows had metal bars to prevent burglaries, and fine chicken wire to divert thrown stones. On the outside was netting to keep out the flies and mosquitoes. An unfriendly environment to say the least.

I learnt a few sentences in Arabic, enough to ask a person if they wanted to buy a book from the Old Testament, but how shocked I was at the opposition we received.

One morning I was out on the road selling books with my co-worker, when we were surrounded by a group of radical Muslims. Under the pretence of a possible sale, they took several from us and opened them. Suddenly they began cursing us and ripping the books apart, then setting them alight.

"Will we be next?" I wondered. Because of my lack of Arabic, their threats and curses fell on deaf ears.

On another occasion Jack Maxson, my co-worker, suggested we go into the Crater area of Aden and try to sell books of the Old Testament, none of which were offensive to a Muslim reader. A short taxi ride brought us to our destination which is steeped in history. Because of the lack of regular rain, King Solomon had built large water storage cisterns in the surrounding hills to trap any rain which might fall. We were told these giant water cisterns could still be seen, although we were never able to verify their existence.

We entered a cul-de-sac where many people were living. The houses were two-storeyed and made from stone which had been quarried from the nearby hills. We had our little briefcase of books and before long a crowd gathered to see what we were selling.

I was beckoned into a doorway by someone indicating he wanted to see some of our books. As I stepped inside, somebody wielding a plank of wood smashed it over my head and I fell to the ground, stunned. Finally I staggered to the outside, calling Jack for help.

Just then we realised a stone-throwing mob had effectively cut off our escape route and were rapidly advancing. We were trapped in the cul-de-sac, with stones falling thick and fast.

Where could we hide? Where could we run?

Suddenly a voice said in English, "Run this way!" Although we saw no person (was it our guardian angel?) we turned around and there, to our astonishment, was an open wooden gate which normally blocked off the narrow alleyway between the stone houses. Although I was nursing a battered and bruised head, we took off in great haste, leaving our books behind.

Miraculously, at the far end of the alleyway another little gate lay open. We flew through that, pursued by the angry mob who were calling for the death of these two infidels.

Just as we reached the main road a taxi drew up. As its sole passenger jumped out, we jumped in, calling out "Maala, Maala," our destination. The taxi driver, unaware he was carrying two Christians or infidels, sped us to the safety of our home. Without a doubt God had saved us that day from becoming just two more Christian martyrs. That was my first and last visit to the Crater.

Only a short time after this incident, a Mennonite missionary, Merlin Grove, was not so fortunate to escape Muslim hatred. He and his wife were both involved in teaching night school in Mogadishu, Somalia. Students were being registered for the new semester when a young man pulled out his dagger and plunged it into Merlin, killing him. Hearing his screams, his wife ran in to help and was herself stabbed, but not fatally.

The perpetrator then ran along the streets of Mogadishu with his blood-stained dagger held high, yelling "I've killed a Christian, I've killed a Christian!" He believed his reward in heaven would be great. God had spared us, and yet had allowed martyrdom for a fellow missionary.

8 More Drama

My second experience of God's protection came just a few days later. One of the missionary couples living in Aden had established a small garden with flowers and grass. Unfortunately this was tempting for the village goats, and despite the barbed wire surrounding the compound the animals still managed to find a way in.

This same couple possessed a dog, however, which objected to the neighbours' goats entering his domain and would chase them out. One day as the dog was chasing a goat the latter became tangled in the barbed wire fence and slit its throat.

That evening when I left to teach at the Air Force Bible study group I was shocked to see the kids jeering at me and throwing stones. Something must be wrong.

At 10pm I returned by public transport to Maala, walking the last few hundred metres, and was suddenly struck by the lack of activity in the area. In fact the place seemed deserted except for a small boy at our gate. Knowing I was a keen stamp collector, he stopped me and asked if I would like some Yemenese stamps in exchange for New Zealand ones. I was delighted as they were hard to come by.

While he waited at the gate, I ran upstairs to collect my stamps which we exchanged. While going upstairs again, I noticed my fellow missionary 'Tok' (short for his surname, Tokalogalu) standing outside the classroom talking to a few night school stragglers.

I had just sat down in the kitchen to enjoy my dessert when Tok screamed for help. With my teaspoon 'weapon' in my hand, I rushed frantically to his aid. I stumbled and then tumbled down the long flight of wooden stairs.

What would I find? His throat slit, stab wounds, or what?

He was lying on the ground, thankfully still breathing.

"Tok, what on earth happened?" I cried.

"After you left, a large group of men surrounded me and their daggers came within inches of my throat," he said. "To avoid the knives, I stepped backwards and fell off the low veranda and yelled for help."

Obviously his attackers must have imagined there was an 'army' upstairs, and escaped in a state of panic.

We phoned the police but there was no answer. Obviously they were in on the deal too and we were on our own. Fearful that the assassins would return, we spent the rest of the night guarding our property. The police did turn up the next day and called for a meeting with the village elders, who quickly admitted they had planned to kill the foreigners (infidels) that night.

Their plan had been carefully worked out. About a dozen men armed with knives had hidden in the darkness just inside our gate, waiting for me to come home. The boy at the gate, asking for stamps, was a decoy for me to stop long enough for them to surround me and do their deed. Somehow they lost their nerve (we know why) and then followed behind me and attacked Tok.

When questioned why they had planned this, they told the police it was because our dog had killed their goat. Accordingly our own blood must be spilt. We agreed to pay a sum of money for this expensive goat, and they in turn agreed to drop their demand for our blood. Without a doubt, we knew God had again protected us from the hands of evil men.

9 Ethiopia, Here I Come!

My visa to Ethiopia eventually arrived. It was now June, my expected four-week voyage having turned into five long months.

I booked an Ethiopian Airways flight from Aden direct to Addis Ababa. What a tremendous relief, first from the extreme heat and secondly from the obvious hostility which had almost claimed my life. Addis Ababa seemed like paradise. How I admired those who continued working in Aden's hostile atmosphere.

As we came in to land I was impressed with the neat little settlements of grass-roofed *tukuls* surrounded by stately eucalyptus trees. Many rivers and streams wound their way down the mountains and through the fields as the result of some good rains.

As I stepped out of the DC3 onto the airport tarmac, the thermometer registered a drop in temperature of fifteen degrees. Addis Ababa had a pleasant mean temperature of 25 degrees centigrade.

Gazing around in both excitement and apprehension, I couldn't help but notice the change in altitude also (Addis Ababa being at 8,000 ft or 2461 m) and the resultant shortness of breath. I felt an overwhelming assurance that this was the place where the Lord wanted us to be.

But first there was a visit to the hospital. I had not felt well during my last few weeks in Aden and continued to worsen once in Addis. Quickly it was confirmed that I was suffering with an amoebic infection and needed treatment with emetine, which landed me in hospital for a few days. This was the first of numerous bouts of dysentery which were to plague me during all the years in Ethiopia.

Then it was off to language school.

10 Language school

Three of us were in the first language class in the new location of Debre Birhan ('Mount of Light') situated some 70 kilometres north of the capital. A fellow New Zealander, Freda Horn, was to be our teacher.

We learned there are 33 letters in the Amharic language with seven different forms of each. This is what the script looked like.

በእርሱ ፡ የሚያምን ፡ ሁሉ ፡ የዘላለም ፡ ሕይ ፲፮፡
ወት ፡ እንዲኖረው ፡ እንጂ ፡ እንዳይጠፋ ፡ እግ
ዚአብሔር ፡ አንድያ ፡ ልጁን ፡ እስኪሰጥ ፡ ድረስ ፡
ዓለሙን ፡ እንዲሁ ፡ ወዶአልና ። ዓለም ፡ በልጁ ፡ ፲፯፡
እንዲድን ፡ ነው ፡ እንጂ ፡ በዓለም ፡ እንዲፈርድ ፡
እግዚአብሔር ፡ ወደ ፡ ዓለም ፡ አልላከውምና ።

John 3: 16-17 in Amharic Language

We were encouraged to visit in the local homes to practise our faltering Amharic. Ethiopians are hospitable people and would always offer us whatever they had in the house (or borrow from a neighbour when they had nothing.)

We took some time to appreciate the sour pancake with the hot peppery sauce which is called "injerra and watt." The injerra is a flat bread made from the grain of a plant called teff. This has a fine leaf and resembles a winter grass we have growing in New Zealand called Poa Annua. It is high in protein.

After the grain is ground to a fine flour, it is fermented with yeast for several days. The liquid mixture is then poured carefully and thinly onto a hot clay plate or pan, covered with a woven grass lid, and cooked quickly over an open fire.

"Watt" is a hot peppery stew usually made of lentils, split peas or vegetables. For special occasions like Christmas, New Year or Easter, chicken, lamb or beef is used. The injerra is served whole with the watt placed beside it or on top of it. With the right hand only, a piece of the pancake is pulled off, dipped into the watt and savoured. Nothing in the world is similar and nothing so addictive. There's no need for utensils either. Ethiopians never seem to tire of this food and often eat it two or three times a day if available. Foreigners learn to love it too and crave for it.

Finances were a struggle in those days. For instance our allowance for the month of September 1954 was E$98.00. But our room and board expenses at the school were just over E$90.00 plus E$40.00 for language helpers etc. A letter home was E$1.50. I'm not sure how we managed, but God provided for us in many different ways.

Saturday was usually free from formal duties and we would go off to market, or head down to the canyon for a hike or catch up with extra study. We were perched on the edge of the Rift Valley, where the altitude dropped more than one thousand metres to the floor of the crater. In southern Ethiopia the Rift Valley might be one hundred kilometres or more across, but in the north the rift was often only a few kilometres wide. Precipitous cliffs created beautiful scenery and were home to many baboon troops throughout the region.

Some of the shepherd boys, in exchange for a little pocket money, were keen to take us from the highlands down into the crater. What a trek. It was sheer joy going down, particularly in the Ethiopian spring once the rains had stopped. The profuse and colourful wild flowers were dazzling. In September the fields were covered with the vivid yellow Ethiopian *meskel* flower. Meskel means "cross," as the stamen is shaped just like a cross. It was amazing to see some of our New Zealand cultivated flowers growing in their indigenous state.

11 Another Royal Visit

In September we were informed His Majesty, King Haile Selassie, was to pay a visit to Debre Birhan. The officials in the local municipality gave orders that all houses bordering the main road (as ours was) must dig out all the long grass in front of the property. Fences were to be painted wherever possible and the whole town was to be cleaned up. His Majesty was to spend several days in the area, and protocol demanded everyone appear on the roadside to welcome him. We were excited. This was the first time most of us had even been able to glimpse this important man. In fact, being a little enclave of foreigners we wondered if the Emperor might stop and greet us.

He arrived as usual with his entourage of officials, guards and servants and swept right past us into the main Coptic church where more than a hundred priests had gathered. Why was he so long in the church, everyone began to ask? After that meeting, he and his entourage were seen climbing back into their vehicles and heading straight back to Addis Ababa.

Why had the visit been so abruptly aborted? Apparently the request from the priests that the foreigners be sent out of the town was not acceptable to His Majesty, so he had left in disgust.

How we thanked God that he had provided this venue for language acquisition for missionaries. In fact for the next twenty years this facility was used for teaching Amharic to hundreds of new missionaries who eventually scattered throughout all of Ethiopia.

Some of the local language helpers eventually did become Christians through the witness of the students and teachers, and established their own little church fellowship. One of those young men later became a close friend of ours. He trained to become a capable lawyer and some years later was appointed to a high government position.

During those first few months in Ethiopia I realised my lack of formal clothes. Having been a student at home and not possessing a great wardrobe I had arrived in Ethiopia with all my clothes for five and a half years packed in one 20-kilo suitcase. (I had brought other equipment besides clothes – important things like tools.) But I quickly discovered there were many official occasions when one was expected to wear formal clothes.

I even started to think about my wedding suit, realising it would be quite formal as we needed to be married by the British Ambassador. I also knew that if I were ever asked to visit royalty or high officials, I would be expected to wear a suit. Even church on Sundays, particularly in Addis Ababa, was a dress-up affair, and I was ill-prepared for such occasions. I remembered Norene had not been particularly impressed by the clothes I had been packing for Ethiopia, and so I ate humble pie by sending her an SOS to buy me a few more suitable garments.

Letters posted in Addis Ababa took up to a month to reach New Zealand. At language school our mail and supplies from Addis Ababa came only about once a month by truck. That was always a red letter day, and all the students would hibernate to their rooms to consume every little detail of news from home (and woe betide anyone who interrupted at such times.) How Norene and I missed each other during that year! I'm sure I would have made much quicker progress with language learning had we been together. (Perhaps some might disagree with that.)

Finally my brief five months of language study were over and my sights were set on our future ministry at Shashamane.

12 Shashamane Leprosarium

Anticipating our ministry was both exciting and scary. We had read a few stories about leprosy sufferers both in the Bible and in literature from the Leprosy Mission. Some missionaries had caught the disease, but that appeared to be the rare exception. We were woefully ignorant as to what to expect.

The Shashamane Leprosarium, as it was known then, was located about 150 miles south east of Addis Ababa on the eastern slopes of the Rift Valley in the midst of the Arussi (now called Arsi) people.

The Emperor of Ethiopia had approached SIM about establishing a medical compound in southern Ethiopia to care for leprosy sufferers, many of whom had found their way to the capital, Addis Ababa. He offered not only the land, but also a daily cash subsidy for each patient cared for. Their disfigured bodies were doubtless an embarrassment to the government.

In September 1951 the Shashamane Leprosarium had officially opened its gates with 200 of these patients. Because these first patients were greatly disabled, the Mission needed to care for them completely. Prior to the opening, SIM had built 50 little corrugated iron roofed huts, each divided into two units.

The leprosarium originally comprised an area of 150 acres which was divided into two sections, a so-called "clean" area and a "segregated" area. A wooden fence divided the two sections.

Even before we arrived in Shashamane we had often wondered what we were letting ourselves in for, yet we both knew clearly that God had called us and guided us to do the training for this special task.

13 On The Way At Last

It was 1 January 1955, and I was being driven down to where we would live and work for the next ten years. SIMers Alex and Theresia Fellows suggested I travel in style with them, rather than suffer a hot, all-day bus trip. Kindly they made room for me in the back of their canvas-sided Landrover.

The road for the first 50 km to Debre Zeit was sealed, but for the next 190 km it was rutted so badly that in many places vehicles just headed off the road to follow tracks which were slightly smoother. The light sandy soil formed great dust clouds behind us which of course, seeped into everything inside the vehicle, including me. Who said something about travelling in style?

But my first drive through the Rift Valley to Shashamane was a thrilling experience even in the dry season. It was uncommonly beautiful as we descended imperceptibly from the highlands of Addis Ababa at 8000ft (2461m) down to Debre Zeit at 6500ft (2000m) and then to the floor of the valley at 5000ft. (1538m).

I was to discover that the so-called "Arsi desert" wasn't a desert in the true sense of the word, although being the floor of the Rift Valley and extremely hot in the dry season, it was often referred to as such. Extending for hundreds of kilometres, it was mostly covered with the thorny acacia tree. These remarkable trees could withstand months of dry weather and within a few days of the falling rains would burst into life with leaves and flowers. The hard red acacia wood made excellent firewood and charcoal.

To my amazement I found the road passed four beautiful lakes– isolated and yet so enchanting. I promised myself we would return again and again to explore these hidden treasures of natural beauty, and over the ensuing years we did. The road was not the smoothest, which meant an average speed of 30km/hr with clouds of dust following the vehicle.

Eventually we began to climb out of the floor of the Rift Valley and noticed a dramatic change in temperature and vegetation. Leaving behind the acacia trees we passed through euphobia or cactus trees. Then winding our way out of the valley we came across many giant ficus or fig trees.

As we continued to climb the eastern slopes of the Rift Valley we noticed the air becoming cooler and the land more fertile. Giant evergreen trees (*podocarpus gracilior*) which were known locally as *zigiba* appeared in abundance. What a perfect place to site a leprosarium.

14 In At The Deep End

"Home" at last, after eight hours of travelling in the back of that dusty Landrover. What a mess I was! I'll make for the nearest shower, I thought.

That was until I met Dr Bob Thompson.

Typical of "Doc," as we later called him, he greeted me with:

"Welcome, Bruce. The kitchen where the patients' food is prepared is completely out of firewood. Do you think you could take the truck and bring down a load of scrap wood from the sawmill, five kilometres up the road?"

"Sure!" I answered.

What else could a young man say? I was keen to get started even though I was filthy dirty. Finally I was able to stumble into my little room for a wash in a basin of cold water. Of course showers were a thing of the past, and as for electricity and hot water, wasn't I now "down country" where such amenities didn't exist?

By the light of my little kerosene lamp I cleaned up as best I could and then enjoyed a tasty meal with the Thompson family. I was starving. That night I slept like a log, until suddenly I was awakened by the sound of someone outside my door. My little abode was only about 2x3 meters and separated from the rest of the missionaries' living quarters by some distance. I thought of all those sharp spears I had seen earlier in the day and admit I was scared. Perhaps they knew I had just moved in. Then the footsteps retreated.

Before I went back to sleep the footsteps returned and just as quickly retreated again. I was pleased when daylight appeared and I could relate my experience to my host and hostess at breakfast. They laughed.

"Don't you know we have night guards on this compound," they said, "and one of them controls your area?"

Did I feel silly! My little hut was actually part of the fence line that ran right across the property effectively dividing the compound into the "clean" and the "unclean" sections.

The seven missionary staff gave a great welcome to this newcomer from Kiwiland. There was the administrator, Dr Bob, and his wife, Hazel Thompson (Canadians) who worked in the hospital and the leprosy baby nursery; Bill and Iris Wallace (Canadians) who taught in the non-leprosy school; two nurses, Mary-Alice Smith (American) and Avis Chennell (British); plus an office secretary/treasurer, Ruth Shustrum (American). I was also to meet the many Ethiopian staff members, especially three young men about my own age, Mulatu Baffa, Beyene Mulatu and Yohannes Mekisso.

Dr Thompson was a busy man and everywhere he went he would have a string of people following him. Nevertheless he promised me about an hour that first morning to show me around the compound, giving me an idea of what my job would involve. "Doc" jumped into his Landrover and roared around the area, pointing out the salient features of our 150-acre property. Within an hour we were back and he was ready to make his hospital rounds.

"What do you want me to do?" I spluttered after him as he hurried off.

"It's up to you!" he yelled back. "I'm busy!"

Now what could I do? I had looked forward to this day for many years and here I was with no job description, seemingly no mentor, no budget and no implements.

Ah, but there was one asset I did have. Around me was an endless supply of willing hands to help me accomplish whatever I wanted to do. Many of them had spent all their lives begging on the streets for their daily bread, but now they were about to learn new skills and have meaningful work. They would no doubt be on a low daily wage, but it would be sufficient to make them feel like "real" people again. Of course I wouldn't be able to employ all who wanted work but I decided each Monday morning how many would be chosen.

15 Sorting Out Priorities

Shashamane Leprosarium was a sprawling complex covering 150 acres, with a further 400 acres added shortly after my arrival. To a newcomer some aspects were a little frightening. The non-leprosy area was where the national employees and missionaries lived, with a day school and clinic for the public.

The other larger part of the complex was where all the main activities of the leprosarium took place. There was housing for 200 incapacitated patients, and a segregation village where 354 other patients were housed. Besides that there was the leprosy hospital complex, the school, the workshop, the church, the "prison" for those who misbehaved and even a cemetery.

All patients who could walk or crawl were given the opportunity to own a good-sized vegetable garden, with the rest of the land being used for growing grain crops. Both Norene and I would be working inside the segregated area.

Gradually my task became clearer. I needed first to teach new skills to those who would eventually be healed and return to their own villages. Secondly there were these two hundred patients who would always be with us and would always need their daily food provided.

My first reaction on seeing some of the patients was shock and repulsion, as I had never dreamed such disfigured people existed. Some had only stumps for feet and needed walking sticks to give them balance while they shuffled along. Others had lost all their fingers or were left with only one or two joints of the finger. Some would drag themselves around on their backsides or their hands and knees.

How will I ever be happy working with such as these? I asked myself. We were told not to shake their hands and to be careful to wash before eating. I knew that once Norene started teaching school, she too would be in constant contact with them. Although we were cautioned to be careful, the medical staff reassured us that the new wonder sulphone drugs were effective and before too long some of the less seriously affected would be cured and able to return home.

As the days went by I would put names to these marred faces and learn to love them as real people.

When I first heard God's call for overseas missionary work I was disappointed at having to give up my cherished ambition of living and working on the land. But now God was opening up to us a lifestyle and challenge way beyond our expectations. Here we were at Shashamane with 550 acres of land to develop into something which could ultimately help untold multitudes of people. And not only could they be helped physically, but we would have constant opportunities to share God's Word with them.

16 Rehabilitating Patients

What would be the best way to rehabilitate patients? we asked ourselves.

We decided to give each one a personal garden plot, five metres by five metres. Once or twice a week they would have a turn to water their gardens from an irrigation system. Regardless of the state of their mobility, they were keen to work and were proud of what they were able to grow. This of course supplemented their rather meagre institutionalised meals which we supplied.

They started growing cabbages, onions, (hot) red peppers, potatoes and carrots, and the competition was fierce. All day long some of them would tend their little plots. Not a weed could be seen. After all, this was probably the first time some of them had been given an opportunity to prove to themselves what they could do.

We also established a small poultry project–but with a difference. We managed to obtain a few Rhode Island red hens and a rooster. We kept them close to our house but agreed to a barter system for eggs. We would give them a clutch of fertilised eggs, if in return they would replace our eggs with their local bantam eggs. Of course the deal was a little lopsided as their eggs were only half the size of ours and the freshness of their eggs was often questionable. We needed to test their eggs in water and separate out all the "floaters" before the exchange occurred.

The plan caught on well and we couldn't keep up with the demand for good fertile eggs. We built a circular community chicken run where the patients could keep their chickens, giving them protection from the wild animals. Everybody who kept chickens built their own little lock-up shed. What fun it was sorting out who owned which chickens! I'm sure there was many a dispute, but I carefully avoided getting involved.

The local soil was sandy and lacked some of the nutrients to grow a good garden. We wanted to introduce potatoes, which most of them had never grown before, and so we called our keen gardeners together and told them we were going to have a competition as to who could produce the best potato crop from a given area. They planted normally but in my plot we added liberal amounts of poultry manure.

Harvest day came. First we dug the normal crop and everyone was well pleased. Then we dug my plot. The results were amazing. The potatoes were much larger and several times the volume of the first plot. What a valuable lesson to all! After that their poultry manure was carefully preserved for the gardens and the increase in production was remarkable.

Quickly the patients began to grow surplus to their own needs. How could they benefit from this situation? Since outsiders were strictly forbidden to enter the leprosarium, we decided to establish a market just outside the boundary of the compound where produce could be bought. This proved a great success as people from miles around would come to buy chickens, eggs and vegetables from our patients.

Those were happy and exciting days as we all got to know each other and built trust and confidence. I was counting the days and weeks before Norene's arrival in Ethiopia. In fact, so were the patients. I had told them we planned to be married at the leprosarium in a few months' time. As this would be the first foreign wedding they had ever seen, excitement was high.

It was now over a year since we had seen each other, and three years since our engagement. I was missing Norene so much and wrote the following note in my diary:

"No mail for three weeks. Today, 8 January 1955, I feel sad as this is my twin sister's wedding day. Dorothy and I have always been close and to think I couldn't be there with her on this important day. Norene is one of her bridesmaids and she will share the events and photos of the day when she arrives in a few weeks."

God knew I needed some encouragement, and unbeknown to me, it was just around the corner.

17 An Unexpected Gift

As you may have gathered, I seemed to be as poor as the people I was working among. Our missionary allowances scarcely met our room and board needs, but I secretly longed to fly to Aden to meet Norene, where she would be disembarking from the ship before flying to Ethiopia. Thankfully her visa was granted.

How I would love to have escorted her into our adopted country. Dream on, Bruce. I didn't even pray about it. I just believed it was in the "too hard basket."

Then it all happened.

About two weeks before Norene's arrival in Aden, her final letter arrived. She wrote,

"You know my Dad was hoping to accompany me as far as Aden, and then travel on to England on business? Well, now he's not able to do that but he wants to send money for your return fare from Addis Ababa to Aden.

I simply couldn't believe what I was reading, and wondered if our SIM director would even permit me to go. The mission felt obliged to restrict the activities of engaged couples, and missionaries were not encouraged to leave their place of work too often. But I decided to write to Addis, anyway. Amazingly Mr Cain agreed to my going as he realised meeting in Aden there would be no stigma for engaged couples to be seen together. A loving God knew the deep longings of our hearts to be able to spend quality time together after a year apart. The verse we had taken together when we were engaged was, "Seek first the kingdom of God and his righteousness and all these (other) things will be added unto you." Now we were seeing God fulfil this promise as he would continue to do through our married life.

By mail I set in action the process of obtaining an exit visa. You might think this would be just a formality. No way. It took days for our Ethiopian business administrator, Ato Lakew, to process an exit visa. We needed the all-important stamp in my passport. Close to Norene's arrival date I made the six-hour bus trip to Addis, praying along the way that we would see another miracle.

I was due to fly out on the Saturday morning and by Friday afternoon the exit visa had still not been granted. Ethiopian Airlines were not permitted to issue a ticket before the exit visa was obtained. At the last minute, before the immigration office closed on Friday afternoon, Ato Lakew was handed my passport and exit visa. He excitedly returned to the SIM headquarters, praising God for answered prayer. We jumped in his car and arrived at the airways office just in time for them to issue my Saturday morning ticket. Wow, that was close, I thought.

As the airline official was writing the ticket he asked to see my exit visa. Frowning, he looked up.

"You can't go tomorrow," he said. "They've given you the wrong exit date. You will have wait until a week tomorrow.

My dreams were shattered. Ato Lakew explained the situation and the official told us we'd have to go back to the immigration office and ask them to make the change.

"But they're closed!" Lakew said. "And the young lady arrives tomorrow morning in Aden."

Finally the airline booking clerk bent over and corrected the date himself.

"I can assure you the immigration official will not let you leave when he sees this alteration," he warned.

"Don't worry," I said, "We'll pray they won't notice the change."

After a restless night and early breakfast I was delivered to the airport. A few passengers were in the queue in front of me and were going through the process of ticketing and immigration. Admittedly I was nervous. Would I be seeing Norene in a few hours time or would I have to wait until she arrived in Ethiopia a few days later? (Of course she had no idea whether I had received her letter and whether I would be there to meet her.)

I prayed as I handed my papers to the official. At that second, the electricity went off.

"Fetch me a candle!" bellowed the official. The flickering light appeared, but the flame was being blown this way and that by the draft. The necessary stamp was added to my passport and I was told to move over to the waiting room. Lord, you've done it again, I whispered. And then the electricity came on. Would the official call me back?

In no time we were up in the air and flying towards Aden. As we came in to land I had a panoramic view of the great ship the *SS Otranto* lying anchored in the port. Obviously Norene had already disembarked. But although this was to be an exciting day for us both, I was conscious she would have had a sad farewell that morning. Her sister Judi and friend Ann had also been passengers on the ship on their way to England. Norene had been grateful for their company, particularly when she was admitted to the ship's hospital with possible appendicitis during the voyage.

18 Reunion

I was impatient to land, clear customs and be on my way. A taxi took me to the SIM Centre and there she was, running out to meet me. In each other's arms at last after thirteen long months!

The following day Peggy and Jack Maxson, the resident missionary couple, suggested we unobtrusively disappear out the back gate and go to the British Swimming Club for the day. Aden was still a British protectorate at that time and had a large air force base there. Those at the club were all foreigners and of course it was nothing unusual for them to see a young couple together for the day. No one even stared.

What a great few hours we had together as we reminisced over the past year. God had brought us safely through many diverse situations. He had helped Norene to do well in her Bible College studies despite having lost her mother and missing me. He had protected me from certain death on two occasions. Without a doubt we knew God had a special plan for us as we were about to enter Ethiopia – this time together.

The promise in Jeremiah 29:11 was much in our minds: *'For I know the plans I have for you,' says the Lord. 'They are plans for good and not for evil, to give you a future and a hope.' (Living Bible)*

Two days later we boarded a DC3.

As we flew I pointed out to Norene the marvellous beauty of the countryside. We saw grove after grove of eucalyptus trees with small villages of round, grass-thatched *tukuls* (huts) nestled together. The green landscape of Ethiopia was a sharp contrast to dry and dusty Aden.

As we walked off the plane my eyes filled with tears as I thought back four long years when we had both stood at the missionary service. Now we were finally together in the country God had chosen for us. It was a dream come true.

A great welcome awaited us in Addis Ababa from our fellow missionaries. I had talked much about Norene and her pending arrival. All had prayed with me that her visa would be granted in time for her to travel directly to Ethiopia without a delay in Aden.

We spent a few days together in Addis as Norene adjusted to the altitude which can be tough on the heart. We travelled around the city by horse and *garry* (cart), but were always careful to have a third person with us. However we were permitted to lock the guesthouse lounge in the evenings and so had a little time together after everyone left.

Norene's father, who owned a furnishing business, had been concerned about the conditions under which his daughter was going to live. He wanted to provide as much as possible for setting up our little home. I had written to Norene's Dad suggesting that one of his 2,000 litre galvanised square tanks (in which china and other goods arrived by ship from England for his shop) would be ideal for use as a rain water tank. No such thing was available in Ethiopia.

Her Dad prepared the tank and packed it full of all sorts of useful items, from small chests of drawers filled with sheets, towels and blankets, to soap (hand and washing) and even toilet rolls for a five year period. The tank was closed with twenty four bolts and weighed in at half a ton. Whenever Norene met a ship's officer as she travelled he would say, "Oh, you must be the girl with the tank."

Transporting this tank caused a few headaches. First it needed to be moved from ship to barge (there were no wharves in Aden) and then by truck to the airport and onto a DC3 for the flight to Addis Ababa. Later we were informed they had to take the door off the freight plane to load the tank on.

19 Back To Work

How we wished we could get married at once. But first Norene had to complete her language study, which could take at least six months. So once again there was another sad farewell.

She was thrilled to find her teacher at language school was New Zealander Freda Horn who had known her mother. Freda informed Norene there was another young lady, Peggy McMillan, who was in a class on her own and had already completed one month of study. She encouraged Norene to work hard and catch up with Peggy. This would shorten her time before our marriage. What an incentive!

There were no telephones, faxes or e-mails, but the postmaster suddenly noticed an increase in the flow of mail between Debre Birhan and Shashamane. Not only were they love letters, but we were trying to organise our wedding by mail. Should we be married at our mission headquarters in Addis Ababa? Or should we try to identify with the people we'd be working with in Shashamane? Bob and Hazel Thompson assured us they would be willing to host the wedding at the leprosarium and we were grateful for their offer.

Before parting I asked Mr Cain, the field director,

"How often can I visit Norene during her six months' language course?"

He stroked his chin.

"I guess we could permit you to go up for one weekend during that time, Bruce," he said. "But you would need to travel up on the Saturday morning and return to Addis Ababa by Sunday afternoon. " It was a disappointing reply, but better than nothing.

Norene now had the formidable task, as I had had, of learning to pronounce and write the thirty odd letters of the Amharic alphabet, each with seven different forms. Gradually they made some sense and eventually she quite enjoyed the grammar classes as she had learned both French and Latin at school. But the speaking was something else. She would visit in the homes most afternoons, sometimes alone, sometimes with other students. All the students had to cope with people laughing at their mistakes.

She wrote from Language School:

"The local people are exceedingly hospitable. They would give their last cup of coffee or their last piece of *injerra* for the sake of friendship. One afternoon as I was walking back alone to the language school, an Ethiopian man called out saying (as I thought), 'Won't you come in and visit today?' I tried to work out my answer carefully and replied, 'I'm sorry I don't have time today. I'll come back tomorrow.' He and some women sitting within earshot all roared with laughter.

The whole way back I said his question over and over in my mind trying to remember his exact words. When I told Freda Horn at the dinner table (in front of the other students) she, too, threw her head back and laughed. She explained, 'He asked you to marry him and you said you were in a hurry today, but you'd come back tomorrow.' I stayed clear of his house after that."

After three months the time came for my permitted visit to the language school. Although we were excited to see each other again, we knew we'd have little freedom to be alone. But Peggy, Norene's class-mate, kindly offered to chaperone our walk down to the canyon on the Saturday afternoon.

"I'm really good at getting lost," she added. And she was.

Somehow on the Sunday afternoon when we strolled to the township to catch the bus, we found it had left without me. How could we have made such a terrible mistake with the timing?

"Come back tomorrow morning," they replied. Another blissful evening together.

The return trip took several hours, and on arrival in Addis Ababa I was barely in the gate of headquarters when the director met me.

"Bruce, I want to see you," he said.

I was on the mat for sure.

"Didn't I tell you to be back by Sunday evening?"

"Yes sir, but I missed the bus."

(We wonder if Mr Cain, looking down from heaven, smiled to himself when that wayward missionary was appointed SIM Ethiopia director some thirty-five years later.)

Chapter Two

Shashamane Leprosarium

20 Wedding Bells At Last

Preparing for a wedding in Ethiopia by correspondence and without the help of any family was no mean task, particularly as we needed to organise two wedding ceremonies. A church wedding in Ethiopia was not recognised as valid by the New Zealand Government, and therefore we were to be officially married by the British ambassador at the British Embassy. This would be followed the day after by a church wedding at Shashamane.

Norene's wedding dress was still packed in its box along with the bridesmaid's dress she had worn at my twin sister's wedding earlier in the year. There were two problems. First she was concerned she might have put on weight at language school and would not be seeing her dress again until the night before the wedding. Hazel Thompson helpfully suggested she would have her sewing machine at the ready in case some alterations were necessary at the eleventh hour.

Secondly I had the difficult task of finding a young woman with a 21" waist to fit into the bridesmaid's dress. Despite my inexperienced judgement of such things, I decided there was only one possibility. Mary-Alice Smith, a nurse from the USA, seemed to fit these measurements. Bravely I invited her to be Norene's bridesmaid and she agreed.

Naturally Norene worked hard on her language studies as she needed to pass her exam before being permitted to marry. We were grateful she passed at the end of five months, thus enabling us to arrange the date of 28 July 1955 at the British Embassy.

The big day finally arrived.

Roy Nancekivell of New Zealand and our American friend, Marion Nagel, were our witnesses at this ceremony which lasted only a few minutes. It was uninspiring to say the least. Following this an Irish missionary couple working in Addis thoughtfully invited us for a special morning tea before waving us farewell on our journey to Shashamane 160 miles south. There our church wedding would take place the following day. The leprosarium had just purchased a small truck and we were excited to be asked to drive this down to the hospital complex. Thankfully, no one suggested a chaperone. After all, we were married now. But we were told:

"No hanky panky on the road. You're expected at the leprosarium before dark for a combined meal and wedding rehearsal. We don't consider you to be properly married until after your church wedding."

Reluctantly we agreed with them. After all, we'd been engaged for three and a half years. What was one more day?

Halfway through the Arsi lowlands the truck spluttered and stopped. Yes, we had filled up with diesel before we left, but for some reason we hadn't watched the fuel gauge dropping to zero. If only we had kept our eyes on that gauge and not so much on each other. A quick check revealed a loose connection in the fuel line. We were stuck between a rock and a hard place.

The admonition about arriving on time was ringing in our ears. But here

Married at last
July 29, 1955

Leaving the 'Tukul' after the Church Wedding

we were in the middle of Arsi and at that time of the day there was little traffic movement. We waited for hours in the boiling sun until an Ethiopian highway vehicle came along and agreed to sell us enough fuel to make it to the leprosarium. Of course we arrived many hours late, to be met with a somewhat hostile reception and no amount of explanation would satisfy our fellow missionaries. The wedding party dinner, although delayed, was special.

After the meal came the wedding rehearsal. During the practice, Bill Wallace, who was marrying us, asked Norene:

"Will you, Norene Winsome Lambourne, take Arthur Rashley to be your lawful wedded husband?"

"No, I *won't*!" came Norene's quick retort.

The whole party burst into laughter. After all, it was nearly midnight. Some months before Bill had married another missionary couple and had omitted to change the names in his little black book.

Not many brides meet their bridesmaid for the first time the night before their wedding. At least both dresses fitted. Norene also met for the first time Dr Bob Thompson who was to give her away. Dr Sam Steeves, who had been at language school with me, had agreed to be my best man and had been permitted to travel down to the wedding.

At one stage we wrote about our day:

"Marigold petals for confetti; a guard of honour of leprosy patients; a round thatched church; the service an hour late and a beaten up Landrover for the bridal car. Even the movie camera failed to work. Where else could such a wedding take place other than in the heart of Africa?"

Saturday was the big day. Our two hundred resident leprosy patients were all invited, as were all the hospital staff along with about twelve missionary friends. In those days missionaries were not permitted to travel around for unimportant events like weddings, so only those working close by could attend. As many as were able crammed into the windowless, grass-roofed, mud *tukul* while all the leprosy patients and some others waited outside.

The bride was due to arrive at one o'clock. But Doc Thompson had trouble with his new 16mm movie camera and arrived an hour late. Poor Norene tried to be patient for that extra hour, as we all did. No one else seemed to mind the delay, as everyone except the bride and groom were relaxed. After all this was Africa.

Finally the "bridal vehicle" was heard chugging along and the deafening joy calls erupted. Norene had to bow low to enter the tukul, which was so dark she was afraid she would end up marrying the wrong man. The service was conducted in two languages, English and Amharic. As a couple we had requested to take communion together which was meaningful to us both. By the time the knot was tied we were all longing for a breath of fresh air. Most of the local folk had never seen a Christian wedding, which was in stark contrast to the local customs.

In the midst of the joy calls the women shouted their blessing:

"Wonde lidge willedu, tolo willedu!" ("Have a son, have a son quickly!")

In Ethiopia a wedding isn't a wedding without lots of feasting. For the 200 leprosy patients we provided sweet spiced tea and bread, whereas for the hospital staff and Ethiopian guests (many of whom were important officials) we organised two sittings of the traditional Ethiopian feast of *injerra be watt*. For several years to come we were paying off these expensive feasts.

Then at about 9pm we sat down with the little group of foreign missionaries to a delicious chicken and salad meal. Norene had baked her own wedding fruit cake at language school in a not-so-friendly gas oven, but it turned out reasonably well.

Near midnight our little reception concluded. Although exhausted by that time we still needed to be driven the eleven kilometres to another SIM compound, where a little grass roofed hut had been prepared for us. On opening our bags we found all our clothes tied in knots as a wedding prank by our fellow missionaries. There was no easy way to iron out the creases either.

21 Honeymoon With A Difference

Only on the mission field would a honeymoon couple be woken at 5 the following morning for a breakfast with friends. But the sole daily bus was due to leave at 6am to transport us to our honeymoon destination some 210 kilometres up the Addis Ababa road.

With much pushing and shoving from other travellers we climbed into an old bus with our suitcases firmly strapped to the roof rack. After some coughing and spluttering our bus roared into life and we were away. But right in the middle of a stream on the outskirts of town the motor died. "Engine trouble!" the driver announced after many "experts" tried to repair the problem. "Come back tomorrow morning!"

Having paid to retrieve our luggage from the roof rack, we waded back to dry land.

"We'll try hitching a ride," I said. All day long we sat on our suitcases on the side of the dusty road, but no suitable vehicle turned up. We wondered what our Ethiopian friends thought about this newly-married couple. It was not quite in keeping with their marriage customs when the newly-weds would be hidden away in the bridegroom's parents' home for several days.

After giving up hope, we were taken the eleven kilometres back to the leprosarium, where our wedding had taken place, and spent that night in someone's attic. The following morning the bus did arrive and we left with some of the missionary children who were returning to boarding school in Addis Ababa. Finally, some five hours later, we reached our hotel in Bishoftu town.

Perfection. A cool room with a stunning outlook onto a crater lake below. We learned the Italians had built this magnificent hotel during the war as a retreat for their officers. Six days of bliss lay ahead of us. Or so we thought.

Hitching a ride on our Honeymoon

"Let's go down and explore the lake shore," I said to Norene.

A steep decline took us to the lake's edge. It was hot but we walked around the tracks for some time. Halfway up the hill on our return to the hotel I announced I had run out of steam and wasn't feeling well. This was unusual for me. With a great effort I made it back, but obviously something was wrong. A worried new wife had to scour the town for some credible medical help.

Miraculously a visiting Swedish doctor in the town was willing to come to the hotel and prescribed a course of antibiotics and bed rest for the next few days. His diagnosis? A bad case of viral pleurisy. Needless to say, we never did explore that particular lake until a few years later.

By the last night I was feeling somewhat better, and so we decided to celebrate by eating together in the dining room. Norene donned a kingfisher blue evening dress she had brought for such an occasion. But no sooner were we seated at the dining room table when she suddenly announced,

"I'm going to be sick! I'm going to be sick!"

She ran to our room, leaving me to enjoy the tasty Italian meal in solitary confinement. Apparently one of the local intestinal bugs had invaded her.

Next day we moved to the SIM rest home, on the adjacent lake. Again it was a stunning vista. Some years before, SIM had obtained permission from the Emperor to rent a small area of land overlooking the lake where a holiday resort could be built for missionaries. The director, Mr Glen Cain of Australia, had a great interest in nature and had introduced many beautiful flowering shrubs and plants which enhanced the whole hillside down to the lake's edge. (In later years I was asked to add more plants and trees to further beautify the area.) Small one- and two-roomed chalets had been erected for sleeping and all meals were served in a common dining room. What a marvellous retreat for busy mothers, who could enjoy a holiday with all meals prepared for them.

There we enjoyed a happy few days that made up for the disastrous beginning to our honeymoon.

Straight after this we set off for a few more weeks at language school. We had both had shortened courses there and needed to work towards our second language exam. How different it was this time, being able to study together and encourage (and correct) each other. Although it was not easy to be back to communal living as a newly married couple, we enjoyed the friendship of other missionaries and visiting again in Ethiopian homes. Once again we realised how grateful we should be that God had called us to work together in this beautiful country with such endearing and hospitable people.

22 Testing Times

Arriving back at the leprosarium all starry-eyed, we were anxious to set up our own little home and eager to start our work together. So many times Norene had said:

"I don't care where we live or how small our home, but I want us to be on our own after all these years of waiting."

Dr Thompson had promised a little house would be available for us.

But the day we arrived back we were told two nurses had now been added to our staff and they, too, needed housing. We felt terribly disappointed that our long promised home was not available. Weren't we entitled to the same? Didn't the mission promise us? Where would we live?

In the meantime the only place available for us was in the unlined attic of the Thompsons' home. A double bed was about all there was with low rafters and only a thin sheet of corrugated iron separating us from the elements. Most missionaries took a rest hour in the middle of the day, but this would prove impossible for us. We would need to have all our meals with the Thompson family. No chance of Norene setting up her own little nest with all the special things she had brought from home. We found ourselves muttering about such poor treatment of a newly-married couple. Surely, we thought, we deserved better.

Slowly, though, we began to realise how we should count our blessings. Weren't we married? Weren't we deeply in love? Didn't we have each other with whom to share our joys and problems? What about those brave single folk who had no partners? They were also there in obedience to God's call on their lives. They didn't always find it easy living with another person whom they hadn't chosen to live with. Weren't they entitled to have their own units built? Of course they were. Later one of the nurses shared with us the secret longing of her heart, that God would one day lead her into marriage. Yet here she was living in Ethiopia with little or no chance of ever meeting a husband.

The Lord taught us to take our eyes off ourselves and consider others. We knew that at the right time, we would have our own home.

Our wedding had taken place the end of July and it was to be the following January before we were able to move into our own home. Those months proved to be an "interesting" experience. Although it couldn't have been easy for the

Thompson family having an extra couple living with them, they were most gracious and loving towards us.

Meanwhile the mother of the home, Hazel, took sick with what was thought to be TB. Already some of their seven children were in Addis Ababa at boarding school and she was sent there for medical help, taking two pre-schoolers with her. We were asked to care for "Doc" and "Paulie" who was about four years old.

Norene:

"I found this hard, as Doc never arrived on time for meals. He was busy in the hospital and seemed to be all things to all people. Most nights we would wait until 8 or 9 o'clock to have our meal, and keeping the wood stove burning into the evening was no mean feat. I remember one night, after keeping Doc's dinner hot for ages, the kitchen worker who had stayed later that night dropped the plate of food on the floor as he carried it to the table.

Taking charge of someone else's helpers in the home was not easy either. I would often find the workers giggling away in the kitchen and I was *sure* it was because of my poor, halting Amharic. Doc was a friendly person and would always be urging people to come and visit him. On several weekends he went to Addis to visit his wife and we were delighted to be on our own at last. But that was short-lived. Almost every time he drove out of the compound, some of his invited guests drove in.

Four guest rooms were attached to the Thompsons' house and the beds needed to be made up continually as visitors, mission or non-mission, would appear at any time of the day or night. All southern roads led through Shashamane and on to Addis Ababa, and so it seemed we were at the hub. "Roads" into many of our mission stations were bad, especially in the rainy season, and missionaries knew that after a hard trip there would always be a bed and a meal when they finally arrived at the leprosarium gates. There was no way of letting us know, and some had large families. There was no telephone, or two-way radio. The kettle was literally boiling all day long on the wood stove, so a "cuppa" was available for thirsty travellers.

Bruce:

At the same time, Norene had started taking charge of the leprosy school. At first there were three grades and three Ethiopian teachers, all leprosy patients. She enjoyed the challenge of working with these needy people and found there was little, if any, problem with discipline. All were keen to make the most of the opportunity to learn in school as they had been outcasts in the past.

The classroom had a mud floor and every Saturday it would be "cleaned" by coating it with a thin mixture of cow dung and ashes. On Monday mornings the smell was quite a challenge.

At times some of her students would regularly go over to the open shutter to spit. This annoyed her immensely. One day she finally decided to ask one of the students for an explanation.

"Well, I'm a Muslim," he answered, "and this month is Ramadan. We're not permitted to swallow even our spittle during the day."

23 Into Our Own Home

We were supremely happy when we could set up our own home about six months later. The two-bedroomed house was built with a wooden frame and the walls and ceiling were plastered with mud. It had a tin roof and wooden floors. There were only bare rooms, with no inbuilt cupboards in the whole house. There was no plumbing, electricity, bathroom or kitchen bench at that stage. But the mission supplied a wood-burning stove and what a boon that was for making all our bread, meals, and for boiling drinking water. For our first term of five years we did not have a refrigerator, which posed some problems in keeping our food fresh. The only place we could buy meat was in the township of Shashamane, eleven kilometres away. Each Saturday we would send a worker by foot to buy some meat and a few other supplies, which would take most of his day. Then we would have to either cook the meat quickly or hang it in our outside safe to keep it as cool as possible.

Weren't we grateful that Norene's Dad had filled our tank with such useful things as two chests of drawers, a formica table and chairs, and some folding cane furniture. The missionaries had also given us a large dish cupboard for a wedding present. Curtain material and a manual Singer sewing machine from home all made our life easier and our home more attractive. Even our pretty china had travelled without incident, and this was useful for all the many visitors we were to entertain (including royalty.)

The joy and relief of living on our own was shortlived, however. One evening soon after we moved in, Dr Thompson came over with a request.

"Bruce and Norene," he said, "would you mind taking care of a missionary lady who is sick and being sent to the leprosarium for medical care? Could she move into your spare room?"

What could we say? We felt like answering, "Please leave us alone." But of course we didn't.

So we welcomed Bernice into our home. After all, we did have a spare bedroom even if we didn't have a bathroom. When we wanted a bath we would drag out a galvanised tub in front of the kitchen stove. After heating the water on the stove we would jump in quickly for a splash before the water cooled off. This worked fine for ourselves and later for our children, but it could prove a little tricky for permanent guests. We had an outside pit toilet.

Even water was a problem. The leprosarium was situated on the edge of a small stream, from which we obtained water by running it through several kilometres of ditches. The water was rationed, as it flowed only to part of the compound at one time. Twice a week we were fortunate to have this muddy brown stream making its way down the water ditches to our house. Then we would rush to fill up our barrels and irrigate our garden. But the water had to go through quite a long process before it was fit for drinking.

First we would add a certain amount of alum which caused the dirt to settle to the bottom. Then the water could be used for washing purposes. But for drinking we needed to strain it through a cloth and boil it for 20 minutes on the wood stove.

Our American house guest proved to be a blessing to us and we grew to love her. Unable to sleep well at night because of pain in her shoulder, she would often sit at the bedroom window overlooking the activities of our small water hole. In the morning we would say to her,

"Bernice, what did you see last night?"

One night she saw a pair of hyenas, then a civet cat and a serval cat. Another night an aardvark (ant eater) came for a drink. We had never ever seen some of these except in pictures.

Our guest's health did not improve and after a few months with us she had to return to the USA. How grateful we were that we had been willing to minister to her in some small way in her time of need.

While Bernice was with us, we were excited when we found Norene was pregnant with our first child. But she suffered serious morning sickness for the first three months, and so teaching in the leprosy school was quite a challenge. Sometimes she would have to give lesson plans and instructions from home to our three trustworthy Ethiopian teachers.

Near the end of the pregnancy we had a six-week visit from Norene's younger sister Judi, who was keen to be with Norene for the birth. Judi quickly settled into life at the leprosarium and we thoroughly enjoyed her visit with us. How interesting it is to see a country and one's circumstances through the eyes of a visitor. The medical work, especially, seemed to intrigue Judi and she found it fascinating to observe the doctor and nurses at work.

"I think I could quite easily stay and work here," she remarked at one stage.

24 Eighth Wonder Of Shashamane

Meanwhile the end of Norene's pregnancy was drawing near and we were not sure where the birth would take place. As we had no medical doctor at the leprosarium (Dr Thompson being a chiropracter), Norene had not been able to have any proper examinations during her pregnancy. We had to trust God that all was well. The mission director said although there was a good hospital in Addis, no gynaecologist was available at the time. He suggested Norene go to Bishoftu, the SIM holiday centre, since Dr Sam Steeves, a medical doctor who had been best man at our wedding, was planning to take some holiday there and his wife Lily was a nurse. At the same time there was to be another missionary, Malinda Veer, awaiting the birth of her baby.

Without a vehicle of our own we had been wondering how Norene and Judi would be able to travel to Bishoftu, a four to five-hour drive. Our baby was due on November 23, but because of the rough roads it was decided they should accept a ride on November 7 with a friend, John Koop. He was also going to Bishoftu after speaking at the Shashamane Conference. I was to follow a week later on my birthday, November 14.

The road from Shashamane was in places like a washboard and the side road into Bishoftu even worse. This had a devastating effect, for at 4am on November 9, Norene's labour started. She called Judi and together they stumbled over the little rocky paths until they found the doctor's cabin. He was as surprised as Norene was.

Although excited, Norene felt upset because I was not present. However, Ted, Malinda's husband, kindly offered to drive to Shashamane and bring me back to Bishoftu. It would be an eight-hour journey for him.

I was out in the field working when I heard Ted calling to me.

Could Norene have had the baby already? I wondered. What a rush to get some clothes together and set off for Bishoftu, praying along the way for a safe delivery. And how we appreciated Ted's offer to drive all that way even though he was concerned for his own wife. But that was Ted, a caring man who had lost his first wife in a car accident before coming to Ethiopia.

That morning Sam rushed over to the air force hospital, a few kilometres away, to borrow a pair of forceps in case of complications with the deliveries. During the labour he and his wife wondered why our baby's heartbeat was so irregular, although they were careful not to voice their concern to Norene. They didn't have to wonder for long. When our infant son made his appearance, after only four hours of proper labour, his cord was tied in a complete knot. Had it been a long labour, he would never have survived, they told us.

Norene wrote home a couple of days later:

"At twelve noon our little boy, Stephen Bruce, made his appearance with Judi at my side. She was almost as excited as I was. Our baby was small indeed, weighing in at about five and a half pounds on the bathroom scales. But how grateful to God I was to have a lovely live babe in my arms when Bruce finally appeared two hours later. It was a bitter-sweet experience without Bruce being

Norene's sister Judi, with baby Stephen Bruce

present at his birth."

The next night Malinda went into labour. A few hours later her little daughter was stillborn. What a devastating disappointment for them and a sad experience for us all. In one guest room we were rejoicing over the birth of our son and in one of the adjoining rooms the parents were sobbing over the loss of their baby daughter. It was another blow for dear Ted and his wife. My task was to build a little coffin in the guesthouse workshop and offer a word of comfort to the parents as we buried the little one under a beautiful flame tree.

Malinda and Ted never had another daughter, although they had five wonderful sons.

After the birth we had intended having a couple of weeks' holiday at Bishoftu, but eight days later a messenger arrived from Shashamane with a request from Dr Thompson.

"I have to ask you to return to Shashamane immediately," he wrote, "as I have been asked to attend a conference and need you to take charge of the leprosarium while I am away. Someone is picking you up late tonight and you'll have to travel all night,"

So pack up we did, and by travelling all night we arrived at the leprosarium around six o'clock, just as the sun was rising. The grapevine must have been active because that day we were visited by 120 local admirers coming to view the eighth wonder of the world ... a white baby.

The Ethiopian women had called out at our wedding "Have a son quickly!" And now they wanted to view the finished product. The wood stove went all day as we served bread and cups of tea to the admirers.

Judi stayed with us for a week or two longer, and then, sadly, had to leave us to return to New Zealand.

25 Teaching Six To Sixty

At first only school-age children attended the leprosy school and we ran it as much like an elementary school as possible. Norene mostly taught the English classes and supervised the teachers who were themselves leprosy patients. As time went on many of the adult patients expressed their desire to learn too, for having been outcasts in their villages, they had had no opportunity to learn. And so it was that we opened up the school to all ages.

We needed different materials for this literacy programme and had to develop much of them ourselves. A Gestetner duplicator for copying was our only means of preparing materials for the new age group. No matter what age or disability, all were encouraged to come and learn to read and, where possible (that is, if they had enough fingers), to write Amharic.

"We have just completed a series of 192 stencils, running off 400 copies of each on our Gestetner machine," we wrote home at one stage. It was not quite as simple as photocopying today.

Half the students learned in the mornings from 8 to 12, and the other half in the afternoons from 2 to 6. Those who were able would work in the fields for the opposite half of the day. The school programme included a Bible period in which Norene and her teachers had a wonderful opportunity to teach the Bible stories and to introduce some of the well-known choruses and hymns with Norene's piano accordion. As the school was being established we were thrilled to find three younger patients who spoke Amharic fluently and were willing to teach with Norene in this new venture. The three of them became Christians and proved to be able teachers.

As Norene's responsibilities with children grew over the years, she worked more from home, supervising the teachers and preparing materials. DVBS (Daily Vacation Bible School) was a regular occurrence during the long holidays ("the rains") and this was voluntary for the students. We were encouraged that many made decisions for Christ during these special classes.

A cute little student carrying water

Norene teaching choruses to Leprosy School children on her piano accordion

How exciting to learn to read!

26 Kebede

One of our young students was Kebede (meaning "he was heavy"). He'd come to us early one Sunday morning, having been dropped off by a truck at our gate. A more miserable and destitute-looking child would have been hard to find. He certainly didn't live up to his name. All he had to his name was a little ragged shirt but no trousers. While having breakfast we had heard him crying outside the main gates, and were grateful our medical staff made room for this little chap to be cared for.

After his shyness lessened he told us his story. His mother was so afraid when she noticed white leprosy spots on his skin that she sent him off to find the faraway hospital she had heard about. He had wandered for several days, terrified of the hyenas' eerie howls at night. Finally a truck driver had given him a ride to our gates.

This bewildered little boy of about seven soon became a confident student in school, gratefully accepting clothes, medicine and the opportunity to learn. After several years of taking leprosy drugs Kebede was considered leprosy-free and could return to his home.

"I am grateful to be cured of my leprosy," he responded, "but I want permission to stay longer, to study in school and learn more about God's word."

This was agreed to.

One day after the Vacation Bible School classes, Norene was at home having lunch when there was a timid knock on our door. Kebede was there, all smiles.

"I want you to know, Mama Bond, that today I have accepted Jesus as my Saviour, and when I do go home to my family I intend to tell them all about him. I remember the day I arrived at the gate, so scared and sick. Today is the happiest day of my life!"

We discovered that many of the young people like Kebede had the gift of acting, and some of our most memorable and humour-filled evenings were those in which they acted out Bible stories in their own inimitable way. Norene loved to train them to put on these plays for the wider group of patients. Perhaps the most memorable was the story of Joseph in the Old Testament.

27 A Place To Worship

It was not the mission's policy to go around erecting church buildings for the national believers. In fact through the years hundreds and now thousands of churches throughout Ethiopia were built by the believers themselves. But in the leprosarium things were different. First, the few believers were all disabled, many in poor health. Secondly, they had little or no money and no way of making money.

So together we set about building a place of worship. In keeping with the rest of the buildings on the compound we built on a stone foundation, with poles and split timber for the walls overlaid with mud mixed with straw. After the mud dried and was smoothed, another layer of mud was added to fill in all the cracks. We used corrugated iron for the roofing. Simple wooden benches were built and we were ready for our dedication service.

By now we had a number of believers. A few were Christian before coming to the leprosarium, but most were new converts. Many different language groups were represented, but all the services were conducted in Amharic, the official language, with various interpreters to translate into other languages.

Twice-weekly we had a compulsory meeting under a huge *ficus* or fig tree, when medicine was distributed. But Sunday's service was different. Numbers quickly grew as many more came to know Jesus as their Saviour. Elders were chosen for this unique gathering of believers who came from many different parts of the country. Little did we realise then that many of these patients, like Kebede above, once cured of their leprosy would return to their homes as God's messengers to establish new churches throughout southern Ethiopia.

28 Munnie

One of those who regularly came to our Sunday services was a young woman called Munnie. She had arrived at the leprosarium when her leprosy, the most disfiguring type, was well advanced. Just looking at her repulsed us. The bridge of her nose was completely gone and she had nodules all over her face. Her fingers and toes were just stumps, but somehow she shuffled around. Most times she covered herself with a white shawl. Fortunately her type of leprosy responded to drugs and so further damage to her body was arrested. For several years she had been in school and had accepted Jesus as her Saviour, growing to be a strong Christian.

Although she was never able to write well because of her lack of fingers, she did learn to read. After a few years of treatment she was given a medical certificate stating that she was healed from infectious leprosy. But being so deformed from the disease she would not have been accepted socially, and so was

Munnie our special friend in Shashamane Leprosarium

given food and housing inside the compound. After further Bible study she became an outstanding evangelist, bringing many women to the Saviour.

Postscript: Forty years later (1994) when Norene and I were due to retire from Ethiopia we decided to pay a final visit to the hospital to say farewell to some of our old friends. During the intervening years the Marxist government had taken over the leprosarium and sadly the compound had deteriorated. Many of the beautiful specimen trees had been cut down for firewood, the missionary and staff houses were a shambles, and the hospital grounds were overgrown with rank grass and weeds. Indeed it was hard to recognise the place we had left many years before.

Amazingly, the church building was still standing. Some of the Christians told us how the building had been appropriated as a storeroom during the Marxist revolution and the believers forbidden to worship. Only in the early 1990s was the building returned to the believers, who were still refurbishing it and had added extra rooms for Sunday School classes.

While we were admiring this new addition, someone came up from behind and gently touched us on the shoulder. We turned around to see a woman, all wrapped up in a large white shawl. She put her arms around us and wept. How dumbfounded we were to discover it was Munnie. We had no idea she was still alive.

"How did you know we were coming today?" we asked.

"When I was praying this morning in my house, God told me to go down to the church this afternoon and there I would find Mama and Ababa Bond."

What simple faith in a loving God!

29 A Mechanical Ox

There was a tension in my mind. On the one hand I wanted to fulfil the government mandate to use the land profitably to provide food for the patients, and on the other I wanted to teach basic and practical things which patients could copy in their own villages.

It wasn't long before I realised that in order to fill the mission's obligation to the government, we needed to buy a tractor and plough. But there was no budget for this; rather it was up to the organiser of such a project to raise the necessary finance from overseas.

I had left a small amount of money in a savings account back in New Zealand, and so as quickly as possible had that money transferred to Addis Ababa. Then by various means the necessary money was provided. Norene, who was pregnant with Stephen at the time, accompanied me to Addis in the mission truck. How proud we felt as we loaded on what was to be the first tractor in southern Ethiopia – a 1955 Massey Ferguson 27 hp diesel. The tractor just fitted onto the truck and we jammed a two-furrow plough between the front and back wheels of the tractor.

Great was the interest at the leprosarium as word spread that Mr Bond was bringing back a mechanical ox so strong it could pull more than four team of oxen. It didn't eat any grass but it was thirsty.

As mentioned earlier, the road to Shashamane was poor and progress was slow. Having left the road for a parallel track, we hit a big rut which caused our radiator fan to gouge a great hole in the radiator. In a few seconds we were drained of water and literally miles away from anyone or any help. Things were pretty serious. Norene prayed while I worked in the boiling sun. First of all I took the sides and tail gate off the truck, and then I tried to untie the tractor.

"Perhaps the nearby bank would be a good place to unload the tractor," I said to Norene.

Pouring our last drop of drinking water into the radiator we made it to our unloading bank. Yes, the tractor was full of diesel and started well. But there was

The Massey Ferguson tractor with a second one bought some years later for Shashamane

no way we could move it off the truck until we could lift the jammed two-furrow plough out from between the front and back tires. The two of us simply didn't have the strength for this, and so we waited and waited and cooked in the heat for several hours.

Finally we saw a cloud of dust coming closer and heard the rumble of a diesel truck making its way towards us. It was no trouble for our truckie friends to pull the plough out from between the tractor wheels. This enabled us to drive the tractor off the truck. After reloading the plough we were soon on our way, with the tractor pulling our damaged truck. It must have been quite a sight as I bounced up and down on the tractor seat with Norene steering the crippled truck. Alas, darkness soon set in and the tractor had no lights. Still, the truck lights lasted our trip home.

Our welcoming committee of Ethiopians had long since given up hope and gone to bed, and so our grand entrance was a low-key affair. Our fellow missionaries were only relieved we had come to no harm.

The next morning we hitched up our plough and headed out to the field. A great crowd of people gathered, both patients and local farmers, to see what our "mechanical ox" could do. There were shrieks of delight as our monster could turn over not just one furrow but two at a time. Their own two oxen yoked together could pull a wooden plough with an iron spike, but it would take many passes and lots of hard work before they could sow a crop.

Before long many people wanted to learn how to handle the new tractor and I had no intention of doing the ploughing myself. We chose several young men to train. Having never had the opportunity to drive a car or even play with mechanical toys, they found it hard initially, but after a few lessons one of the young men told me he could manage. So off I went to do something else.

It didn't take long before someone ran up to tell me to come urgently.

"Icussie's had a terrible accident!" he cried. "He came to the fence and forgot how to stop!"

The fence was pretty flimsy and no harm had befallen the driver, but the bonnet of my new tractor was ruined. That caused some reaction amongst the onlookers. Obviously my mechanical ox refused to listen to any commands. After that expensive mistake, my new driver went on to become an expert and was able to teach many others.

30 Smallpox Strikes

Of all the injections and vaccinations needed before one could contemplate going to Ethiopia in those days, smallpox was perhaps the most important. Were we grateful for that little scratch on our arms, leaving us with a round scar that showed we had been vaccinated.

Arsi girls receiving smallpox vaccinations

In most of the world smallpox had become a scourge of the past due to effective vaccinations, but for parts of Africa it was still something to be feared. In May 1957 rumours started spreading in our district that some terrible disease was killing hundreds, and people started arriving in droves. It was obvious that a smallpox epidemic had started. There was little our medical staff could do for those already infected, but we contacted the Ministry of Health who immediately sent down large supplies of smallpox vaccinations to our hospital.

Panic broke out in the district. People from miles away arrived by foot at all hours of the day and night begging for this powerful medicine. The desperation of the crowd became so great that the medical staff could not possibly handle the stampede by themselves, and so it was all hands on deck – teachers, housewives, office workers and even the agriculturist.

We quickly built sturdy rails, so that when people came they would be forced to line up to receive their vaccination. The noise, even at nights, was deafening as people waited for help. The Arsi women and girls wore only decorated cow hides tanned with rancid butter, and the odour was something to experience. Thousands upon thousands were vaccinated and so that terrible epidemic was stayed. Many who had become infected either died or were left with permanent scars all over their bodies.

31 Mitchell And Devers

We made some life-long friends while working at the leprosarium. Hedley and Thelma Waldock from Canada were one couple we admired very much when they were appointed as administrators, and we worked together for several years. Other Canadians Gordon and Norma Creighton were also great friends to us. Another couple, Charles and Lucille Anderson from USA, lived just eleven kilometres from the leprosarium.

Several little Arsi churches had been established by earlier missionaries, and Charles and I would drive a vehicle or trek out together to a different church each month for a fellowship meeting Two district elders from each church would come as representatives, and we would arrive in the late afternoon to a welcoming committee.

One month Charles and I headed out in a small pick-up with some of the Arsi elders to a distant place called Seraro. The first part of the metal road was good, but after thirteen kilometres we turned off to follow a dirt track which was designed for animals only and barely passable. We hadn't expected such a long journey, and the gathering darkness made the last part a nightmare. The lights of our vehicle obviously warned the whole district of our arrival.

We were given a great welcome, with the usual foot washing ceremony, and then came the more formal programme of hearing the various reports from the different churches.

As this was the first time Charles and I had been to this particular area we were keen to ask the local believers about their history.

"Do any of you remember the day a large party, including two white people, passed through this area on their way to the town of Alaba?" we asked. "Do you remember what happened to those people?"

Although almost twenty years had passed, many of the believers remembered it well. They told us how a large party of armed Arsi men had attacked the group, killing everyone including the two white men. It was 9 May 1936 when the massacre took place. (The Arsi had a custom that before a man was eligible for marriage he had to kill a man from a different tribe and present the evidence to his fiancée.)

Cliff Mitchell was from New Zealand and Tom Devers from Canada. They had been establishing a new SIM outreach at Tutitti which was on the border of the Gedeo and the Goojee tribes. Myrtle, Cliff's wife, and her little son had gone ahead to Addis as had Tom's fiancée, because travelling had become increasingly dangerous with the Italian army advancing towards the capital.

Postscript: Years later I met many times with Myrtle Mitchell in Invercargill. Never once did I hear a trace of bitterness, despite her husband having been martyred and her only son killed in a motorbike accident in his early twenties. Each time we met she would always ask about the Goojees, the tribe they had expected to work amongst. Had any of them become Christians yet? Had SIM established a mission station in that region yet? She died in 1976 and left what little worldly possessions she had to help establish an outreach amongst the Goojee tribe.

32 Arrested

I'm sure we were about to hear more from these Arsi believers, when suddenly the door of the church was flung open violently and we were facing the barrels of loaded rifles.

Was this to be our time? The attention was aimed at us foreigners. Several policemen marched in, pointing their rifles at us.

"You're under arrest!" they announced.

But that posed a problem. Since it was late at night, what would they do with us? Would they lock us up? Many arguments followed between the police and our Arsi hosts. No way would they allow the police to harm us in their presence and so being greatly outnumbered, the police agreed to a compromise. We could sleep with our friends in the church but in the morning we'd be taken to the police station. The police positioned themselves at appropriate places around the church so their prize prisoners could not steal away in the night.

There was little sleep that night for us and as day dawned we committed our way to the Lord. Looking back I am only sorry we didn't have a camera to record the events of the day. Like two criminals we were marched along the path to the police station, perhaps a distance of two kilometres. Charles and I were in the front, the armed police walked behind us with their loaded rifles, and behind them all walked the local Christians and their families.

The local police headquarters proved to be a collection of little grass- and tin-roofed buildings. We were ushered inside and told to sit on a flimsy stool while copious hand-written notes were recorded about us and our so-called misdemeanours. Whether we were considered spies, or whether the police had been warned to look out for two dangerous foreign criminals, we will never know. Obviously they seemed satisfied and rather smug that we had been captured.

Finally it was announced that because of the severity of our crimes we were being passed on to the district police station which was some fifty kilometres away. But there was no transport available.

Not a problem. We assured our captors we would drive ourselves to prison, allowing our guards to accompany us lest we try to escape. The police captain counted out a number of bullets for each guard, and with our crimes fully documented and our guards fully armed, we set off back to the little church, picked up our sleeping bags and set off in our own truck.

Because of the state of the track it took several hours to drive to the district police station. We were tired and not a little apprehensive but knew God would somehow work out this problem for us.

Our guards were first off the truck, clutching their dossier of our so-called crimes and organising a cell in the lockup. We were then ushered into the slightly more modern station to await the captain's presence. After some time he stepped into the room.

"What's all this about?" he asked angrily, after taking one look at his prisoners.

With obvious embarrassment he called for decent chairs for us and a drink to quench our thirst. Immediately I recognised him as one who had been an invited guest at our recent wedding. At that time he had viewed some of the work we were involved in at the leprosarium and had been greatly impressed.

"There must be some *terrible* mistake!" he groaned.

He called our police guards and gave them a tongue lashing, but I guess the poor fellows were only following someone's instructions.

"You men go home," he told us. "When the case comes up in court, I will personally be your guarantor and the case will be dismissed."

Although we were worn out when we arrived home that night, we were thrilled to trace how God had so miraculously gone before us by providing the only person who could possibly have sent us home as free men.

Postscript: The number of believers in that district has grown by leaps and bounds, and today there are several churches established.

33 Royal Visits

His Majesty, Haile Selassie, was King of Ethiopia and all powerful. It was by his permission that SIM was allowed to work in Ethiopia. How important it was, then, for good relationships to be built up between the missionaries and himself. Being a progressive man he sought to unify Ethiopia into one country. Previously the land had operated under a feudal system, with several powerful chiefs in charge of different regions of the country.

A visit from the Emperor

In 1958 the Emperor made a visit to the Sidamo people. There were no government buildings in the area, and so hundreds of Sidamo men came together to build a large complex. These outstandingly beautiful bamboo-woven *tukuls* were built right on the shores of Lake Awassa.

Soon after the King's arrival at Lake Awassa he sent a royal invitation inviting Dr Thompson and ourselves to the mid-day meal on Sunday. How exciting! What would we wear? What appropriate gift could we take? Out came our glad rags, cleaned and neatly pressed. As for a gift, we needed to take something unique – perhaps something we had grown. When establishing the Rift Valley nursery we had built a little propagating shed. Someone had sent us some begonia tubers which we had planted in this shed. These had flowered with beautiful huge blooms, and so we decided to prepare a large bouquet of them for the King. I suspect there were no other begonias growing in Ethiopia at that time, and so it seemed an appropriate gift.

Quickly we were ushered into his banquet tent where a series of small tables had been set up. We wondered about the seating arrangement, but everything had been carefully worked out. At the top table Dr Thompson and the King were seated. Next came a larger table where the Crown Prince sat with the younger Prince Mekonnen. I was taken to that table. Further down the pecking order, at the third table, Norene was seated with Princess Tenagnework and three of her five daughters. We wondered how we would cope with the language, but all were fluent in English except for His Majesty who spoke Amharic and French. Just as well we weren't at that table. We were all quickly put at ease and able to enjoy an exotic meal of the best injerra and watt it was possible to make.

We spent a memorable few hours together and marvelled that we had been chosen to share a meal at the King's table. We thought of the lovely chorus which says, "He brought me into his banqueting table and his banner over me is love..."

Another day stands out in our memory. One of the missionary families working with us at Shashamane was leaving for furlough and we arranged a farewell morning tea at our home. Just as we were all ready for the visitors, a black shiny Mercedes drove up and stopped outside. Norene ran out to see who the visitors were and was taken aback to see Princess Tenagnework and one of

Becky on Princess Tenagnework's knee. 1964 visit

her granddaughters. She stammered a greeting and without hesitating said,

"Your Highness, would you like to come and have a cup of tea with us?"

The princess readily agreed.

"Oh, how did you know I was coming?" she remarked as she entered our little living area.

On another planned visit by Princess Tenagnework at the leprosarium, we organised for the younger children on the compound to gather together some flowers for posies to present to her.

34 Rift Valley Nursery

Mr Glen Cain, the SIM Director for Ethiopia, had passed on to me a large quantity of ornamental and tree seeds for trial, to see which varieties would be suitable for the highlands of Ethiopia. The seeds were a gift from a representative of United Nations, and so we needed to take good care of them. We had remarkable success in that most varieties of seed germinated and were transferred into seedling boxes or individual clay pots. At that time PVC plastic pots had not been heard of and so we found ourselves needing thousands of clay pots.

There was a tribe of people in Ethiopia who worked with clay to make all sorts of water and cooking pots. They were experts in their trade. We enquired as to where we might find some of these people and were delighted to find we already had some of them living as patients in the leprosarium. We quickly became friends and offered them a contract to make thousands of suitable clay pots for our seedlings.

The seedlings shot away, and before long we needed to find a good market if the project was to become viable. We quickly put together a simple catalogue, calling ourselves The Rift Valley Plant Nursery. We offered a variety of tropical and sub-tropical fruit trees, flowering shrubs and a large number of forest trees, both indigenous and exotic.

As word spread, people representing many agencies and from different organisations enquired about buying trees and shrubs from us. We began to realise we had established the first plant nursery in Southern Ethiopia, if not in all of Ethiopia. Previously all plants had to be imported from Kenya. Certainly clients came from all corners of Ethiopia to buy their plants for landscaping different projects. They came from Addis Ababa where the Jubilee Palace was being built, from Jimma for a new agricultural college just commencing, from Harare, from Debre Zeit, where the Swedish were helping to establish an air force base, and from many other towns. We could hardly keep up with the demand.

After three seasons we reluctantly closed the nursery because it was growing too big and taking up more time than I could spare. We were happy that later on some enterprising Ethiopians took up the challenge, opening their own little plant nurseries in different parts of the country.

35 Second Addition

At our wedding in 1955 the Ethiopian women had blessed us with the refrain, "Have a son, have a son quickly!"

Everyone was happy that another son, David Brian, was born on Valentine's Day 1958, only fifteen months after his brother. Once again we drove to Addis well before his due date, "just in case." Sure enough, the next day he decided to make his presence known. The British doctor, Margaret Fitzherbert, had now returned to Princess Tsehai hospital in Addis and so we had a "proper" birth in a hospital and I was present for the great event. There were few mod cons in the hospital, but the medical expertise was tops.

I had a few scary moments though. After being with Norene for some time I had brought Stevie back to our mission headquarters and put him to bed, telling Norene to phone when her labour started in earnest. Around 2am I was startled by a telephone ringing in the hall near my guest room. A nurse from the hospital said in Amharic (as I interpreted it):

"Mr Bond, your wife says, 'Please come quickly, I'm dying.'"

Leaving our little toddler and trusting he would not waken before I returned, I sped to the hospital. As I dashed into the ward Norene wondered why I looked so concerned. She assured me all was well and that she had sent the message her labour had started again and would I please come. (The words for death and labour are a little similar to an amateur.)

David, being considerate of his brother (as always), arrived before 6am, and so I was back again when Stevie woke up. We did not believe there could be such a placid baby in the world. Unlike his older brother, David even loved to sleep. What a blessing! We returned to Shashamane soon after the birth to resume our work, and our Ethiopian friends were all impressed with our second male child. The closeness in age was to be such a blessing, as they were great pals and a comfort to each other when they first started boarding school.

36 Sickness Strikes

In March of that year, SIM was starting a new mission station up in the highlands at a place called Adaba, nestled in the foothills of the Bale mountains which rise to 14,225 feet (4,377m). I had to make a trip by Landrover to complete formalities for the building of this new station. The only way into the property was from Shashamane, over a dirt track which was difficult even in the dry season, but impassable during the rains. The 120 kilometre trip took my co-worker and me about eight hours. I believe this was one of the scenic wonders of Ethiopia.

After a few days we completed our business at Adaba and started our return trip to Shashamane. Unfortunately I developed severe abdominal pain. This became unbearable, but it seemed we had only two options. Either we continued, or we stopped in the wilderness to wait for the pain to subside. Obviously the pain was increasing, and so after committing ourselves to God we pushed on.

That must have been one of the longest and most uncomfortable trips I have ever made. I was in agony and for almost eight hours was jolted from side to side in the car. On arrival at the leprosarium Norene was shocked to find me in such pain. I was then examined by the medical staff who concluded I had appendicitis and needed immediate surgery. But we were still five or six hours away from Addis Ababa and a surgeon. It was already dark, but after a shot of morphine to dull my pain we set off with Doc Thompson as driver.

Our friend Lucille kindly offered to care for Stephen. We were most grateful for her offer, even though it was difficult for Norene to even consider being separated from either of our boys. David was only two months old. The road to Addis was improving daily as there was a large American company with a contract to seal the entire road. This meant we made the trip in just over five hours. Dr Fitzherbert, who had delivered David, kindly offered hospitality to Norene and our baby in her own home and then proceeded to find the necessary staff for the immediate surgery.

We were told we had just been in time to prevent serious complications. Norene wrote home later:

"I had such a scary experience as I was waiting in the unfriendly hospital for news of Bruce's surgery. Of course it was on my mind that it must have been 'touch and go' when Bruce had been waiting so long for surgery. Standing near the operating theatre, waiting for them to wheel him out, I heard one of the nurses call out, 'The patient in the theatre has died.'

Before I keeled over, another nurse ran over and explained there were two theatres in the hospital."

Later in the same year sickness struck again. Both feeling extremely tired, we decided to go to Wando Valley, about twenty kilometres from Shashamane, for a few days to a little hideaway. One of our missionaries drove us there. At that stage there was a little hot spring nearby and lush forest all around. The hut had concrete floors, a wood stove and a couple of beds but little else, and so it was rather difficult to care for two little boys there.

The following morning we made a devastating discovery. Our urine was black and we knew what that meant. We must have both contracted infectious hepatitis. But how to get back home? Calling a local Ethiopian boy, we asked him to find some transport for us. Shortly a truck came bouncing up the dirt road and the two of us climbed into the cab each with a child on our knee. There were no car seats or seat belts in those days.

How sick we felt as we bounced along and were both relieved to be in our own bed again. We had a young man to help in the kitchen and the missionary nurses kindly offered to take the boys at night. Doubtless they had some broken nights with our Stevie.

Back then the medical people thought two weeks in bed was sufficient, but unfortunately Norene's symptoms returned after a few months and she was put on complete bed rest for eight tedious weeks.

37 Homeward Bound

Early in 1959 we had a visit from Norene's Dad and his new wife, Kate. Once again we found it interesting to see our work through the eyes of visitors. Norene's Dad, being a top-notch photographer, took several reels of 16 mm movie film which we often used in our deputation ministry in later years. He was horrified to discover we didn't own a refrigerator in the hot climate, and promised we would have one when we returned for our next term. By this time we were more than ready for a furlough. We had been plagued by recurring dysentery and our little boys had suffered eye infections from the ever-present sticky flies. Back then mission policy was that a couple had to serve a full ten years between them, before going on furlough. This meant five and a half years for me and four and a half for Norene.

Our third child was on the way at that stage and Norene was not so well as we were packing up to leave. We flew on a DC3 to Aden where we connected with our passenger ship. Ruth Cremer of New Zealand accompanied us and we enjoyed good fellowship along the way. The boys and I enjoyed ship life but the constant movement made Norene's nausea worse.

"Welcome home, Bruce and Norene!" said the SIM rep who met us in Sydney. "You'll be glad to know I've booked you on this same ship to return to Ethiopia eleven months from now."

We laugh about it now, but at that moment Norene never wanted to see another ship for the rest of her life.

A pleasant surprise awaited us in Sydney, however. After almost four weeks on the ship, as we drew alongside the wharf we spotted Norene's Dad walking towards us. He revelled in surprises and had flown over from Auckland to meet us.

Being the generous and thoughtful man he was, he took one look at his daughter in her five-year-old outfit and offered:

"I know some lovely clothes shops here in Sydney and I've already chosen one or two suits for you to try on."

My brother Grahame and his wife had sent money to buy me a new suit as well, and so we all looked rather swish a day or two later when we alighted from the plane at Auckland.

"Is royalty arriving today?" someone at Whenuapai airport was heard to remark.

No, it was just an ordinary missionary family returning after a long separation. What an overwhelming welcome we received from family and church friends! But just as we walked out to meet everyone, a little fight ensued between our two boys, both under three. They both ended up crying their eyes out, with one bloody nose to boot. Rather humbling for the parents!

Arriving for first furlough with Norene's Dad

During the next eleven months we did not live on our own, but Norene's and my family members welcomed us into their homes for various lengths of time. We were ministered to physically, spiritually and emotionally, certainly needing every bit of that tender loving care.

Rebecca Wynne made her entrance into the world in a "real" maternity hospital five months later, in January 1960. How grateful we were to God for a little daughter to join our family. The irony was that the doctor didn't even arrive in time, when it seemed we had come all the way to New Zealand for a "proper" birth.

We spoke at meetings around the Auckland area and later did some deputation work as a family in the lower North Island. We were based in Palmerston North for some of that time, living in two small caravans on the property of kind friends, the Jenkies. It was not so easy with a young baby, but we coped.

And yes, eleven months later we were on a ship heading back to Ethiopia. Our relatives, especially Norene's older sister Jean, worried we wouldn't have any rest, with five of us (including a five-month-old baby) in one cabin. But we enjoyed the trip immensely.

Chapter Three

Return to Shashamane

38 The Coup

Following our furlough we were permitted to attend language school for some weeks while we worked towards our second language examination. Even with three pre-schoolers Norene was still able to attend most classes and we both benefited from this time before returning to work at the leprosarium.

Wednesday December 15, 1960 was a day to remember. That day our nearest foreign neighbours, Seventh Day Adventist missionaries, drove into our compound with the frightening news that serious fighting had broken out in the streets of Addis Ababa and suggested we listen to the BBC for accurate information.

In those days Shashamane was about six hours south of Addis on the main road. The regular bus had not passed by and we realised there hadn't been a single vehicle either. Emperor Haile Selassie was on a state visit to Brazil and had wisely appointed two official bodies, the army and his Imperial guards, to watch over the country in his absence. But some of his most trusted men turned against him in an attempt to seize power. Fortunately there was strong opposition and jealousy between these two bodies, so when the Imperial guards staged their coup, the army remained loyal to the Emperor. A bloody battle ensued.

On December 21 of that year we wrote to our family in New Zealand that excitement had been reverberating around the country, not because of Christmas drawing near but because of war.

We continued in our letter:

"We possessed no radio ourselves. So as soon as the children were in bed we listened to the BBC at our neighbour's house. The news was frightening. Serious fighting had erupted in Addis Ababa with many people killed. The BBC warned all foreigners to stay put and not attempt to move around the country."

We ourselves were in no danger – or so we thought – as we were two hundred and forty kilometres from the scene of the fighting. So we slept peacefully that Wednesday night. Unfortunately, many of the missionaries from Shashamane were in Addis Ababa as the boarding school was breaking up for the term. As a consequence I was the only male missionary on the station. Naturally the women whose husbands and school children were in Addis Ababa were concerned for their loved ones.

All day Thursday and Friday not a vehicle passed our gates. The clinic and hospital continued to function normally, but somehow there was a restlessness among the local population as rumours spread that the government had been overthrown. Our letter home continued:

"The local tribal people started to arm themselves with spears and guns, gathering together into large groups and roaming the countryside. We were warned by our friends to increase security around our compound, as looting and killings could erupt if they thought there was no government control. Rumours flew. Armed groups started circling the leprosarium, threatening to destroy the compound."

The leprosarium had been established for more than ten years and during the last six we had made many friends, some of whom had become Christians. They assured us of their protection even, if necessary, against their own fellow tribesmen. We knew they meant it.

The BBC reported that nineteen government officials and up to two thousand people had been killed in Addis Ababa. As a group of missionaries we continued to pray for those in the capital and for protection for ourselves and our national staff at the leprosarium. Some of our staff, being from other tribal groups, were just as vulnerable as we were.

Rumours of an imminent attack on our compound increased. Chanting continued day and night, with boasting of what would happen to us individually when they looted our property. To our relief, on Friday we heard His Majesty had suddenly returned to Ethiopia, taking up the reins of government again.

Because the coup was officially over and only the ringleaders were being hunted, I decided it was safe to leave our compound to work on other land we were leasing up the main road. Because the main crop we were growing was *teff*, it was critical that it be harvested when ripe. Early in the afternoon a runner came to tell me the alarming news that Arsi locals had attacked the leprosarium. We tore back down the road, not knowing what we would find.

On arrival at our main gates my worst fears surfaced as I encountered a large number of men trying to force their way past our armed guards. Uncertain of what to do for the best, I revved up our truck and charged towards the gate. Miraculously the crowd parted, allowing the vehicle to enter. Obviously the rumour had been false, as nobody had yet broken into the compound, but none of us knew how long we could hold out against these determined thugs.

Within a short time vehicles were again travelling down our road from the capital and the troublemakers gave up their evil intentions. The men and schoolchildren from Addis were given a heartfelt welcome on their return. But sadly some of our leprosy patients, who had left the relative safety of the hospital compound to return to their own villages, were killed on the way.

39 Prayer at the Orchard

October 1961 was a lovely month in the Rift Valley. The rains had come and gone, leaving the promise of an abundant harvest. Our little family was growing quickly. Stevie was almost five, and great company for his younger brother David. We often said, though, they were little partners in crime.

One day we found a good children's book in the outside fire where our bath water was heated. We called the two boys over to ask about it and Stevie reported proudly his little brother had thrown it in. We then reprimanded David for doing such a naughty thing. He was upset.

"But Stevie told me to…!" he said between sobs.

Later we heard the following conversation:

Stevie: "David, Jesus isn't in your heart 'cos you threw the book in the fire."

David: "Well, he's isn't in your heart either, 'cos you told me to."

The little children certainly opened the hearts and homes of the local folk. Rebecca (or Becky as we called her) was loved by all her little Ethiopian friends.

And now Norene was expecting our fourth child, due April 1961. But even before we had informed our New Zealand families we started to have complications. We went into Addis Ababa to the hospital there and were told our half-term baby had died.

Norene writes: "I was devastated to lose this baby I had carried for nineteen weeks, but was willing to accept the loss from my heavenly Father who loved me and knew what was best. This experience gave us an empathy with others too. Some of our missionary friends were not able to have any children and our Ethiopian friends often suffered the loss of children."

Drs Hamlin and Nicholson were a husband and wife team who had established the fistula hospital in Addis and have written the book *Hospital by the River 2001.* They decided to operate, although they knew it was a dangerous time of the pregnancy.

Norene haemorrhaged seriously and (as they told us later) was at death's door. She remembers feeling as though she were in a dark tunnel with only a speck of light at the end, and hardly able to find her next breath. We sent an SOS to our friends around Ethiopia to pray for her.

Some days later we returned to Shashamane to continue our work. Mail day was always a highlight, but it was never regular as we had to wait until a truck brought supplies from Addis. After some weeks a letter arrived with unfamiliar handwriting.

"Dear Bruce and Norene," the letter began. "The other night I had a strange experience which involved you folk. I have to write to ask you if there is any validity in this experience. I was woken from a sound sleep and a voice seemed to be saying to me, 'Pray for Norene.' I knelt at my bedside and prayed for her. A long time later I had the assurance all was well and I was able to return to bed. Please write and tell me. On this particular day, at this particular time, was Norene in some great danger, needing God's protective hand?"

Checking back in our diary we found it was the time our surgeon friend had been so concerned about Norene's condition. You can imagine how grateful to God we felt when we realised that in some mysterious way he had touched our friend thousands of kilometres away.

Yes, we were separated from our New Zealand friends and family. There was no telephone or other means of instant communication, but we were hooked into God's network. After that experience we asked the Lord to make us more sensitive to hear his voice when he wanted us to pray for others.

We were reminded of a Bible verse: *The earnest prayer of a righteous man has great power and wonderful results. (James 5:16, The Living Bible)*

40 Number Four

The following year we were overjoyed to be expecting another child into our family. On top of this we received letters from home saying we were to have two special visits. First, Norene's Dad and his wife Kate were planning to come again for several weeks to be with us for the birth, which was to take place at the leprosarium as we finally had a resident doctor. Then my parents, who had been planning a trip for some time, decided to come after the birth and stay for six weeks over Christmas.

The only sad aspect was that Stevie had to begin boarding school in Addis in early September. The rule was that children had to be a full six years old by the September when they started grade one. He would be just under six at that stage, but the Bingham Board (of which Norene was a member) had made an exception because in our "down under" schools children started at five years. No homeschooling was permitted in those days, and so we had no choice. From the time our children were born we had tried to condition ourselves for this painful separation. But even now, after all these years, just writing about it brings tears to our eyes.

In those days the rules were strict. First the school staff asked parents not to visit children for the first two months. Secondly, missionaries were expected to remain on their mission stations for continuity of the work, and so travel to and fro was discouraged. Stephen was homesick, and this was hard on us as parents. The only contact we had most of the time was a little weekly letter he dictated to an older student until he could write himself. These letters arrived spasmodically, as all our mail did. How grateful we were that our boys were so close in age, as David would be joining his brother a year later.

After the two-month period our schoolboy was allowed home for a long weekend, and so was able to spend time with us and his visiting relatives. This happened to be just a few days before his new little brother arrived.

One of our missionary friends in Ethiopia, Lila Balisky, wrote the following touching poem. We could certainly identify with her.

He's Only Seven
He's home again, my boy, my son
Oh, dear God, he's been gone so long.
Tonight I sat beside him on the bed
While he was sleeping
Just to look and watch,
Thinking of times past and times to come
And cried praises that now – tonight – he's home.
His place at our table makes the family circle full.
The food to cook is more and there are the extra
dirty clothes on the floor
Like it used to be.
He's grown up so much since he left home –
Knows much more of living, knowledge, humour,
Knows you better, too, I sense.
Has grown in confidence,
Strong, but still so young,
To be away from home.
My mother-heart begs that he might stay
But when he's gone we always keep a place his own.
His bed made in his room
So he could come at any time.
But tonight, he's home.
God numbs a mother's heart so while he's gone
We all get used to an empty bed
And it's almost – dare I say it – like he's dead.
What does my boy think to come home again?
And will he go away in peace?
Does it tear his heart these comings and goings
Like it knifes a mother's soul?
God keep him.
Many times again he will come and go,
Always keep him and may he always know
You love him and we love him too.

Keep him in the right way;
Make him strong and tender, brave and true,
Honest, humble, a man like you.
May he KNOW you, God,
That's all I ask.
I give him to you.
Thank you, God, for Hannah,
She gave her son to you;
It's also all that I can do.
And maybe, God, maybe –
You know all about it?
For you sent your only Son away from home,
And He didn't have to go,
But you loved us and we don't have to send ours –
Except that we love you and want others in the world
To know you, too.
God, you turn my tears to joy,
You'll be always with my boy….
But, he's not a man yet, God, or twenty-one;
He's only seven, my little son

The resident doctor at Shashamane was planning to deliver our baby and so we had no worries. But a couple of weeks before the due date he mentioned he was going away for the weekend. Norene tried to tell him our babies had all come early, but he decided to take the risk.

As was our custom on a Sunday night, we met with our missionary colleagues in one of the homes for a singsong and taped message. One of the hymns we sang that night was *When all my labours and trials are o'er….* Norene wrote home as follows:

"As everyone sang this verse and glanced at me they all got the giggles. At midnight my labour did start and one of the nurses, a midwife from England, stepped in and did a good job of delivering our little boy, Philip, after less than two hours of labour. There was no need for a doctor. It turned out to be a real family affair as my Dad kept the wood stove going and made us all a cup of tea before the birth. Then we all had another one after it. Kate, his wife, was in the room as was Bruce during the whole procedure. (When the doctor arrived back a day or two later, with a sheepish grin he asked, 'Would it help if I tied the cord again?')"

What a great time we had during those three months when our wider family were visiting. I was so grateful my parents (72 and 62 respectively) had made the effort of the long sea journey to be with us. My Dad loved to work in our large garden, but the minute he picked up a spade or shovel the Ethiopian workers would rush over and offer to do it for him. Norene's Dad, who had won prizes for his films, made the most of his photographic skills as he shot many reels of 16mm film. These were again useful during our furloughs at home.

41 Wando Valley

Not far from where we lived was the lush, fertile Wando Valley. It was aptly named "The Garden of Eden" and we always took our visitors there. The dirt road passed through an area which was the border between two tribes, the Arsi, and the Sidamo. To the south lived the Goojie tribe. It was truly no man's land, and any male who valued his life would not walk down that road. In those days the Arsi tribesmen still practised the custom of killing a man from another tribe and producing the evidence before they were considered fit for marriage. But travelling by vehicle, as we did, posed no problem.

Princess Tenagnework owned land in this beautiful valley, and early on she asked us to help her develop some of it into a coffee plantation. Ethiopia is famous for its coffee, which has a distinctive, strong flavour and is still the country's main export. For centuries it grew wild before it was discovered to be a valuable cash crop. Farmers would gather the coffee berries from under the trees, dry them in the sun, and sell them. Later on the beans were picked and taken to the local coffee mills before being exported.

Until 1950 coffee was rarely cultivated in a plantation but simply grew wherever the birds would scatter the ripe berries. Things began to change when it was found that conditions in Wando Valley were ideal for coffee cultivation.

The new plantations infused new growth into the whole area. Since they were labour intensive, many people were able to find work. Coffee buyers arrived from Europe, suggesting that washed coffee would be a more favourable method of preparing the beans for sale and would bring a better price. The coffee bean was picked when it was ripe – a deep red colour – and immediately passed through a hulling machine. Then for twenty-four hours the beans were soaked in water and thoroughly washed before being dried on trays in the sun. Once dry they were ready for sale.

During those early days we had some interesting experiences, like the time the men were digging with their hoes between the coffee bushes, to get rid of the long grass, and they disturbed a large python which had obviously lived in the area for a long time. It rose up several feet in the air, ready to strike down the man who was closest to it. Fortunately the workmen surrounded the reptile and were able to kill it with their hoes. They skinned it and found it was almost six meters long, big enough to have easily swallowed a man.

42 Thermal Pools

On the Princess's property we discovered a hot spring which after a few hundred metres ran into a crystal clear, cold water stream.

Wouldn't it be wonderful, I thought, if a thermal pool could be built for people to enjoy in this magnificent setting of tall forest trees?

As mentioned earlier, we sometimes went down to the Valley for a couple of days of R and R, and had built a grass-roofed tukul and a small tin-roofed shed so that we and others could spend the night in this serene tropical setting. The first time we went down it all seemed magical, and we thought we had woken up in paradise. During the night all kinds of sounds echoed from the dense tropical bush in the hills around us. Then as dawn approached, various troops of black and white Colobus monkeys perched in their favourite resting places and greeted the new day with a frog-like croak. As the noise would become deafening there was no chance of our sleeping any longer, and so we had to welcome in the new day too.

Along with the Colobus monkeys were the Vervet monkeys with their chattering noise which grew louder when a leopard approached. To add to the dawn chorus were myriads of bird calls, especially the raucous hornbills with their loud brayings.

Daylight quickly followed dawn, with a slight mist hovering over the forest. We became aware of what appeared to be plumes of steam rising from many different places within the valley. But most appeared to be in areas where the forest was impenetrable. So here we were in the middle of a thermal area which had never been developed.

The next time we met with the Princess and told her of our discovery, she became excited.

"If I provide the finance," she said, "would you be willing to supervise making a pool for me?" This wasn't exactly part of our missionary job description but it was tempting to think how we might spend some of our free time. We organised a good stonemason and before long he and his crew, with a little help with the plumbing, completed the pool which measured four by ten meters, and one metre deep. It was far too hot to swim in the daytime, but in the early morning or the cool of the evening the temperature was perfect.

Talk about God's spoiled children! Often we would be relaxing in the pool and look up to see the monkeys or baboons eyeing us suspiciously. Just before retiring was our favourite swimming time. We had to be sure to take some sort of lamp to show the way and to scare the nocturnal animals. One evening Norene was walking around the edge of the pool, holding the lantern for all to see, when the light temporarily blinded her and she took a fatal step

Hyenas

into the pool, lantern and all. We then had to grope our way up the windy pathway with one wet mother and a ruined lamp.

Not only was it a treat to go swimming in the pool and have a picnic nearby, but the trip down from the leprosarium was often exciting. Most times we would see wild animals in the car lights. In one area, where the hyenas obviously had their den, we could always count on seeing several of these night scavengers. In Amharic the word for hyena is *jib*, so the children aptly named the area "Jib Alley."

Over the years we were privileged to see a variety of wild animals. One early morning we spotted a lioness sitting on the side of the road, and one evening a tawny yellow leopard, temporarily blinded by the car lights, just sat and looked at us for some minutes. Of course the effect of development is that when human beings move into the habitat of wild animals and birds, they quickly disappear for ever. In the 1950s when we first went there it was largely uninhabited, but today, with thousands of people living in this valley, the roaring of lions and coughing of leopards is, sadly, a thing of the past.

43 The Princess's Bear

Princess Tenagnework was happy when she had a holiday home built in the middle of the coffee plantation at Wando.

On one of her visits, she sent a messenger asking if we would join her the following day for the mid-day meal. Our children, except for Philip, were at boarding school so the three of us set off with a few other missionaries to enjoy our meal. We had instructed our young son to be on his best behaviour.

While we were being entertained in the lounge before the meal, Philip showed a particular interest in a large bearskin stretched out on the floor. The mounted head of the bear with its glassy eyes seemed to peer at everyone in the lounge. Philip's interest finally bubbled over as he asked many different questions. The Princess explained to him this skin had been a gift to her from the Indian government. Obviously our little boy's curiosity was not fully satisfied, as we were shortly to find out.

Later we all enjoyed a large variety of dishes of injerra and watt. Some were made with meat and some with vegetables, but all were typically spicy.

The meat in one of the dishes was rather tough and Philip was having trouble chewing it.

In quite a loud voice he said, "Mummy, this must be the *bear's* meat."

44 Midwife with a Difference

Our close Ethiopian colleagues, Mulu and Alemai, were expecting their first baby and wanted a break from the leprosarium, and so we decided to go together to Wando Valley. On our first morning there, Mulu and I decided to be brave hunters and trek up the hills behind us to explore. We left the women in the two tukuls. The bush was unbelievably dense, and much of the time we had to scramble over undergrowth and vines several feet above the floor of the forest. Of course we were so noisy that every animal from miles around fled before we ever reached the top of the hill.

Finally, exhausted, we did reach the summit and were taking a well-earned rest when we were startled to hear cries from the valley below where we had left our womenfolk. Ethiopians have an amazing way of communicating with each other, even over great distances. Although I couldn't understand what was being said, Mulu told me he was urgently needed. He assumed Alemai had gone into labour, but returning was a problem. It had taken us several hours to trek up through the bush and there was no quick way back. Mulu, urged on by the news, fought his way through the bush at such a pace that I begged him to leave me to descend in my own time.

In the meantime, down at the tukuls there was plenty of excitement. After we men had left for our morning hunt, Alemai had sent an urgent message to Norene.

"Please come quickly," she said. "I think my labour must have started."

She had been afraid to tell Mulu as she wasn't sure it was real labour and didn't want to unduly spoil his hike up the mountain.

Norene grabbed her crawling child and hurried across the dirt track to Alemai's tukul, praying all the way it would be a false alarm. Before coming on the holiday, however, she had jokingly asked one of the nurses:

"Just in case Alemai should go into early labour, please tell me what I should do."

"Oh, it's easy," Nurse Peggy had answered. "You just tie the cord in two places and cut it."

They had both laughed, but now reality was setting in.

"Norene, you can deliver my baby, can't you?" Alemai said. "You've had one of your own."

"But Alemai, you don't see your own being born!" she replied.

After a brief examination, Norene was convinced the arrival of the baby was imminent and so asked their worker to rush out and call Mulu who had some medical knowledge. That was the message relayed up the mountain.

Like all babies they come when they are ready, and long before Mulu had reached the "maternity unit" the baby girl had made her appearance. The nurse had advised Norene that the cord needed cutting, but where? And with what? and how quickly? Ever resourceful, Norene ran back to pick up her sewing kit which she had been using just that morning. Sewing thread and small scissors would have to do. With a shaky hand she cut the cord.

Minutes later Mulu came bounding through the door to see the new midwife cradling a beautiful little girl, his first child. Norene had hoped some of the local women would come and take over, but they expected this missionary teacher to know all about delivering babies. How grateful she was to hand over the live baby to the father.

They named her Mezan and she was the first and last baby Norene ever delivered. We met Mezan many times over the years and she always addressed Norene as her "second mother."

The following day, in the early afternoon, the local evangelist rushed over to tell us his wife, too, was in labour. Because there was little progress, he asked if I would drive them to our mission hospital back at the leprosarium. This seemed like a better option than another home delivery, and so off we went. The track was pretty bumpy, but a number of women were in the back of the Landrover cradling our mother-to-be and trying to shield her from the worst of the jars. Halfway up the hill the woman cried out:

"It's coming, it's coming! Please stop!" I was happy to stop, as things were becoming a bit hectic inside our birthing unit. All the passengers piled out and within a few minutes the joy cry went up announcing the birth of another live baby. With everyone on board again, we continued to the hospital for a final checkup.

45 Lake Shala

Camping

We were certainly spoiled with the choice of lakes near Shashamane. There was Awassa to the south and then Shala, Horo and Langano to the north and west of us. In time we tried them all.

We were so busy at the leprosarium that we felt these

little trips away with the family kept us sane.

One year we decided to explore Lake Shala, a unique volcanic salt lake. We had little camping equipment – just one tent between us and sleeping bags for all. (In fact one of our missionaries once said to us, "We seem to have all the equipment, but you people seem to have all the fun!")

At one place a small river flowed into the lake where the water was shallower and less salty. There were shoals of fish and thousands of birds feeding on the fish being swept into the lake. As this was a remote place, for safety's sake we invited another missionary family, the Al Bergens, to join us. Both families had Opel station wagons and four children.

As it was hot down at the lake's edge we decided to camp under some of the many thorn trees, the best ones being across the river. So after lightening our load of people, we crossed successfully. What an idyllic spot for camping! Not a soul was around, the shade was lovely, the river teemed with fish, and swimming in the river was safe. It was an ornithologist's paradise. We set up our spartan campsite and enjoyed the afternoon. The evening was fun too, with a large cheery campfire.

Early next morning I was horrified to notice the river rising, owing to rain back in the hills.

"Abandon camp!" I yelled. "We'll have to cross the river and set up on the other side."

All hands helped dismantle our campsite. Our vehicles were not made to negotiate rivers, but with careful coaching we made it to the other side. Our friends, encouraged by our success, followed us, but then got stuck in the middle. What could we do? The situation was critical, and so we backed our car into the river once more, attached a tow rope, and pulled. At last there was progress, with both vehicles emerging before the rising water level made it impossible. Unfortunately, by the time we were out of the water I realised I had burned out my clutch and could go nowhere.

The enthusiasm of that camping holiday dissipated somewhat as we wondered how we would ever get home to Shashamane. We usually took one of our farm workers with us on such trips, so he could communicate with the locals who spoke the Oromo language. He offered to walk back to the main road (five to seven kilometres) and then catch a bus to the leprosarium and deliver a letter to our tractor driver, asking him to come with a tow rope and pull us back to Shashamane. It worked.

Most of the next day was taken up with a slow tow home. I then had the task of draining the excess water and changing the clutch plate, a first for me.

We had learned a big lesson: on a camping trip in Ethiopia never cross a river, even in the dry season, and expect to be safe. We'd often read to the children the Dr Seuss book *The Bike Lesson*, and so they grabbed the chance to chide their dad saying this was a good lesson for him.

In January 1964 my youngest brother Ken was returning from England after sharing in our brother Ian's wedding. He decided to break his journey in Aden so he could visit us in Ethiopia. That he could come without too much extra expense delighted us. We always wanted to make such visits memorable for our visitors, since their coming required a tremendous effort. I think we achieved that for Ken.

After showing him around the leprosarium, we decided to take him down to Awassa for a short visit. Ken was a keen ornithologist and Lake Awassa was a paradise for hundreds of different species of birds. We borrowed the Brants' three-metre dinghy. One beautiful morning we decided to go for a little trip around the lake and had an enjoyable time. Until we got home. Then we discovered Ken's tent had been slit at the back and all his possessions stolen. This included all the photographs and slides which he had taken on his trip since leaving New Zealand. He had his camera in the boat, so that was safe. What a sad conclusion to his visit with us!

Chapter Four

Highlands of Bale

46 A Move To The Highlands

Our August 1964 newsletter started off this way:

"Goba News. Surely you must have made a mistake, some of you will be saying. Don't you mean *Shashamane* News?"

We had been working in Shashamane for almost ten years and knew it was time to offer for a different type of ministry until our furlough. A Canadian couple, Gordon and Norma Creighton, were capably taking over our work at Shashamane. We were appointed to work in Goba, the capital of the province of Bale (pronounced Barley), east of Addis Ababa, while Australians Bob and Joy Jarman went on furlough. This was considered to be a church planting ministry in the highlands of Ethiopia. We moved on April 15, 1964

What a contrast to Shashamane! We felt we were in the 'sticks' now. We had the company of only two other missionaries living in the second little house on the compound. Marjorie Langford was the Australian nurse and Doris Lacy the American teacher. We proved to be a great team together.

There was a dry weather track which was fine for the old Italian Fiat trucks which lumbered slowly through the mountain pass, and for four-wheel drive vehicles. But since we had no suitable form of transport ourselves, flying was the only means of travel into the province. This was expensive, and the twice-weekly Ethiopian Airlines flight was unreliable because of the unpredictable weather.

Goba was 2,770 metres up (9,000 feet) on the slopes of the Bale Mountains which peak at 4,377 metres (14,225 feet.) Billowing clouds would often descend on the town, hiding the grass runway from the air. Often in the rainy season one could hear the Ethiopian Airlines (EAL) plane flying overhead, searching for a break in the clouds in order to land. But it would have to abort the descent and fly back to Addis Ababa.

47 The Water Tank

As mentioned earlier, the crew of the SS *Otranto* had come to know Norene as "the girl with the tank." Little did we realise this would be one of the most useful items we could have brought to Ethiopia. We set it up at Shashamane, to catch 400 gallons of precious drinking water, and then brought it with us to Goba.

We rebuilt a stand for the tank there and were doubly grateful to Norene's Dad for his kindness in insisting his daughter bring it with her. Goba had a heavy rainfall but there was no way of storing the water apart from a few old 40-gallon drums which were popular with the village thieves. Once the dry season came, we would have to hire a local water carrier who would fill up old four-gallon kerosene tins from the river, tie them to a saddle on the back of a donkey, and bring them up to our compound to fill up the larger drums. We felt pretty secure with our 400-gallon water tank full of rainwater. No one could pinch that. But even that would run out in the dry season.

When it came time for us to leave Goba eventually, we didn't have the heart to disconnect the tank and so we left it for the use of the next missionary family. (Thirty years later when we re-visited Goba we looked outside the back door and there it was – our 400-gallon water tank.)

48 Cows On The Runway

One Tuesday the plane had landed and taken off on schedule, but was not due to return until Sunday. That night four-year-old Becky developed excruciating abdominal pains and our first thought was appendicitis. The missionary nurse was absent from the compound and we desperately needed help. We had no communication at all and the next plane was not due for another five days. How vulnerable we felt! But our heavenly Father was with us. We took Becky into bed with us and spent time praying for relief from her pain. As the new day dawned she was much improved and able to sleep. How we thanked God for healing her.

Steve and David were schoolboys now, needing to fly to and from Bingham Academy, their boarding school. Coming home was exciting for them as the school staff would take them to the airport, see them airborne, and an hour later they would be landing on our grass runway in Goba. There being no fences to protect the runway from trespassing pedestrians and no lawnmowers

Cows on the runway!

to keep the grass down, hundreds of local cattle did a marvellous job. On approaching the airfield the pilot would circle once to give the shepherd boys time to chase their livestock off the runway, and then make a final approach to land. At 9,000 feet (2,779m) when the DC3 came in to land, there weren't many options and we sometimes imagined what might happen if the runway were not completely cleared. What excitement as the plane came to a stop and safely disgorged our two boys.

Of course, going back to school was another story. We were not far from the runway, but when it rained the track to the plane was tricky. Fortunately we had our own transport – three horses. Becky would ride with Norene, Philip with me, and the two schoolboys would ride together. Quite exciting when everything went well. *(See coloured photo)*

The children off to school

The airfield at Goba from where our boys left for school. About 1964

Separation was hard on us all. For the boys it could mean up to five months before they would see us again and for us parents it was heart-wrenching. We often wondered if the school staff might forget to be at the other end to meet our seven- and eight-year-olds.

While in Goba we had problems with thieves breaking into our buildings. In the end, when they started trying to steal our horses, we had to provide our night guard with a gun.

In each mission house where we lived, we had the traditional attic for storing extra goods and our children knew this was always out of bounds for them. Why? Because we kept birthday and Christmas presents up there. On each furlough we would be given extra gifts for our kids and would hide some of them away for the future. How exciting it was to bring them down and wrap them for the special occasions.

Philip riding his homemade Christmas present. 1963

Our Goba Christmas happened to be the fifth one in a row away from New Zealand and our store in the attic was painfully low. We were not sure what we could do about it. We went to the local Arab shop and bought anything we could find, like torches for the older boys, a little car for Philip and some hair ties for Becky. We weren't too excited about these purchases and thought the children might feel the same way.

Outside our home in Goba. 1964

But necessity is the mother of invention. I had brought out a pattern of a rocking horse for such a time as this, and so decided to make that for two-year-old Philip. Then Norene suggested I make a rocking bed for Becky's dolls. But what about the two older boys? How about a kite for them to play with in the Goba wind? We had to search for suitable light wood and finally accomplished that task fairly successfully. Our children were understanding of our predicament and appreciated the hours we spent in preparing for these special personal gifts.

All missionary children seem to have fond memories of pseudo-aunties on the mission field. Our children were no different, having many of these dear single ladies as "aunties" to spoil them. They had several in Shashamane, Goba and Dilla. Aunty Jewel, who was engaged to be married to Warren, was one of their favourites. Jewel asked if Becky and Philip would be flower girl and ring-bearer for her big day. What an honour! Jewel wanted the two of them dressed in traditional Ethiopian clothes, and so we visited the local tailor who was only too grateful for some extra work. *(See coloured photo)*

The wedding was to be at our SIM Rest and Holiday Centre at Bishoftu, one hour's drive from Addis Ababa, and so we arranged to have our two-week holiday at that time. Becky was allowed to come out the night before, but Steve and David were not permitted by the school staff to come to the wedding as they would have missed half a day of school on a Friday afternoon. That was hard for us all to accept!

All went well and Jewel was excited to have her parents and sister visit from the USA to celebrate her big day. She looked like a real jewel, and Becky looked sweet in her Ethiopian dress with a green border which complemented her auburn hair. On her arm she carried a little basket of rose petals to scatter up the aisle. Philip was conscious of the precious rings tacked on to the little lacy white cushion as we had instructed him to be careful with them. During the solemn ceremony he called out loudly, "Mummy, the rings are *still* here!"

After the ceremony Jewel gave them each a thank you gift. Becky opened hers first and was excited to receive a cute Ethiopian doll wearing a dress just like hers. She thanked Jewel and Warren appropriately. Philip then opened his parcel which contained an Ethiopian male doll dressed just like he was. The look of chagrin on his little face was comical.

Going over to the couple he said, "Thank you Aunty Jewel, but I just wish it was a car!"

49 Awakening of the Infant Church

After the hustle and bustle of Shashamane, Goba felt isolated. Nobody turned up. Our Australian missionary colleagues, Bob and Joy Jarman who had worked many years in Goba, left us a great example. Norene still had Becky and Philip at home, with little help in the house. But that didn't stop her from having an active ministry with the women and in the girls' school. Let me quote from our prayer letter written in January 1965:

"Thirty young girls are attending our girls' school here. The academic subjects, up to about standard four, are taught with special emphasis on Bible and handwork. Our aim is to prepare these girls to become better wives and mothers in the future. In Ethiopia most girls are given in marriage, and until the present there have been few Christian girls available to marry the Christian young men. It has been Norene's responsibility to teach Bible and handwork in the school along with her ministry to the women in the area.

"Every year the girls make a knitted garment for themselves, and then a crocheted cloth and a skirt or dress. Becky, five years old, likes nothing better than to sit with these girls, doing her own simple knitting. Lots of helpers are at the ready to fix up her mistakes.

"We have already mentioned to some of you that thirteen girls have come to know the Lord since the school year commenced five months ago. Many are from broken homes, and so this is a real encouragement to us. Norene and one of the Ethiopian teachers have now started a group along CE (Christian Endeavour) lines. This is separate from their daily Bible lesson and the girls are learning to take leadership."

When we arrived in Goba there were about fifteen baptised believers who formed the core of the emerging national church. It was with this little group that I spent much of my time. During the school term, one night a week we would meet together to pray, one night was for Bible study, another was for discussion on church matters, and the fourth was for teaching English to any who desired it. In the rainy season that meant sloshing through a sea of mud in the dark to meet in the various believers' houses.

Up until this time all our church activities had been held on the SIM compound – a situation typical of many small mission stations. This compound consisted of a medical clinic which Marge was in charge of, an elementary school which was Doris's domain, and two small missionary homes. There was also the multipurpose building where the girls' school was held and where the few believers held their Sunday services. The whole compound, which SIM rented from a local landowner and where our four horses grazed, was surrounded by a barbed wire fence and prickly cactus trees.

Since there were signs of political unrest, we deemed it wise for the believers to purchase their own property to build their church somewhere outside the mission compound. This was not an easy task for this small group who were despised by the Orthodox church officials and hated by the Muslims. But eventually the believers were able to buy a small property not far from the mission compound.

Despite limited resources they were able to erect a small building for their Sunday worship. The roof was built with a thin grade of corrugated iron and the mud walls were plastered with a mortar mixture of chopped straw and topsoil. The door and window shutters were made from pit sawn cedar planks. Although the building was quite small, about 75 people could squeeze inside, Ethiopian style.

Postscript: In the end we had to leave for furlough before the official opening, but we departed happy in the knowledge that the believers now had their own place of worship.

50 A Visit to Sof Omar Caves

We were fortunate in that the government office for the whole of the province of Bale was in Goba. The Governor had become a personal friend during our time at Shashamane and had warmly welcomed us to Goba and helped us out whenever we had problems. I was overjoyed when he invited me to join him and his entourage to visit the beautiful caves of Sof Omar. Being a progressive man, he wanted to visit the caves himself in order to ascertain the possibility of opening this remarkable site to the public. His initial plan was to build a tourist hotel and airstrip near the mouth of the caves, where visitors could come for guided tours to see this spectacular sight. I knew this was the chance of a lifetime to see one of Ethiopia's natural wonders.

In a tourist brochure, *Guide to Ethiopia*, by Briggs we read:

"This sixteen-kilometre network of limestone caverns lies 100 kilometres east of the Bale mountains at 1300m. These have been carved by the Web river in its descent from the Bale highlands. They remain an important site of pilgrimage for Ethiopian Muslims."

I had read about these caves, but never dreamed it would be possible to visit them. Being in disputed territory where there was much unrest and bandit activity, it was not safe for small groups of nationals, let alone foreigners, to visit. But travelling with the Governor meant we were accompanied by armed guards.

We drove through to the caves and on arrival the guards jumped out, set up their machine guns and rattled off a few rounds, just to let any *shiftas* (as they are known locally) know they had better keep a low profile or be killed. As we descended towards the caves I was amazed to see the Webeshebele (or Web) river one minute meandering along its riverbed, and then suddenly dive into the caves in front of us. There was a sense of awe, excitement and fear as to what we were going to find. This was the dry season but we all knew that in the wet season this river became a raging torrent and somehow disappeared into the blackness of the caves ahead.

We stopped to light our pressure lamps and with armed guards going before us entered the mouth of the caves. Inside the entrance were hundreds of objects left as offerings by visiting Muslim pilgrims. But did they smell! Normally nobody dared enter into the blackness of the caves and we couldn't blame them. What would we find? It could be a suitable spot for a leopard's lair or a family of hyenas. Even a lion would find shelter there. The entrance stank, not only because of all the decomposing offerings, but also because of the droppings of thousands of bats attached to the roof of the caves. In fact we needed raincoats.

But once inside, we were blown away by the intricacies of the cathedral-like amphitheatres which had been carved out by the raging waters during the rainy season. As if by some master carver, the sandstone had been fashioned into beautiful designs, with over twenty-metre high ceilings. Even the light of our pressure lamps was insufficient to illuminate the vastness of some of these caves. Some were so large that hundreds of men could hide inside and never be noticed. On we pushed, until we were halted from proceeding by a steep bank with the river flowing at the bottom. We realised that without a boat we would never make it through to where the river exited on the other side of the mountain range.

Fortunately our party was willing to trek over the hills to the exit. According to our tourist guide, the river ran underground for about sixteen kilometres. We re-entered the caves at the exit, to take a few coloured pictures to record our visit. Its breathtaking beauty could only be ascribed to our amazing Creator. *(See coloured photo)*

51 Trekking and "Fool's Gold"

I felt like a true pioneer missionary, preparing for my trip into Dello, Angetu and Orborso. Not that I was the first missionary to have ever travelled that way before, as Bob Jarman had made at least one trip into the region. But I was in good company, as Ato Lemma, the local resident evangelist, and two Sidamo evangelists were with me. Lemma was well acquainted with this part of the country, as he told me his father had been a rich slave trader and would often bring slaves from Sidamo via Dello up to the highlands of Goba. Lemma had been wonderfully converted to Christianity and had a great desire to spread the gospel to those who had never heard it. He was our guide and had various contacts along the way.

But first we had to obtain permission to travel to these remote regions. This turned out to be a relatively easy procedure because of our friendship with the Governor.

At the time Bale was considered one of the remotest provinces of Ethiopia, having few all-weather roads and only a few dry-season tracks. The government had established airstrips at various strategic towns and the

Ethiopian Airlines DC3s would make regular trips to these outlying places. At 2,770m (9,000 feet) Goba must surely have been one of the highest airstrips in Ethiopia. Dello, on the other hand, was only 900m (2,925 feet.) Even if the plane took off from Goba it might not be able to land at Dello which was only a few flying minutes away on the other side of the Bale mountains. Flying for those few minutes was scary, for no sooner had the plane taken off than it began to rapidly descend to the dirt airstrip at Dello. Whenever the cloud coverage was too great the trip would be aborted. The Dello airstrip existed to fly out the coffee which grew in abundance in that area. Here again, coffee trees had never been planted or cultivated by man but were growing wild and spread by birds.

The three evangelists and I took off about mid-day Saturday, 30 May 1965, waving goodbye to a rather sad three-some, Norene, Becky and Philip. We could not say exactly when we would be home again. Our luggage was carefully weighed in, as the rule of 20 kilos per person was strictly adhered to. In fact at the last minute we had to reduce our luggage and leave valuable food supplies behind.

The contrast between the high altitude of Goba and the lowlands of Dello was unbelievable. In just a few minutes we were transported from the crisp, rarefied air of the highlands to the hot steamy jungle of Dello, where we quickly shed our warm clothing.

We introduced ourselves to officialdom and registered our presence at the local police station. Everyone was polite, assisting us in every way they could. Since it was a market day we noticed with interest the different ethnic groups. Many Somalis had travelled long distances with their camels, bringing rock salt to trade for coffee and grain. Then there were the Oromos, selling grain, honey and coffee, and the Amharas who ran the government offices and police force. There was little we could buy except for a few local pawpaws and bananas. As we were about to embark on a long trek by mule in the next few days, we realised how limited we were for weight.

A local believer kindly offered us a place in his house to set out our sleeping bags. The evening was the best part of the day, when it seemed the entire population went down to the local river to bathe. A simple evening meal followed. Were we starved! We had eaten nothing apart from a little fruit since we left home early that morning. Our luggage included a battery tape recorder and a series of gospel tapes. After the meal we played one of these to our hosts who were most interested in hearing the message. There was neither electricity nor pressure lamps – just little wick lamps. By nine o'clock everybody had settled down to sleep. Or so we thought.

At midnight the death wail started. We were told two people had died, probably from typhus. This did not encourage sleep. Sunday morning dawned, with hot sweet tea and dry bread plus some sweet bananas. We invited our host and a few of his friends to hear our tapes again. Some were interested and asked many questions. Later we went for a walk through the little village and I was amazed to find wild orange and lime trees growing. The oranges weren't sweet, but the limes were genuine. Wild coffee was growing everywhere, with ripe coffee beans dropping to the ground. Men gathered the beans into baskets and sold them to merchants in the market. I noticed a tree similar to wild plums, but its fruit was hard and sour. While I was enjoying my nature walk, the other members of our party were trying to negotiate a price to hire five mules from Monday morning.

Again it was early to bed and early to rise, as the mules were due at daybreak. What a pathetic bunch of animals finally arrived to transport us and our luggage to the next town! We were quickly assured they were the best mules in the whole town. After much argument we loaded our goods, mounted our beasts and started off at a quick trot. Talk about uncomfortable! In the highlands of Goba we rode horses all the time, but nothing could have prepared my back for this constant thumping. After a while I would get off in desperation and run behind the mules, and then mount again until I could stand it no longer.

Apart from the mule ride, that day must count as one of the highlights of my time in Ethiopia. We passed through a pristine forest with trees towering twenty to thirty metres. The diversity of bird calls and abundance of wild animals gave me the impression we must be passing through the Garden of Eden. At one stage I noticed the mules' hocks were covered in gold dust and for a moment I thought we'd struck a goldmine. I jumped off and carefully scooped up some of the fine dust, carrying it with me for the rest of the trip. Later I was deflated to hear it was just "Fool's Gold." To me it had certainly looked real.

52 Of Bedbugs and Cow Bells

Six hours later we finally arrived at the little village of Angetu, having seen no houses and no people along the way. We were able to rent a filthy little cattle hut to sleep in, but were grateful for some protection from the afternoon sun and the dangers of the night. I was given a slightly raised mud platform to keep me away from the pools of urine from the accompanying cattle. How desperately sore and tired I was from the trip. (Lemma the evangelist had kept urging me on, telling me we were not safe unless we reached the shelter of the village that night.) As darkness fell we gathered together a few people and shared with them the gospel. Finally I fell asleep on my little raised platform.

About nine o'clock I was woken and told to eat. But I rolled over.

"Tomorrow!" I murmured.

What a restless night. Bedbugs nibbled at me constantly, cow bells clanged every time an animal moved, and early in the morning the roosters perched above us started crowing. At any rate everyone was up before daylight and I was grateful to get outside and away from the stench. Norene had packed my food and included some small packets of porridge which I quickly boiled up and ate, not knowing when or where our next meal would come from.

We spent the day contacting people. In the afternoon we wandered down to the river to wash out some of our clothes. While down there a large group of Sidamo women came and started a little fire. We watched in disbelief as we realised these folk had come to offer a sacrifice to the river god, by boiling coffee and pouring it out as an offering. They chanted and danced by the edge of the river before scattering some newly-cut grass on the water. We asked what their problem was, but they were too scared to tell us. Later one of the men told us an entire family of seven had been wiped out with possible typhus and they had come to the river god to beg for mercy and healing.

We returned to the village by 5:30 to be met by a group who had gathered to hear our message on tape. The following hours were spent sitting under the stars, sharing the story of Jesus. Some people became interested and asked if we could send them a teacher. At 10pm we decided it was bed time and wandered back to our little cattle hut. Our five mules had been tethered outside our hut to graze in the cool of the evening, but to our horror we discovered two of them had had their tethers cut and seconds later would have disappeared for good. How we thanked God for his protection as these animals would have cost us much more money than any of us carried.

My three fellow travellers were able to eat the local food made from plantain or false banana, but my stomach had never learnt to tolerate it, and so I went inside the hut and boiled up some water for a packet of soup to sip with my dry bread.

Lemma told us our next town of Orborso was a good twelve hours away. We must arrive there before dark, he said, as there was no overnighting in the bush in that area. So at daylight we loaded our animals and, without stopping for breakfast, headed west. Apart from the discomfort of the mule's bony back, the trip itself was enjoyable and picturesque. Occasionally I would dismount to stretch my cramped legs and to examine some of the fauna I'd never seen before.

One thing we had been able to buy at the Angetu market was sugar cane. By cutting it into fifteen- to twenty-centimetre lengths we could strip the outside layer and chew contentedly for hours to quench our thirst.

As planned, we arrived at Orborso before sunset, grateful to be in the shelter of the village for the night. But where could we go? There were no hotels, motels or boarding houses. I almost wondered if we had entered Sodom or Gomorrah. The young men were drunk, rude and abusive. As darkness fell we finally managed to rent a room. But then two young men started fighting outside and it wasn't until the village chief came along and tied up the men that it was safe for us to enter the building which had just a mud floor and four bare walls. We were famished but couldn't buy any food. Finally we boiled up some sweet tea and with stale bread it seemed to satisfy our hunger. We often thought of the extra food we had to leave behind in Goba because of the weight restraints. Of course no ceilings and only partial walls caused us to hear everything going on in the next room which turned out to be some type of brothel. A sleepless night followed, but nevertheless we were grateful to have reached our destination safely.

The town of Orborso was about as isolated as one could find and we were told it had been a Mecca for hunters. All the large animals such as elephant, lion, buffalo, giraffe and rhino had been found there. We decided we had arrived a few decades too late, for only the smaller animals had survived the onslaught of these hunters.

About 8:30 the following morning an official-looking man poked his head through the window and demanded to know who we were and whether we had permission to be there. He was not pleasant to begin with, but after reading our letter from the Governor of the province, cooled down somewhat and asked us to report to the police station. Once formalities were over and we were duly registered in his book of visitors, we discussed the possibility of the mission working in this area by helping to start a school. He became interested and our relationship improved dramatically. We discussed the best route to get into this area and he suggested that another time we enter from the south, via Negele, which was at least a three-day journey. Land would be available for us and water would be no problem. But without the services of Mission Aviation Fellowship we decided it would be impossible for a missionary family to work there. The three evangelists who were with me agreed that in the meantime a national evangelist could come in and establish a base. This town was the meeting place for several ethnic groups, none of whom had ever heard the good news of Jesus.

On market day many people from various groups were present. Hundreds of Somali men trekked in with their camels, Oromo men brought grain to sell, Goojie men came to trade animals for coffee, and Sidamo people brought produce, chickens and spices to trade. The local Amhara people who, as usual, were the town administrators and policemen, came to buy their weekly supplies. What a volatile mix! No wonder each group was suitably armed. We understood now the need to be safely in this town by nightfall.

We were told a large river lay just to the south of us, and so we made the two hour trek in the afternoon. We washed all our clothes and enjoyed a refreshing bath. On arriving back in the town we were visited by about ten Sidamo men who wanted to know more about our message. Our three evangelists who were travelling with us knew the local language and had no problem sharing it with them.

Again our evening meal consisted only of bread and tea. From the market we managed to buy a scrawny live chicken and decided the following day we would celebrate. The bed bugs were voracious that evening, and thus we spent a restless night. Our two Sidamo evangelists decided it was time to leave us and head back to Sidamo. They had travelled so lightly. For their journey of several days they had nothing apart from their cotton blanket or *garby*. But knowing the local language they were assured God would protect and provide for them on their way home. After a time of prayer and discussion we commended them to the Lord and they left. We never met them again, and so we'll have a lot of catching up to do in heaven.

Our chicken was suitably prepared and boiled.... and boiled..... and boiled. Finally it was declared fit to eat and was put aside for our evening meal. The water in which it had been cooked provided lovely soup for our mid-day meal. We were on our own now, Lemma and I. Our bread was so mouldy I could eat no more or it. There was a real shortage of water and we could buy nothing, for there wasn't a shop in the town.

People kept coming to us, however. In the evening after we'd eaten our rather tough chicken, six more Sidamo men came to hear our tape and learn more about Jesus. They stayed the night and all we had to give them was tea and the mouldy bread. But they appreciated their time with us, even if not the food. Before they left they rededicated their lives to Christ, for they told us they had believed some years before, but had nobody to teach them.

The following days passed quickly, with lots of visitors and many further opportunities to share. On Sunday we had a little service and a number of people attended which encouraged us. The administrator of the town had become quite friendly and that evening invited us to his home for a delicious meal of real food, injerra and watt. What a meal for two starving men!

53 Of Lizard Soup and Home

Sunday night was our last night in that little village. With the hyenas howling outside our door and a distress cry somewhere in the town, we spent another restless night. We were up at five o'clock to pack our mules and be on our way by six. It was good to be heading towards home. I had constantly prayed that the Lord would undertake for Norene, Becky and Philip at home in Goba and for Steve and David at boarding school.

Another twelve hours sitting on an Ethiopian mule's saddle was a marathon, but again it was a great time to enjoy the beauty of God's creation and to marvel at God's goodness in allowing me to make this trip, the results of which will be known only in eternity.

We were about to cross a big river when two of the mules, the ones carrying our supplies and sleeping bags, bolted up the hill with me in close pursuit. First of all my cap was snagged in a low lying branch, and then my shirt was ripped off my back, but there was no stopping lest those mules disappear in the bush. What a chase!

Finally I won the day and the animals were brought under control. We constantly prayed for protection that day as there had been rumours of *shiftas* or bandits along the way. We would have made easy pickings with our animals and no visible protection. We were told later that one notorious *shifta* had been hiding near the path where we travelled, but on seeing the foreigner, let us pass.

It was almost dark by the time we arrived in Dello and unpacked our mules. They needed to graze if we were to continue our homeward journey in the morning. I offered to prepare our evening meal with the last remaining packet of soup Norene had sent along. The water was nicely boiling and I was about to pour in the soup powder when I heard a plop. Asking for a light I was given a burning faggot from the fire. In the dimness I was horrified to see a large floating object in the water. On closer inspection it proved to be a fat lizard which had fallen from the roof. Even although I was craving for some meat, I extravagantly poured water and lizard out and started afresh to make our soup. It tasted good!

There was no problem dropping off to sleep that night. But at 9:30 I was awakened and told the evening meal had been prepared. This proved to be a type of maize meal mixed with unboiled milk and water. Unfortunately it seemed to be riddled with fine particles of stone from the grinding stones and I just couldn't get it down.

During the night it rained, and next morning we discussed our situation. If we dilly-dallied the rivers would rise rapidly and mud would become a major problem. The mules and riders were tired but move we must. We started off at a fast trot (mules can't gallop) and although I begged to slow down, my fellow traveller urged me on. It was a hard ride for me, but we managed to cut our travel time by an hour to Dello. To our great surprise our Goba nurse, Marge, was there conducting a clinic and welcomed us with a "real" cup of tea. Ethiopian friends invited us for the evening meal, but first a bath down in that wonderful warm river water. Good food, clean water and safe travel made us so grateful as we listened to the rain pouring down that night.

Now it was time to make that scary but inspiring trip from the lowlands to the highlands. Would our DC3 arrive? And would it have room for us all? There were many clouds around and although it was reasonably clear where we were, no one could see the mountain peaks. So we waited. Finally we picked up the noise of the plane and before long it was circling our airstrip. Having decided it was safe to land, the pilot swooped down and after only a few minutes on the ground, took off again for Goba. In no time it seemed we were landing in the rarefied air of the Goba airfield. What a welcome Norene, Becky and Philip gave me!

Before we could even contemplate another trip to the lowlands, ethnic fighting broke out and the Somali *shiftas* captured the three towns we had visited with all the people either being killed or fleeing to the highlands. EAL stopped flying and it was not safe to consider travelling even by foot. We never heard precise details, but we believe all the Sidamo people fled back into their own province, with some taking the message of Jesus in their hearts.

54 Yeshi – A Remarkable Woman

Yeshi was born in 1946 in the Bale province and was married at twelve. This is her story:

Weizero Yeshi

"Although I was nominally an Orthodox Christian, I regularly worshipped ten different evil spirits. In 1972 both my husband and I accepted Christ as our Saviour and the evil spirits were cast out of our lives. As a married couple we moved to the town of Goro where we were persecuted by the Orthodox community because of our faith in Jesus. God gave us some lovely children and we were happy as a family. We continued to witness to others and our little group of believers grew to sixteen. We rented a house to use for worship, but during one morning service the building was surrounded by police and we were all marched off to prison. Our place of worship was closed, our domestic animals taken and the new believers scattered.

A year later our youngest child died, but the Orthodox priests would not permit us to bury him in the area consecrated for burials. After much delay and heartache, we secretly buried his body in our backyard in the middle of the night. Shortly afterwards my husband was forced to join the militia and within two weeks he was dead, leaving me with five children and a sixth about to be born. I prayed that my husband's body would never be found, for I knew the authorities would not allow me to bury him in the proper place. Even although other soldiers' bodies were recovered from the woods, his was never found. I cried out to God constantly for help. Many people begged me to turn back to my old ways to gain relief from persecution, but the Lord enabled me to remain faithful to Jesus my Saviour.

The next ten years were difficult as I sought to provide for my children. My only daughter was forced by the Communist Youth Movement to join their organisation where she had to sing Communist slogans, denouncing her Lord and Saviour. She refused and was taken outside and stoned until she was almost dead. Some of my boys also suffered the same fate later on. During these years we worshipped God as a family in our own home and after ten years one or two others secretly came asking if they could join us. Our home was on the main street, directly opposite the police station. We pasted newspaper over all the windows and cracks in the door so that no light could be seen from the outside. About one or two o'clock on Sunday mornings we worshipped together. No singing, no talking, just whispers. Long before the roosters started crowing, people would disappear into the darkness of the night.

Our numbers started growing and in 1989 there were twenty-five attending the worship service. But obviously the officials had their spies out, for one morning, there in the market square, lay two of my precious goats with their throats cut. The warning was ominous. They made it known that those who followed Yeshi's religion would suffer the same fate."

There was no turning back, however. The group decided to appoint three elders, with Yeshi the first to be chosen. A year later some of the new believers wanted to be baptised and after a period of instruction, Yeshi was to baptise them. In the middle of the night a small group left for the nearest river where she had the privilege of baptising those first ten believers in the icy cold water. The whole group continued to believe Romans 8:28 –*And we know that in all things God works for the good of those who love him, who have been called according to his purpose*.

Things changed dramatically with the overthrow of the Marxist government in 1991. The new officials were much more lenient towardsYeshi's new group and they were permitted to rent a property for weekly services. They were even granted an area of land for a cemetery for the believers. Numbers started to grow, and in 1993 two hundred were attending worship.

These reports were hard to believe after all the suffering Yeshi and her family had gone through. Norene and I determined that before we left Ethiopia we would visit this remote area to see for ourselves what wonderful things God had done through the faithful witness of this one woman.

In 1991 when I became Ethiopia Director, many church leaders from all over Ethiopia would come to my office. They would usually seek assistance from SIM to help in the reconstruction of their properties after the devastation caused by the Marxist regime. What a privilege it was to hear some of their stories. In fact I sensed I was listening to the story of the Acts of the Apostle being re-enacted in the 20th century.[1] The only female church leader who came during the four years I was in the office of Director was Yeshi, who came on several occasions and enabled me to write down her story.

After an absence of nearly thirty years, we revisited Goba and the Bale area in 1994. First of all we witnessed the changes to our old station at Goba. In the intervening period a Marxist regime had been in control for seventeen years. Our old home had been appropriated and used as the headquarters of the Communist Youth Movement. We could barely recognise the house, daubed with communist slogans inside and out. That regime had been ousted and the local people wanted the missionaries back. As mentioned previously, our 400-gallon tank was still in use outside our old house. We met up with some believers from the past and heard amazing stories of how God had cared for them through the communist years.

We then made a quick detour to visit the town of Goro, where Weizero Yeshi lived. Her house wasn't hard to find as she had previously told us it was opposite the local police station. We were ushered inside and sensed we were walking into a holy place. Here we were, sitting in the room where for fifteen years worship services had been held each Sunday in the dead of night. Tears came streaming to our eyes as we thought of how Yeshi's husband had been martyred, how her only daughter and some of her sons had been stoned and how her goats had been slaughtered. Under such circumstances would we have remained true to our Saviour? we pondered.

Her windows were still covered with the same old newspaper and her front door remained firmly closed. Truly this was a little taste of heaven for us, as we realised that because of Yeshi's faithfulness, a large number of people from this little town of Goro will also be in heaven.

55 Farewell Goba

Now let us go back to mid-1965. After only fourteen months at Goba, our five-year term had come to an end and we were due to return to New Zealand. It was a real balancing act for us, trying to do what was best for the children's education and what was best for our work. Because our two boys were studying under an American system we considered it wisest to go home in June at the end of their school year, returning a year later for their new school year. Of course that meant it was difficult to place them in the appropriate class in New Zealand, mid-year.

"Wouldn't it be a bonus if we could fly home via Kenya?" I remarked to Norene one day.

On making enquiries we found it would be no more expensive to fly that way, and so our dream of visiting some of the game parks in East Africa seemed to be feasible.

Arriving at the airport all six of us were so excited, until one of the motors on the plane refused to start. What an anticlimax! We then had to spend the night in an Addis Ababa hotel and return at daybreak for a successful take off.

Our first stop in Nairobi was to book a car for our long safari through East Africa. The bigger the car, the more expensive it was, so we decided the six of us could squeeze into a little Volkswagen beetle. Any luggage and food supplies had to go under the bonnet. Philip, under three, fitted in the luggage compartment behind the back seat.

Norene and Becky headed for the Nairobi supermarket and had a great time buying food items, some of which had not been available in Ethiopia. We tried to pay in advance all our accommodation and game park fees, as we were on a strict budget and didn't want to run short of money during our trip.

56 To The Game Parks

Early next morning we headed off to visit our first game park at Amboseli, 250 kilometres away. Immediately we started spotting wild animals– a great sign of things to come.

After entering the gates of the park we travelled another 80 kilometres to our accommodation. We had booked two *bandas* – two-room thatched cottages that were cool and comfortable. We were told the best time to see the wildlife was either late afternoon or early morning. Of course we were all keen to make a start, and so off we went at about 4pm across the dirt tracks which criss-crossed the massive park. We were warned not to depart from them. Hardly had we started when we came across a mother cheetah and her three grown cubs. No doubt pangs of hunger had gripped them and they were out hunting for their evening meal. What a spectacular sight and how exciting! In the distance we could see Mt Kilimanjaro with its snow cap glistening in the setting sun.

Excitement ran high again as we caught sight of three large-tusked bull elephants trudging towards the forests on the slopes of Kilimanjaro. No doubt their position of authority had been usurped by younger males in the herd, leaving these retirees to eke out their own living. They appeared to be quite aggressive and we were grateful we didn't have to compete for the right of way.

One of the herds of Elephants we saw in the Game Park. 1965

The black-maned lion we 'met' in the Game Park. 1965

Most kills take place at night, so the lions, leopards, cheetahs and hyenas are out in force, chasing their prey. What a fun "sleep" we had, as all night long wild animals thundered past our door. The park was vast and most animals would stick to a certain geographical area, and so the next morning we decided to hire a guide to make sure we saw as many animals as possible. His fee was reasonable, but how would we fit him into our little vehicle? Seat belts had not been thought of, but even so it was a tight fit with Norene squeezing in the back with the four kids. To our delight our guide led us to hundreds of animals. A large pride of lions, a herd of elephants, a small herd of cape buffalo, wart hogs, and all the usual grazing animals. By 10:30am the temperature was rising, the animals were retiring to the shade, and we were ready for breakfast.

After a day or two at Amboseli, we moved on to the highlight of our trip, a visit to the famous Ngorongoro Crater in Tanzania. Often we had read about this famous spectacle, where thousands of wild animals congregate in a vast crater. We crossed from Kenya to Tanzania at Arusha and passed through lush country, climbing to 2,300 metres (7,475 feet). After reaching the rim of the Ngorongoro crater, we were delighted to settle into the Crater Forest Lodge for a couple of days. Not only did it have a spectacular view of the crater, 615m (2,000 feet) below, but we also had a most accommodating host. He owned an old Landrover and we were able to hire this and a driver to take us down into the crater the following morning.

I doubt any of us slept much that night as we contemplated the next day's excursion. The crater was vast, at 102 square miles. The pamphlet read, "We guarantee (or your money back) that you will see 10,000 wild animals. This will include all of the big five -- lion, rhino, elephant, hippo and buffalo."

At daybreak we started to wend our way down the mountain track to the floor of the crater. As we drew closer we could see what looked like great herds of domestic animals grazing on the plains, but in fact they were different species of grass-eating wild animals. By mid-day we had seen all the big five, plus our 10,000 quota of wildlife. We could imagine we had been travelling through a huge zoo without any fences. It seemed to us there was a perfect balance enabling each species to maintain its presence in the crater.

But our driver was not ready to go home yet.

"Ngorongoro crater is famous for its black-maned lions," he said, "and I'm determined to search for one today. You're such an appreciative family!"

It took some time, but we all tried to be patient. The grass was quite long in places, restricting our view. Then we saw him! The driver was nearly as excited as we were. Here was this beautiful, sleek black-maned lion gorging himself on a newly killed wildebeest. Driving within a few meters we watched the amazing spectacle of the "king of the jungle" tearing the tough skin and devouring kilos of fresh meat. Obviously his meal hour would extend over a considerable time, so we opened *our* lunch and munched away on our tasty sandwiches. Initially the driver left the motor running, but as time went on it stalled.

Eventually, having gorged himself to bursting point, our hero stretched himself and slowly waddled up the hill to take a well earned siesta. Our children were getting restless, and so we suggested moving on.

The driver just stared at us.

"And who will volunteer to get out to crank the car?" he asked.

We had no idea the starter was broken and the car had to be hand-cranked. Just as he asked the question, we were amazed to see two lionesses suddenly appear out of the long grass seeking their share of the kill. It was another full hour before they had had their fill and moved up the hill to join their mate. Only then did the driver jump out to crank the car.

What an unforgettable day, and how privileged as a family to see this glimpse of God's amazing creation.

And to think that in heaven "the lion and the lamb will lie down together."

57 Tsavo

A day later we crossed back into Kenya and headed to Tsavo National Park. Two memories stand out from that visit. First the large number of lions, and secondly the huge herds of elephants. On our first evening, just as the sun was setting, Steve and David were sitting on the verandah, arguing over how many elephants and zebra they could see. Since there was no fence between us and all the wildlife, we wondered what would happen if the elephants decided to visit us that night. No wonder all the children decided to sleep in our *banda*.

After a trouble-free night, we set off early in the morning to take a few close-up photos of the elephants. We closed in on a herd of at least fifty adults with all their offspring. After taking some lovely shots, we noticed that the guardian of the herd, a massive male with droopy tusks, suddenly decided he'd had enough of these intruders. With ears flapping, his trunk held high in the air and trumpeting at the top of his voice, he charged towards us. Talk about an eye-to-eye encounter! Without a doubt that little VW had never taken off so quickly in all its life. From 0 to 100 mph in seconds! Having safely escaped from the elephant's fury we made it safely back to the camp. We thought we should report the incident to the manager, who listened sympathetically.

"Oh, you were fortunate," he said with a smile. "Last week some tourists, also in a VW like yours, had a similar experience, but couldn't get away in time. The elephant tipped the car onto its side, kneeled on it, crushed it, and then left in disgust, leaving the occupants inside petrified but unharmed."

In our prayer time that evening we had good reason to thank the Lord for his safety and protection.

On our last night at Tsavo, the manager came asking us if we were interested in hiring one of their little boats to watch the elephants coming down for their evening bath and drink. We were enthusiastic, but our budget had been spent and we reluctantly had to turn down the offer. The manager returned a little while later, however, telling us he would take us all at his own expense.

What a sight awaited us as we chugged out about 100m from the shore and waited. Just at sunset the peace was shattered as herd after herd of elephant arrived, squealing and trumpeting as they rushed into the water. They drank gallons, and once their thirst was quenched they playfully squirted one another. After an hour or so they headed back into the forest to give the next herd a turn. Later from our *banda* we could hear the sound all night long of different herds coming and going. By morning there was absolute silence, with no elephant visible anywhere.

Missionary life might have some disadvantages, but there were many advantages, too. I'm sure you'd agree!

58 New Zealand Again

Our return to New Zealand took only a couple of days, compared to the previous boat travel of four weeks.

What an exciting reunion with family and friends! The cousins were most impressed with the older boys' American accents which they had acquired from boarding school. The Howick house we were intending to rent was not available immediately, and so for the first six weeks Nola and Grahame Bond took pity on this homeless Ethiopian family. There were four adults and eight children altogether, and our host and hostess even gave up their own bed.

Our furlough proved to be traumatic in several ways. A few months after we arrived, Norene's older sister Jean (aged 38) who had been like a mother figure to us, went into hospital for unexpected surgery. She appeared to be making a good recovery, but the day she arrived home a blood clot suddenly took her life. Her husband Charles, was left with the care of four young children, aged twelve, eleven, nine and seven. He was devastated, as was Norene and all the other members of the family.

Then, a few weeks later, I was told I would not be able to return to Ethiopia before I had surgery as I had suffered much ill health over the last few years. And so it was that shortly after this bereavement I went into hospital for abdominal surgery. Although the initial surgery seemed to go well, complications set in and it was some months before I was well again. This was a stressful time for Norene, with her concern for me and four young children to manage in a tiny house in Howick. But later on, a larger rented home in the country area near some of our family did wonders for us all.

SIM had recently introduced a new system called "Forty Fellowship" for supporting missionaries. This was based on the system of forty people giving six shillings (60c) a week. In this way a missionary would be fully supported in terms of their transportation to and from their area of service, their daily food, housing requirements, medical needs and administration. This worked well, providing enough people were willing to commit themselves. Of course for a couple this amount had to be doubled, with a smaller sum for each child. The concept was new to the New Zealand Christian public, but friends and family members alike offered to support us. Many of these people became lifelong friends and continued giving to our work until our retirement in 1994.

After a year at home we were well enough to make plans to return to Ethiopia. Our family and friends helped tremendously with preparing our outfits for the next four-year period. Because the four children would all be in boarding school at various stages, many more clothes were required than in the previous years. Howick Baptist Church, our new home church, was also a great encouragement to us during the furlough and in the ensuing years.

Family group about 1966

Chapter Five

Dilla

59 Ethiopia Bound

After a little more than a year at home, August 31, 1966, saw us flying to Sydney where we boarded the Italian passenger liner, *Fairsea*. With that name we were sure to have a great trip, we thought. The children were six years older than they had been on our previous sea voyage (now nine, eight, six and three.) We all looked forward to what we were going to see and do aboard this huge ship.

The first part of our trip was fabulous as we travelled from Sydney to Singapore via the Barrier Reef. From there on the weather deteriorated and our fair sea turned into rough sea. Norene often succumbed to seasickness, feeling quite miserable with the constant rolling of the vessel. But the children quickly gained their sea legs and were all over the boat, to the concern of their parents who were sure at times they must have gone overboard.

Since we were travelling on an Italian shipping line, it was customary to have an early morning Catholic mass in the main lounge on Sunday mornings. But there was no provision for a Protestant service at all. Plucking up courage, we asked the purser if we could hold a Protestant service in the lounge at 11am. We mentioned we were missionaries returning to Ethiopia and would speak about our work there. He granted permission.

Sunday dawned in the middle of the Indian Ocean, with atrocious weather. How many people would come? we wondered. Could we possibly stand upright to conduct the service? Norene was still feeling sick but was determined to do her part. To our surprise, just before 11am the captain and officers, dressed in their smart uniforms, marched in to the lounge in military style and sat in the reserved front rows. Passengers followed until there was standing room only.

We were both dressed in traditional white cotton Ethiopian clothes. Some of what we said must have touched a chord of sympathy in the captain's heart for, at the close of the service, he stood up to thank us and suggested an offering be taken for the Ethiopian missionaries. We were later called to the purser's office and presented with a sizeable cheque to help with our work. Rather ironically, Ethiopia was the country where Italy had been defeated and greatly humiliated at the beginning of the second world war. From that day on we were well known, and many passengers were keen to chat to us and hear more about our work.

On entering the Gulf of Aden, the captain announced we would shortly be seeing the coast of Africa. We passed within 200 meters of the lighthouse and gave the lonely keeper a blast from our siren. All the passengers, eager to see land again, rushed to the port side to catch their first glimpse of Africa. But it looked barren and most uninviting.

A few hours later we reached Aden. Later we were to write in our newsletter:

"As we were the only ones to disembark in such a hot, barren place, the passengers seemed to shake their heads as if to say, 'That poor disillusioned family. Fancy taking those lovely children into such a hostile environment!'"

Little did they know that beyond that barren coastal strip lay the fabulous and fertile country of Ethiopia, where many were in need of both physical and spiritual help.

What a welcome we received in Addis Ababa as our C47 touched down! Flags were flying and the army band was playing. Even a red carpet was rolled out, and a great number of people were waving. But something was different. We were not permitted to taxi to the front of the airport building. Another larger and more prestigious plane was taking centre stage. Out from the terminal building marched none other than President de Gaulle and his entourage, leaving after a state visit. Only after his plane had taken off and the red carpet been rolled up, were we permitted to disembark!

The next day was a sad one for us all. Let me quote from our newsletter which we wrote home at that time:

"Today saw the opening of the mission boarding school for the new year. We were grateful we had arrived just in time for the three older children to start. However, it was not an easy day for any of us, as little Becky (6½), who was entering boarding school for the first time, clung to us tearfully and begged us not to leave her. Her brothers stood by, trying to comfort her and be brave themselves, and yet they were well aware of what the separation would mean.

After all, doesn't the Christian life demand some sacrifice from us all? We often turned to Matthew 10:37: *He that loves son or daughter more than me is not worthy of me.*

God had given us these precious children as gifts, and yet we knew we must not clutch them to ourselves, but rather hold them with an open hand so he could continue to use us in his service. We prayed often that our children would eventually understand and not become bitter because of their parents' commitment to God's work."

When the first short letters arrived from the children a few weeks later we were so touched to read all three had cried under the bed covers for the first few nights until they adjusted again to being separated. Stephen wrote a little later, "You might notice my writing is a bit smudged in some places, but that's because of my tears which are dropping on the page as I write."

How could a parent have a dry eye at such a time?

David wrote, "Often when I am left at the meal table by myself just trying to get the food down somehow, I sit and dream about the wonderful juicy peaches we used to pick from Mr Bridge's orchard in Waiuku. Then it's a bit easier to get the food down."

The boys told us that when they were a little older they would sometimes go (with or without permission) to the local market and buy corn on the cob which they would roast on an outside fire. We're sure they haven't told us all they got up to, though. We hear more snippets as the years go by, and the punishments which ensued.

60 Dilla Bible School

Our assignment was now to Dilla, Gedeo, an area about three hours south of Shashamane (or seven hours from Addis) in the Sidamo Region. We felt privileged to be appointed there. Brief reports about the miraculous events which were taking place in that region had come from friends, Albert and Evelyn Brant, who had first opened the work there in 1949. Back in 1954 Albert had driven me down to the town of Dilla as soon as I had completed my language school studies. A new church was just being born. In fact I attended the first communion service, little realising that twelve years on we would actually be working in this area.

Our good friends, Ken and Shirley Craig from Australia, were now in charge and did all they could to welcome us to the team and settle us into our new ministry. My initial assignment was to teach in the Bible school.

But am I not a trained agriculturalist? I protested inwardly. Isn't that beyond my natural gifting? How will I have all the vocabulary necessary to teach in Amharic?

On the other hand Norene was a born teacher, and her assignment to teach in the women's school was just right for her. With Ken's encouragement I accepted the challenge.

Bible school started just nine days after we arrived at Dilla. Although my health was still causing concern following the previous surgery, I determined with God's help to teach well. This meant studying for many hours. The students were sympathetic to my poor language skills. They understood my predicament as Amharic was not their first language either and they were still learning. They made some terrible faux pas, as I did, but somehow we understood each other.

I remember one such time at an evening meeting. I was praying (as I thought) that God would "bless our hearts" as we met together. Later they rather sheepishly told me I had asked God to bless our thieves tonight. (There was just a slight difference in the vowel sound.)

We and our missionary colleagues made many funny mistakes over the years. One of our rather plump single missionaries, still sitting on her mule after a medical trek, asked her guide (as she thought) to help her down. She had to repeat this several times as he couldn't do anything for laughing. Finally the penny dropped and she realised she was saying, "I want to give birth, I want to give birth!" (This time there was a difference in just one consonant.)

Some months later we wrote:

"Bible School exams have started. Unfortunately, several of the 78 students have been tied up in prison because of false accusations regarding their faith. But the others were able to take their exams and did quite well. Some of the subjects we have been teaching are Genesis, Exodus, Job, John's gospel, Acts and Doctrine. Many of those in Bible School are already in positions of leadership in the church. At this time of year their coffee is ready for picking, and so it is time for a long coffee break. (Like several weeks!)"

61 Some Background

Let us go back some years. We mentioned Cliff and Myrtle Mitchell of New Zealand in chapter 31, under the title *Of Mitchell and Devers*. Early in 1936, because of the unsettled conditions in the country, the missionaries from the three southern stations met at Yerga Alem, to decide what they should do. Myrtle Mitchell and her baby, along with Tom Devers' fiancée and a few others would trek through to Addis Ababa. Allen Smith, another New Zealander, decided to join the Norwegian Red Cross. Within a few months, however, law and order were breaking down everywhere so on 7 May 1936, Cliff and Tom left Yerga Alem with a party of some twenty well-armed Ethiopians to try to reach the capital, Addis Ababa, where their loved ones waited. Tragically they were all massacred two days later.

Thirteen years later, on 2 February 1949, Albert and Evelyn Brant arrived in Dilla, a few miles northeast of where the Mitchells had worked previously. Now a mission station was being established amongst the Derassa people (now known as the Gedeo.) The Brants' story is an amazing one and can be read in the SIM publication, *In the Wake of Martyrs*. Albert and Evelyn were mentors to many younger missionaries like ourselves and used to inspire us with their fascinating stories about their early days in the Dilla area.

Now with all this history behind us, we ourselves were appointed to work among the Gedeo people. During that first year in Dilla I learned as much as possible from Ken Craig, the station head. Dilla was situated on the eastern slopes of the Rift Valley and a more beautiful vista of mountain ranges, covered with highland trees, would be difficult to find. Closer to Dilla the hills were covered with coffee bushes, and these were shaded by different species of large trees such as zigiba (*popcarpus falcatus*), wanza (*cordia abiscinica*) and dogma (*syzygium guineese*). Interspersed among the coffee bushes were bananas, pineapples, pawpaw and many other tropical crops. Interestingly, the early missionaries were the ones who first introduced many of these fruits.

Visit to a Church

62 About The Gedeo Church

What a joy it was to travel with Ken Craig to monthly church meetings with the leaders of the various churches. These meetings were a time of fellowship and sharing, as opposed to the monthly business meetings which were held on the SIM compound. The churches were growing so rapidly that it was hard to keep up with all that was happening. The first church in Gedeo was established in 1950, soon after the Brants arrived there. Five years later the number had grown to seventeen. By 1960 there were twenty-eight. In 1965, shortly before our arrival, there were seventy-four churches, and by the time we left in 1970 the number had grown to more than a hundred.

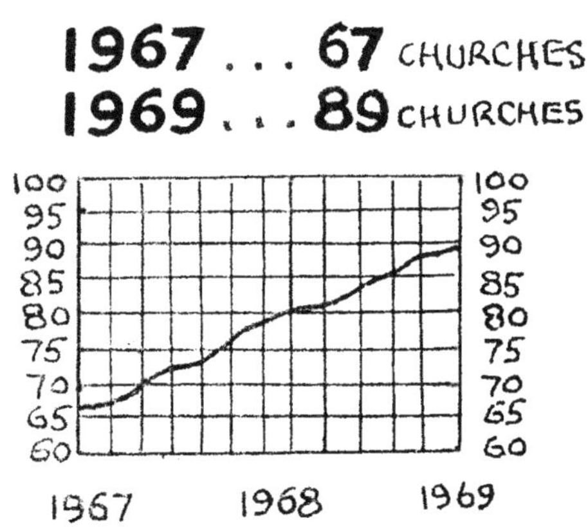

Gedeo Church Growth

The congregations were divided into twelve districts. At our monthly fellowship meetings, only three representatives from each district were permitted to attend, plus the elected executive officers and two missionaries. These district meetings were hosted in turn by each district. Each church was fully autonomous and would choose its own eldership, appointing one of these men to represent them at the district level. Then at the district level three men would be chosen to be their representatives at the monthly fellowship and business meetings.

These monthly fellowship meetings were occasions that Ken and I looked forward to, for it was then we learned what was happening throughout the district. Our mules were our means of transport, which meant we could go up and down the mountain tracks without too much effort. We carried with us our own sleeping bags, some boiled water, a flashlight, our Amharic Bibles, and some TP. On arrival we were welcomed at the gate and our animals taken care of. Having been ushered into a small shelter, we would be seated for the foot washing ceremony (or should I say, the foot *scrubbing* ceremony.) We foreigners had such soft feet compared with those of our Ethiopian brethren, and we'd sometimes have to plead for less rigorous treatment. From there we would be led into the church, which had been generously strewn with freshly-cut grass or banana leaves, to rest with all the other delegates who had received similar treatment.

As the sun went down (about six o'clock all year round) our formal meeting would begin with a time of prayer and singing, followed by district reports. This was a most interesting time as we listened to the reports, both good and bad, of how God had worked in the district during the past month. We used to say it was like reading the book of Acts all over again. as similar miracles seemed to be taking place. Many evil spirits were cast out, witch doctors were dramatically converted, and people were healed from sickness. But along with these blessings Satan's opposition continued to be fierce.

About 10pm the evening meal would be served. Hands were washed Ethiopian-style by water from a jug being poured over the hands into a basin beneath. Then another person would follow with a towel. Once all the guests had washed, a blessing was given and the food served. What a meal it would be! Our hosts would go to so much trouble to prepare the best and tastiest they could afford. As was the custom, everyone was urged to eat plenty. The food was the national dish of injerra and watt which I always found extremely tasty, until some of the local spices reacted adversely on my delicate digestive system as a result of my earlier surgery. Invariably for the next day or two after returning home, I would have some reaction. Strong coffee followed the meal, after which it was time to get some rest before the morning light.

With thirty to forty people stretched out on the floor of one small building, sleep was almost impossible for us foreigners. Long before daybreak someone would start praying aloud and gradually others would take their turn. As dawn was ushered in, there would be a scurry of activity outside as our hosts prepared our breakfast. There was firewood to chop, fires to light, water to collect, coffee to pound and water to heat for washing. Following prayers, the guests would all make their way into the coffee bushes to relieve themselves, and then have a quick wash in preparation for our next session.

This was the time for more formal teaching, and Ken or I would be prepared to share a message from God's word. Breakfast of sweet spiced tea and bread would follow, and again guests were urged to eat well as most of them would possibly not eat again until the evening. Our mules would have been watered and fed and brought round to the front of the church for us to mount and make our way home.

During the four years we were in Dilla we continued this routine, gaining a tremendous appreciation for these diligent people who had mostly become Christians within the last decade. When home from boarding school, our two older boys loved to accompany me to these meetings. The whole experience was an adventure for them, and they, too, craved the local food.

63 Other Ministries

The second main monthly meeting was held on the mission compound, being strictly a business/ finance meeting to which the representatives from the various districts would bring their financial contributions. These gifts would support their own missionaries or evangelists working either in remote areas within the Gedeo province or in other tribal areas.

There was no bank in Dilla at that time and all the cash, which was largely in coins, would be stored in the office of the house where the missionary in charge lived. For our first year this was in Ken and Shirley Craig's home, but after they left we were the custodians of all the cash. It was quite a responsibility! During our four years in Dilla a branch of the Bank of Ethiopia opened and we helped the church establish its own account.

At this monthly business meeting we spent time discussing various church problems and praying together. This was our opportunity, as foreigners, to show hospitality to our Ethiopian friends. At noon we would buy large quantities of Ethiopian bread rolls from a nearby Arab-owned shop and boil up a huge urn of sweet cinnamon tea. A happy and worthwhile day for us all.

Following our first year of teaching in the Bible School, the Craig family left for furlough and we were asked to take on their responsibilities as station head. Peter and Eileen Jenkins, from Australia, were assigned to teach in the Bible School. We had excellent relationships with them also. For most of the time we were a staff of nine missionaries on the Dilla station.

Our ministry was diverse, with a large elementary school headed up by New Zealander Ruth Cremer. A small hospital was established, with a doctor, two missionary nurses and a large Ethiopian staff. This meant we took care of people's physical, mental and spiritual needs. The hospital served a large area, with a number of in-patient beds, and much surgery was also carried out.

The two doctors who worked there with us were Nathan Barlow and Lindsay McClenny.

At one stage Nathan Barlow himself needed an abdominal hernia operation, and decided to use the surgery as a training exercise. He told his medical team to administer a local anaesthetic so he would be wide awake and able to give instructions as they went along. All went well with the operation (there was no key-hole surgery in those days) and the team learned a lot through the procedure. The patient even lived to tell the tale.

As a staff we met together every morning for prayer and discussion before our day's work and each Sunday evening we met for singing, a Bible message, and fellowship over supper. Socially we met together on birthdays and special holidays.

64 A Summons

One afternoon the elders and I had an official summons from the government administrator in Dilla, to appear in his office the next morning to answer charges being made against us. The total population of the Gedeo people at that time was estimated to be about 500,000. The believers numbered between six and seven thousand and were growing rapidly. We wondered what new accusations had been brought against us.

The administrator called us into his office and after the normal greetings began telling us about the unrest that was being caused by this new religion the foreigners had brought to Dilla.

"There is a lot of fighting among the people," he said. "This religion is dividing families and communities."

Because of a whole string of false accusations he ordered us all to stop preaching and teaching and to return to the previous ways. I wondered how we should answer this man who was genuinely seeking to maintain peace in the region. The oldest man in our group, illiterate and almost blind, stood up.

"Sir, are you not aware of the changes the gospel has already brought to our community?" he said. "Those of us who have believed in Jesus have given up our old drunken ways. Before we believed, when we sold our coffee we would go into the drinking houses around the markets and drink until we were drunk. We would fight amongst ourselves and go to the prostitutes. We would go home and beat up our wives and children. Because our money was spent in drinking and at the brothels, we would live in poverty and squalor for the rest of the year. Our kids never went to school, never had any decent clothes, never had much medical help. and our houses were leaking and rotting.

"Now, since accepting this so-called 'new religion,' our way of life has completely changed. Instead of wasting our money as before, we are now able to build good houses with tin roofs. Our children are becoming literate. We're able to go to the clinic for medical help. We are able to dress ourselves in decent clothing, as you can see today. Furthermore, for the first time we now know that God loves us and sent his son, Jesus, to be our Saviour. Our sins have been forgiven and we are children of the heavenly King. There is no way we will ever give up preaching and teaching this new religion. No matter what you do or say to us."

Silence.

God had indeed "used the weak of this world to confound the wise." The governor knew what the old man said was true. Fearing further rebuke, he let us go with a word of caution. We wondered what he said to his superiors after that meeting.

65 Martyred For Christ

Tesfaye was a teacher's delight and an outstanding student. First, because he had an unquenchable desire to learn the Scriptures. Secondly because he was an Amhara, knowing the Amharic language perfectly, compared to most of our students for whom Amharic was a second language. He would ask the right questions and was able to help the teacher out when language problems arose. What an encouragement to me! He would always sit in the front desk and was always alert. Both Norene and I sensed from the beginning the Lord was going to use this young man in some special way in our area.

This was confirmed to us at one of our annual conferences. When an appeal was made for those who would be willing to take the Gospel to unreached people, Tesfaye was one of the first to volunteer.

(We well remember him visiting our home the week of 29 May, 1969. Why? Because this was a sad time for us. I was away on a preaching trip on one of the islands in Lake Margureta when Norene was called to the hospital to answer the only phone on the compound. On a crackly line from New Zealand she was only just able to decipher a message from my brother Grahame. My dear Dad had passed away. Poor Norene had to keep this news between herself and young Philip (six years old) until I arrived home two days later from my trip It was a sad time for us, being so isolated from the rest of our large family.

Our thoughts went back to 1966 when on the way to the airport after our furlough we had visited my Dad in hospital following his stroke, and said our sad farewell. Naturally we wondered if we would meet again on this earth. We had offered at one stage to stay in New Zealand until he improved, but he would have none of it.

"Please return on time," he insisted, "for I know it is God's will for you to be in Ethiopia."

Luke tells us: *Anyone who wants to be my follower must love me more that his own father, mother, and children, etc.* (Living Bible translation.) I loved my Dad so much and had he, himself, been bitter about our returning, perhaps the Lord would have guided us otherwise. We also knew there were other family members who were more than willing to care for him in our absence. So bearing all this in mind, we sensed God wanted us to go ahead however hard the parting was going to be.

As mentioned earlier, my Dad and Mum at age 72 and 62, had both made the long journey by ship to Ethiopia to visit us for six weeks at Shashamane in 1962. They had been most impressed by all they saw and experienced, and both wrote constantly about that visit. So we knew Dad really wanted us to return to our work.

The children loved their grandfather and he seemed to have a special place in his heart for auburn-haired Rebecca whom he called "my little Goldilocks."

After my arrival home from the lake the word got round about my Dad's death and many Ethiopian friends came to comfort us. We followed the local custom of having our doors open from morning until night, serving tea, bread and roasted grain to whoever came. It was normally a three-day mourning period. In fact within a few days 160 people had come to comfort us.)

Tesfaye, our special student and friend, was one of our comforters that day. As Norene chatted quietly to him that day, she felt this would be a good opportunity to write down some of the details of his life's journey so far. This is what he said;

"I was born in the mountains above the town of Dilla, where my father was a wealthy landowner. My parents were Amharas, and so they brought me up in the strict Orthodox faith. My education was at the priest's school, where I studied both Amharic and Ge'ez (the language that all Orthodox priests learn.) After my father died I developed a real longing to know exactly what the Bible taught and finally sold my expensive jacket for seven dollars and bought a Bible. Now I was able to read the truth for myself and after much reading and praying accepted Christ as my Saviour. But my family turned against me, disinheriting me and forcing me to leave home. I wanted to live with an evangelical Christian family, but like Paul in Acts they thought I might be spying on them, and so they turned me away. I became absolutely destitute and was sick for twenty-two days before the believers finally realised my sincerity and accepted me as a fellow believer."

It was after this that God called Tesfaye to enrol in a four-year Bible School course, and during that time both Norene and I had the privilege of teaching this outstanding young man. In his second year of study he again became sick and was diagnosed with hepatitis. He was too sick to study and for two years wandered from church to church, teaching and preaching although he received little money.

"It is only food I worry about," he said. "As long as I have one shirt, a pair of jeans and a pair of running shoes, that is all I need. After all, when they bury me they will take my clothes anyway. I can't take them with me."

It has often been asked why the Orthodox Christians were so opposed to the evangelical believers. Dr Brian Fargher, ex-SIM, has ably answered this question as follows:

"*Theologically* Orthodox Christians really do believe they are the only ones with the true teaching of Jesus. All the rest are heretics. *Historically* they say they were there first and this is their country. *Socially,* in every Orthodox country the church has the authority and maintains some sort of social order. *Politically,* all non-Orthodox in an Orthodox country like Ethiopia consider religion and patriotism as one. So to be a non-Orthodox Christian was an oxymoron; it was like being a traitor. *Ecclesiologically,* in the minds of the Orthodox in Ethiopia, all of the non-Orthodox people were potentially Orthodox and eventually they would be pulled into the church. So when outsiders came along and preached you could be a Christian without being Orthodox, no wonder they got mad!

"Praise the Lord Haile Selassie was there to protect the missionaries. Personally the power of the local priests was undermined. They could no longer exercise control over people through baptism and burial.

"With all this opposition in mind it was nothing less than a miracle that SIM was able to continue a ministry in Ethiopia and establish thousands of churches."

Postscript: The next part of Tesfaye's story was told to us after we left Dilla in 1970. Tesfaye married Kibabush, whose mother was from Goojie land and whose father was from Gedeo. The Gedeo elders assigned him to work down by Lake Margureta amongst the Goojee people. This was a difficult and dangerous assignment. The Goojees were semi-nomadic, living in large areas in southern Ethiopia. They were well known for their custom of killing men from other tribes and bringing the evidence to their future wife in order to prove their manhood. A Goojee wife proudly wears a coin in her ear when her husband attains the status of a murderer.

Despite being aware of the dangers of working among the Goojee, Tesfaye sensed this was where God wanted him to serve. He knew their language well, having married a Goojee wife, and was not afraid to accept his assignment. The couple moved to that area at a time of great unrest in Ethiopia. Tesfaye started a little school for the local Goojee children, and one by one people started to accept this new religion. Before long the new believers had built themselves a place of worship. Fighting then broke out between the government forces and the Goojees, and in the ensuing unrest, Tesfaye was murdered and his body mutilated. The murderer demanded all his possessions from his wife. When this happened their little five-year-old son ran off in terror, but he was quickly caught by the murderer's teenage son, who promptly killed him and mutilated even his little body.

This wicked man tried to kill Kibabush too, but the local Goojee women intervened and she, along with her two little daughters, was saved. For four long weeks the grieving Kibabush tried to hide from view as she struggled to walk back to her own family. Finally, almost delirious from hunger and dehydration, she reached the safety of her own area and was able to notify the believers of her calamity. Peter Jenkins drove down and brought her back–a sad and distraught woman.

We met up with her shortly after this when we returned to Ethiopia in 1976. Kibabush and her two girls were cared for by the Gedeo Church and some years later she was remarried to a Christian man.

We thank God for Tesfaye, who laid down his life in order to bring the gospel to the Goojee tribe. We know he did not die in vain. We believe that the sacrifice of this man's life has become the "seed of the church" for today there are many Googie believers in that area.

66 Baa Baa Black Sheep

A morning church service was held on our Dilla compound only once a month, and so we could go out to the more remote churches on the other Sundays. There were no roads at all, apart from the main south road leading to Kenya. But everywhere there were tracks used by people and animals when going to the markets. When the church we were intending to visit was within reasonable walking distance, we went by foot. Sometimes, though, we would be invited to a more distant church and were advised to travel by mule. Before Philip, our youngest, started boarding school he welcomed the chance to trek into the lush countryside. The area was densely populated with houses, dotted throughout the coffee trees. Bananas, avocados, pawpaws and pineapples were also in plentiful supply. Forming a canopy of shade over the coffee trees were several species of indigenous trees, a marvellous environment for the birds and monkeys.

One Sunday we had been invited to attend a baptismal service about a three-hour hike from our compound. We had left home at 7am, but on arrival at the river were amazed to hear the baptism had been cancelled. The reason? A messenger came running to tell us that two churches had been burned down in the night, and so the members were all out guarding the other churches from destruction. Later on, when things became a little more settled, we attended a service where 130 people were baptised, followed by communion which always took place after a baptism. We were away from home for eleven hours that day, but felt privileged to be in the midst of one of the greatest spiritual movements Ethiopia had yet experienced.

Sundays seemed to be the loneliest day of the week, the day we missed our older children the most. Norene often said she felt this dreadful heartache (an actual pain around the heart) when she thought of the children. So when we were invited out to different churches most Sundays, this took our minds off ourselves and our loss. Usually the church folk would send a guide to make sure we didn't get lost. Philip always had so much energy and would run twice the distance the rest of us did by dashing off along all the little side tracks to investigate. He had a special interest in birds, which has continued until today.

Once we arrived at the round grass-roofed church, special low stools would be arranged at the front of the church for the visitors, whereas most of the rest of the congregation would be sitting on the low forms or grass mats. The services were long, the stools hard, and the Gedeo language still rather foreign to us. My message in Amharic would always be translated again into the Gedeo language. Looking back I don't know how Philip survived, but he was always keen to come with us. Sometimes he would mutter things like, "I wish this old man would stop praying so long."

One particular day I was invited to give the message, after which people brought their prayer requests.

A young couple, whom we had never met, came forward asking us to pray they would have a child. Having been married for a few years they were still childless. Among unbelievers, custom permitted the man to divorce his wife in such circumstances. But with both being Christians, they wanted their marriage to be for life and therefore asked the believers to pray with them in this difficult situation. We all prayed for God's intervention.

A year passed and another invitation came from that same church. After I had spoken, the usual invitation was given. A couple came forward. The wife was draped in her white Ethiopian *netela* (shawl). I did not recognise them.

"You will all remember," said the husband, "that last year we stood in front of you asking for prayer for a baby. God has graciously answered your prayers."

The wife unfolded her *netela* and there, lying in her arms, was a beautiful baby boy.

"This morning we have come to give thanks to God for answering your prayers," the husband continued, "and to dedicate this little boy to the Lord."

He then ran outside and untied a black lamb which he led to the front of the church where his wife was standing.

Philip, on seeing the protesting black lamb, broke out in song:

"Baa baa black sheep, have you any wool?"

Norene and I could hardly contain our laughter, but as the rest of the people didn't understand English, the joke went unnoticed.

"We have only one sheep at home," the husband continued, "and she gave birth to this black lamb, which we have brought as a thank offering to the Lord."

I was then asked to dedicate the child to God.

We will always remember this touching story because of Philip's little ditty, "Baa baa black sheep."

67 "For Such A Time As This..."

Sometimes we do wonder why certain events happen in our lives.

As explained before, we had become close friends with the daughter of the Emperor, Haile Selassie. Princess Tenagnework accepted us for who we were and for the work we were doing in Ethiopia.

I suspect that many times Queen Esther, a Jewess, must have wondered why she had been chosen to be the wife of King Ahasuerus. We know from reading the story in the book of Esther that the King appointed Haman as his Prime Minister. Haman used his position to seek to destroy all the Jews who were living in the Media-Persia empire. He almost got away with it, except he hadn't reckoned on God being in control to protect the Jewish people. Esther's uncle alerted her as to what was about to take place and told her she must act on behalf of her people or they would all be destroyed.

Esther, although Queen, did not have access into the King's presence as a matter of right and told her uncle so. He sent back word to her saying, "Who knows whether you are come to the kingdom for such a time as this?"

Esther learned that day one of the reasons why God had brought her into the palace. The events that followed caused the reversal of the decree to annihilate all the Jews.

Why do I mention this story? There seemed to be a parallel for us in the Gedeo area. From time to time terrible persecution would break out amongst the new Gedeo believers. This was mainly instigated by the Amhara landlords and the Orthodox coptic priests. They did not want the Gedeo people to hear the gospel or to be educated, as this would loosen their power over those who were virtually their serfs.

One day the church elders came, asking us to pray for them as they went to Addis Ababa to try to have a decree reversed. This decree stated that 27 of their churches were to be closed. The church buildings were used for both worship on Sundays and school classes from Monday to Friday. The closures had happened as a result of false accusations, and so the elders tried to see the "landlord" who lived in Addis Ababa. After a month they returned without having been able even to get through the gates.

They shared their frustration and sorrow with us as all the churches remained tightly closed and the pupils learning in the church schools were not able to continue their education.

"Mr Bond," they said, "we understand you know our landlord well. Therefore we believe you should go to Addis and plead on our behalf."

I was flabbergasted when they told me their landlord was none other than our dear friend, Princess Tenagnework, the daughter of Emperor Haile Selassie.

I reminded them our mission did not normally become involved in political matters. Furthermore, I secretly didn't want to spoil our friendship with the Princess by bringing up a hot political issue. But the elders reprimanded me by suggesting that perhaps, just perhaps, like Queen Esther who had been appointed Queen for saving the Jewish people, God had brought me to Gedeo to intercede with the Princess for such a time as this.

"Aren't you aware of the suffering so many of the new believers are facing," they asked me, "and aren't you willing to share in their suffering?"

What a rebuke to my pride! What a lack of faith and trust on my part. And so I agreed to go.

First, though, I made two requests:

"Please ask the elders to call the believers to set aside time for specific prayer, and please choose three elders who can accompany me to Addis."

By now we had our own car, and so I decided to drive the seven hours up to the capital with the three elders. We arrived in the late afternoon, not knowing just how long we would have to remain in Addis while we sought an appointment to see the Princess. I phoned Her Highness's office and her secretary answered. Amazingly he returned to say, "The Princess will see you tomorrow morning at 9am."

Once I shared the news with my friends they were overjoyed. We all spent a sleepless night, praying and wondering what Her Highness would do and say.

The next morning we arrived some minutes before our appointment. The armed guards at the gate had been advised of our coming, and so ushered us into the car park. No sooner had we stopped, when a servant came running out.

"Mr Bond, come immediately," he said. "The Princess is waiting to see you."

With Ethiopian royalty there was a considerable amount of protocol and I had carefully rehearsed in my mind how and when I should bow and how I would introduce my subject. On entering the spacious, regal-looking lounge where Her Highness was sitting, I was surprised to hear her say:

"Mr Bond, what is wrong? Why are you looking so sad?"

Startled, I forgot all the diplomacy with which I was to introduce my problem.

"Your Highness, many of our churches on your land in Dilla have been closed," I blurted. "People are not permitted to worship and all the school children are not able to learn."

The Princess immediately challenged me.

"By whose authority has all of this happened?" she asked.

"By yours, your Highness," I quietly replied. "I have brought with me three Gedeo elders who will testify to you regarding this edict"

Immediately she clapped her hands together (an Ethiopian custom to call somebody) and her secretary came running.

"Fetch those three men from Mr Bond's vehicle," she said. "I need to talk to them."

They arrived and politely bowed and stood waiting, wondering what was going to happen. The Princess questioned them at length, and then asked for proof as to the truth of the accusations.

"We brought the letter regarding this edict," they said, "and it is signed by your Highness."

Again she called her private secretary, who was the one responsible for all her properties scattered throughout Ethiopia. I had met the man before, under different circumstances, and knew he was anti- mission and anti- evangelical believers. He scowled at me when he walked in and was absolutely disgusted when he saw the three Gedeo elders, whom he considered as dirt. The Princess waved the letter at him.

"Who signed this?" she asked.

Lowering his gaze, he confessed "I did."

She then proceeded to reprimand him before dismissing him from the room. She looked at us and apologised for causing us so much trouble.

"Go home," she said. "Within seven days another letter will be sent, rescinding the previous orders and giving full permission to worship and to reopen the schools."

We could hardly contain our excitement as we realised God had so miraculously answered the prayers of his people.

In seven days time we received the promised letter, the churches were reopened, and the schools recommenced their classes. On reflection, we began to understand why the Lord had allowed us to have such a good relationship with the most influential woman in Ethiopia "for such a time as this."

68 Malaria Control

Malaria was endemic in the Dilla area, and so we regularly took prophylactic pills to keep us free from the dreaded disease. In our houses we either slept under mosquito nets or covered our open windows with mosquito screens. But as for the nationals it was not so easy to protect themselves, as prophylactic medicine was not always available or was too expensive, and they had no way of keeping the malaria-carrying mosquitoes out of their houses. Many did build up some resistance to malaria, although a great number suffered from recurring bouts and some died.

The government initiated a malaria control programme which was funded by the World Health Organisation. This consisted of teams going around the countryside spraying DDT on the inside walls of buildings every six months. After an area had been thus treated the incidence of malaria would be greatly reduced for a few months.

For some years we had been travelling to Gedicho Island on Lake Margureta, about thirty kilometres away, to seek ways to help the people with their needs. After much effort a small school had been established, and many of the children were becoming literate. A national evangelist from Dilla was their teacher. His assignment was difficult, as he had to learn the island language and adapt to a totally different culture and environment. Furthermore, most times when we visited him he would be either sick with malaria or recovering from a bout of it.

"Please," he pleaded, "can't you do something to help the people with this terrible scourge?"

We were determined to do something, and so began to make plans.

Dr Nathan and Doris Barlow had now joined our staff and were keen to

Malaria control

use their medical expertise to help not only the local people but also those from more remote areas who had no help whatsoever. They were willing to join me on a combined venture of malaria control for the island population of Gedicho.

The government authorities in charge of the malaria control programme for the district told us they had no plans in the near future to help these people, but gave us their blessing to help as much as we could.

I was always loath to tell a rather lonely Philip that I was planning another trip away, as he always loved to accompany me. But this was certainly not the trip for a six-year-old with lots of energy. So he had to make his own fun. He was quite an organiser and loved to call his little Ethiopian friends to a "feast." He'd go with a worker to the nearby Arab shop and buy a few local buns and a few boiled sweets. Then he'd ask his mother to make up some sweet spiced tea, cut some bananas off the bunch hanging in our back verandah, set up the table tennis table under the huge ficus tree, and hey presto! A feast was ready for his gang of Ethiopian friends. (One of these friends, Worku, still keeps in touch to this day [2004.] He's a keen believer in the Lord, a trained physiotherapist, and is married with three children.)

But to get back to our trip. We bought 600 pounds of DDT, a spraying machine, and enough anti-malaria pills for all the people. Together with our food and drinking water for four days, plus a couple of mosquito-proof tents, we waited for our hired Landrover to arrive. Finally the Italian owner and driver chugged up to our compound in a decrepit vehicle which they assured us was reliable and safe. We had no option, and so crammed in with all our luggage. Nathan and Doris sat in the front with the Italian driver, while I was in the back with the car "mechanic," sitting on the cartons of DDT.

"Hope to be back in four day's time!" I called out as we were leaving.

"Don't let the crocodiles bite off your toes in those balsa boats!" Philip called back.

Although only a fifty-kilometre trip, it took us ten hours to reach the lake's edge. This included a three-hour delay beside one river while we waited for the water level to go down.

Finding reliable transport to cross to Gedicho Island was a real drama. Our own motor for our twelve-foot dinghy had broken down and we were waiting for parts to arrive from the USA. We therefore had to rely on the island people coming across in their boats to the local market to take us and our baggage over. Just imagine travelling two or three kilometres in crocodile infested waters, in a boat made out of balsa wood. I suspect "boat" is the wrong term to use for these crafts which were simply basla sapplings lashed together and shaped in such a way that the bow protruded high out of the water. The stern was open and the heavier the load, the further it settled into the water.

The rafts were cleverly constructed, but unfortunately didn't last long before they became water logged. They were propelled not by paddling or poling, but by a plonking action, whereby a solid chunk of balsa wood attached to a long pole would be thrust into the water as far as it would go and pushed backwards. Progress was slow. It was exciting and scary at the same time and we were relieved to make it safely to the island, having passed several large menacing crocodiles eyeing us suspiciously.

69 Gedicho Island

Our Dilla evangelist gave us a great welcome and introduced us to the chief to whom we explained how we would help them. We discovered there were three distinct villages, each with slightly different customs although all spoke the same language. The malaria control people had asked us to record the number of houses on the island and the number of people we would treat. Everyone received us joyfully, agreeing to have the walls of their houses sprayed with DDT as we had been instructed to do. When it was discovered Nathan Barlow was a medical doctor and would treat any who were sick, they came out of their huts in their dozens as they had never had a doctor on the island before.

Soon we were to discover there were only two who opposed our coming and would not allow us into their huts. They wouldn't take any of the prophylactic medicine either. These were the two local witch doctors.

"Why would we take your medicine?" one of them said to us. "We have our own medicine which is much more powerful than yours."

But still many people had died.

We gave anti-malaria pills to an estimated 1000 people who were living in these three villages. In the smallest of these lived the renowned hippopotamus eaters. There was no mistaking their houses, for the whole village exuded a stench of drying meat. (At least to us it did.) Some time later we had the opportunity to witness part of their hunt for this delicacy. All the men of the village travelled in their balsa wood rafts to where the Bilatey river flowed out into Lake Margureta. At this confluence, a huge delta of some kilometres had formed where large balsa trees were growing. There were a few narrow channels of open water where the hunters were able to manoeuvre their rafts to shoot the hippos. After a couple of days the bloated carcasses would float and were dragged out into the open water and eventually onto the shore of the lake. Then the hunters cut the meat off into long thin strips to dry under the scorching sun. At night they would light fires around their drying meat to keep away lions and hyenas.

By our fourth day on the island we were more than ready to return home, what with our spartan meals, our constant fighting with feasting mosquitoes, and our restless nights. We had had many opportunities to share God's message, but always received the same reply:

"We'll think about what you've told us and tell you tomorrow."

We felt sad about leaving our evangelist on his own and realised anew the sacrifices some of our national missionaries made in seeking to reach these isolated tribes. Some years after we had left Dilla we heard that a number of these people had become believers.

Our trip home was something to be remembered. The Landrover spluttered to a stop at least ten times. Then our travelling "mechanic" would get out each time and dismantle the carburettor. The fuel line would be blocked, and so he would take a mouthful of fuel and squirt it out expertly through his lips into the carburettor and off we would go. Finally the fuel tank was abandoned altogether, and a can of fuel was placed on the roof rack to feed the motor by gravity. There was no hand-brake and the foot-brake hardly worked. No starter, but the crank worked fine. The oil all ran out of the front differential, and so we chugged home on the back drive. In muddy places it was a case of all passengers out to push.

Many times we thought we were stuck for the night, but amazingly we arrived home at 11pm to a wonderful welcome and sumptuous meal. Our Italian driver and Ethiopian mechanic were so proud they had made the trip safely. So were we. But between the mission compound and the town of Dilla (about two kilometres) they were forced to abandon the vehicle with a third flat tire.

Enough was enough. They went on home by foot.

70 Their First Visit To Dilla

I was driving our three older children home for their first visit to Dilla for a three-week Christmas break. After stocking up on essentials in Addis, I arrived at their school and was met by three excited children. A long, dusty trip of seven or eight hours lay in front of us. The children had often travelled the first 240 kilometers to Shashamane, but for the next three-hour journey they were entering new territory.

The region of Sidamo was lush and heavily populated. Coffee, bananas, sugar cane, sour oranges and pineapples could all be bought from roadside vendors. They would rush out of their houses, waving their wares and hoping to make a sale. Of course if we stopped then the haggling started until a price was agreed upon. Sometimes no agreement could be reached and so we would start to drive off. But not wanting to miss out on a sale, the vendor would dramatically drop the price.

Seeing the children were not permitted to leave until after lunch, we couldn't make it all the way to Dilla in daylight hours. After dark we stayed alert, looking for the eyes of wild animals which would show up in the light of the car, and they became experts in recognising animals by their eye colouring.

Finally we could see the lights of Dilla town twinkling in the distance. What an exciting moment for the children arriving in the dark (there was no electricity yet on the mission compound), meeting Mum and Philip, and then running outside with a pressure lamp to check on all the pets.

Did I say pets? Yes, there were lots of pigeons, chickens, a pet deer, a tortoise and the family mule. I guess we could have expected to have at least one vet in the family, and David would fulfil that role in the future.

Early next morning they would all be up exploring the compound with their slingshots slung around their necks. The boys had made these at school and were permitted to kill one type of bird, the "mouse" bird, which tore to shreds any living plant in the vegetable garden and every ripening fruit in the orchard. These mouse birds were experts at eating mangoes, pawpaw, custard apples, guavas, and even had a go at the ripe pineapples The boys were compensated for every mouse bird destroyed, and they carved notches on the handle of their slingshots to denote the number shot. However the more they shot, the more others seemed to arrive, until finally we gave up trying to grow a decent vegetable garden.

At night during the mango season we would take our torches and watch the fruit bats devastate our ripe mangoes. It was a struggle, but somehow we managed to harvest a share of the crop as well.

A little airstrip had been built close to the compound at Dilla where MAF could land their Cessna planes. One day we noticed a dead donkey lying on the airstrip. Dead animals were never buried as our nocturnal rubbish cleaners would do the job for us. We promised the children we would drive down to the airstrip about 9pm to see if any *jibs* (hyenas) had started their clean-up job. The airstrip was alive with hyenas fighting between themselves over the last morsels. Where did they all come from? we wondered. Nothing was left. Even the skeleton had been ripped apart and taken away. We shuddered when we thought what would happen to a lone human being, walking at night. We'd heard some gory stories at times. No wonder when darkness falls in Ethiopia, outside activities cease.

Steve and Dave after the Mouse Birds

71 A Brush With Death

Steve had suffered many times with throat infections and tonsillitis, and so our SIM doctor convinced us his tonsils should come out. He said he would operate in our local hospital if we gave permission. We asked eleven-year-old Steve what he thought.

"Sure," he answered bravely, "providing you, Dad, will come with me into the theatre."

This was arranged during the holidays.

Everything was duly prepared and Steve and I went into the operating room where he was put to sleep. When the doctor was putting in the mouthpiece and administering the ether something went wrong with the procedure and Steve suddenly stopped breathing. Things became desperate. The doctor tore off his face mask and immediately started mouth to mouth resuscitation. It was really touch and go as the minutes ticked by with Steve turning a distinct shade of blue before starting to breathe again. After some time the doctor decided to continue with the surgery (although I wanted to pick up my son and flee from the hospital). One of the nurses told us later it took about 45 minutes for Steve's breathing to return completely to normal.

Even as I write this story, some 36 years later, I have a panicky feeling, wondering if we made a mistake having surgery in this bush hospital with less equipment on hand. I know our doctor friend felt badly, and we were all conscious the Lord was watching over us and saved us from tragedy.

Many of our missionary friends were not spared the tragedy of losing a child, as we were that day. We also knew Steve had been spared for a special purpose.

Norene tells her side of the story.

"While Steve was in the hospital I had a definite urge to call the other three children and we prayed for him again on the steps outside our home. We had all prayed in the morning, of course, but this was a strong urge from God to pray again at that moment."

72 "I'm Going Fishing"

So said Peter Jenkins, our co-worker. Even from his youth in Australia Peter had loved to fish, and so he and I formed a good team. On many evenings from our mission station at Dilla we would watch the sun setting over beautiful Lake Margureta and promise each other that one day we'd organise a fishing trip.

Real fish stories abounded about huge Nile perch inhabiting those waters. "Bigger than a donkey," one man said. We'd never seen a Nile perch, but one day a fisherman brought us a single scale which they claimed was from a perch. This fired up our imagination and we resolved to prove for ourselves exactly what did swim in those waters.

And so a trip to Lake Margureta began to be hatched. The government was pushing tourism at great expense and had bought a ferry which could carry a couple of hundred people plus several vehicles. The ferry was assembled on the far side of the lake at Araba Minch. Once it was launched, a daily crossing was inaugurated from Araba Minch to Lante which was the nearest point to Dilla. In order to make the connection, the dirt road was now graded right to the lake's edge. This meant we could now drive down to the lake in just one hour. What a bonus for us fishermen!

Once at the lake's edge, there was the problem of finding clear water where we could throw out a line. The shoreline of the lake was shallow for about a hundred meters, where a dense mat of reeds and water grasses grew. It was an ideal habitat for the hippos to feed and for crocodiles to lie in wait. We had loaded our dinghy onto the roof rack of the Landrover to make sure we could get our lines out into the deeper water where we suspected the perch would lurk.

Our greatest problem was not the hippos or the hundreds of monster crocodiles basking in the sun, but the millions of mosquitoes waiting to bite any warm-blooded creature that ventured into their domain, particularly at daybreak or sundown. So the area was uninhabited except in the middle of the day when the Goojees would drive large herds of animals down to the lake for water. At dusk their hum sounded like swarming bees, and so a mosquito-proof tent was our number one priority.

We spent a sleepless night with lots of animals prowling around us, but dared not go out of the tent knowing the mosquitoes were waiting. A quick breakfast and we were ready.

We had read previously that the best way to hook Nile perch was to use live bait. We were prepared with a small drag net and fishing rods. Nobody was keen to take the far end of the drag net. (I wonder why?) Once the sun had warmed the shallow water and the mosquitoes had retired for the day, we started catching some tilapia, the ideal bait fish. Excitedly we baited our lines, rowed out to deeper water, dropped the lines over the side and came back with the ends of our lines. Taking no chances, we tied these to something solid on the shore and waited.

It happened about mid-day. One of our floats went mad. Obviously one of our bait fish was being chased and then there was a huge splash and one line went taut. Peter was given the honour of trying to land our first catch of the day. It was exciting as the Nile perch, similar to some game fish like marlin, leapt into the air, attempting to throw the hook. We saw that beautiful silvery flash and knew immediately we had hooked the real thing. It took a while to reel in, and as it got close to the shore, Peter made a dash into the water, all fear of crocodiles gone, and carried the fish to dry land. Success at last. How many years had we planned and dreamed of catching a Nile perch!

We weighed it as best we could and discovered it was a disappointing 20 pounds – just a baby. But where there were babies, there were sure to be adult fish. Our first priority was to get the fish back into the water to keep it breathing. We had no way of keeping it cool, and in that temperature we knew it would only last for a short time. We had brought with us a collapsible wire netting cage which we assembled and tied in the water, knowing that any fish we caught would be safe from the crocodiles. As the sun heated up, the number of strikes increased. Sometimes the perch were able to throw the hooks, but by late afternoon we had all had the thrill of landing at least one fish. And the size greatly increased with each fish caught. The last fish of the day was absolutely huge – well over 100 pounds and two of us could hardly lift it. As our cage was full, we needed to make a dash for home before some of our catch deteriorated. We pulled down the tent, gutted our fish, and after securing them on top of the roof rack under the dinghy, headed for home.

Phil and Mark weighing the big Nile Perch

73 A Mother's Dilemmas

Norene writes:

After all these years I still have nightmares remembering the many times we had to say our goodbyes to our children. We used to say to people we made no sacrifices worth talking about other than the sacrifice of leaving our children in boarding school in Ethiopia or leaving them in New Zealand when we returned to Ethiopia.

On furlough when I mentioned these experiences, women would sometimes say to me, "Oh, I could *never* do that. I could never send my children so far away to boarding school."

I used to answer, "No, neither could I, but for the grace of God."

I could not have been more sensitive about this issue, and yet God continually assured us we were in the centre of his will and making this sacrifice for his sake. Each time we drove out of the school driveway, leaving a child sobbing, was emotionally excruciating. At times like this God seemed to say, "I have given you these children as a gift. Please don't clasp them to yourself selfishly, but hold them up to me on an open palm."

Several episodes stand out in my memory. Stevie (as we called him when he was small) had just started school a few weeks earlier when we went to Addis to farewell my Dad and his wife, Kate, after they had been visiting us. We took Stevie out for the weekend at SIM headquarters and when taking him back, he was extremely upset. We left the following morning with heavy hearts to return to our work at Shashamane.

Another time I remember was the morning Bruce left with the two boys when David was entering school for the first time at five and a half. As mentioned earlier, children entered school after their sixth birthday but our boys were permitted to start earlier because of the New Zealand system.

My heart was in an absolute turmoil that morning. Where else could I turn for comfort but to my normal Bible reading of the morning? The passage

Life in the Dorm at Bingham Academy (our sons David and Steve on top bunks) about 1970

for the day was Mark 4:35-41. Yes, it was the story of the storm on the lake. I was definitely in a rocking boat that morning. I felt like the disciples when they asked Jesus saying, "Lord, don't you even care that we are (I am) drowning in (my) our sorrow?"

Jesus arose from sleeping and calmly said, "Peace be still."

The Living Bible says in verse 40, "Why were you so fearful? Don't you even have confidence in me?"

The Lord did calm my heart that day, but I have to admit the storm often blew up again on my lake.

David wrote one time, "Steve and I sometimes get into bed with each other when we're homesick. One night the dorm supervisor, who was strict, came in and found us in the bottom bunk together. We saw him coming so decided to pretend we were praying. We prayed for every relative and cousin we could think of, opening our eyes from time to time to see if he'd gone. The trouble was, Mr Reimer was determined to stand there and hear us out. Near the end some of our relatives were imaginary ones."

Bruce and I both needed to assure each other from time to time that God had definitely called us to be missionaries and that we must accept this separation as part of the job. In those days there was no alternative. The mission rule was that all children attended boarding school and there was no homeschooling.

One evening when missionaries came from Addis Ababa and were having dinner with us (or "supper" as the Americans called it) they waited until we had all eaten before giving us the bad news. David had broken his leg in two places above the ankle – our poor little boy who had been in school only a few weeks. We were heartbroken and of course wanted to leave immediately to see him. The couple who broke the news said they also had word from SIM that we were not to travel up to see David as I, Norene, would be going up to Addis for a school board meeting in ten days' time and I should wait until then.

How does anyone expect parents to go to bed and sleep at night when their dear little boy needs them? We found this a tremendous trial, but in those days one did not travel around without permission. What an eternity those ten days seemed!

Later David explained what had happened. He was in a little cave in the playground when some girls were rolling rocks down a hill. He evidently ran out at the wrong moment and a large rock hit him with force above the ankle.

Becky was the one who showed her homesickness even more than the boys. Because of furlough, she was six and a half before starting at Bingham Academy in grade two. For the first year she was upset every time we left her, but after that she had a teacher whom she loved dearly and who understood her difficulties, and so things were a little easier for her and for us. Sometimes we had special permission to have her home for extra time so we could help her with her school work. We were also given special permission to teach Philip for his first year at home as the staff were becoming a little more lenient about homeschooling.

Becky often suffered from car sickness and always longed for tomato sandwiches when she travelled long distances. At one stage we had grown a few little tomatoes in our garden and tended them carefully so there would be a few for sandwiches when the children returned to school. We made the sandwiches from our home-made bread and had them sitting on the bench.

After the children and their Dad had left, Philip and I went inside and what did we find? You guessed it. Those precious little sandwiches were still sitting there. What kind of a mother was I to forget to put them in with the lunch? All I could do was pray that God would care for Becky on the way and help her when she realised the sandwiches were missing.

I had to wait many weeks before I heard the outcome, as their school letters were pitifully short and simple. When she came home again she said, "Mummy, do you remember when my sandwiches were left behind that day? I was so sad when I saw they were missing, but just at that moment the McClennys' car drove up and when they took out their lunch to eat with us, 'Aunty' Marion opened the tupperware and said to me, 'Becky, would you like a tomato sandwich?' She didn't ask anyone else – just me – so I knew God was looking after me."

My loneliest days, of course, were when Bruce also had to be away from home for two to three weeks at a time. The Lord graciously brought to us a winsome young teenager named Tirunesh who became like a daughter to me while helping me in the home. What a blessing she was. She later married a young man who also worked for the missionaries and they are ably bringing up a family of seven in the Christian faith.

74 The 'Bug' Bookshop

Seventy-six churches had now been established amongst the Gedeo people and on Sunday morning the church bells echoed throughout the hills and valleys, calling people to worship. For most people the time of the day was determined by the position of the sun, as only some adults could afford a wrist watch. But each church had its own bell. In fact it was our task to buy old brake drums from the markets in Addis Ababa and bring them down to Dilla for those building new churches. We could count the approximate number of churches in the district by the number of brake drums we had sold.

The churches all had a dual role, for on Sunday they were a place of worship and on weekdays they served as the local primary schools. The government had established schools in the larger towns, but nothing in the countryside. So in some areas the mission and the local church provided this primary school education. Admittedly the schools lacked even the most basic facilities, but we did keep dozens and dozens of blackboards and chalk for the various church schools.

Norene opened a little bookshop which she ran from our back porch at first and later, with gifts from supporters in New Zealand, a small bookshop was built.

We started off our *Dilla Diary* newsletter in February 1970 like this:

"Have you ever been having a meal when a knock has come to the door? We ask ourselves, 'Have we ever been having a meal when a knock has *not* come to our door?' The reason? From the back door, front door or even the little side door, comes the call, *Baytorch, baytorch, metsehalf, metsehalf!* ('People in the house, book, book!')

Or more likely we would hear *bug, bug!* ('Sheep, sheep!')"

Norene often replied, "I'm sorry we don't sell sheep here; go to the market." This would usually bring peals of laughter.

On the first page of the first reading book in Amharic was a picture of a sheep, with the first word in the book being *bug* or sheep.

We continued our letter:

"You might laugh if you saw our assortment of stock. In our mule shed we keep old brake drums and these are eagerly bought for church and school bells. In our car shed we have a variety of blackboards and plenty of blackboard paint. We have quite a trade with the blackboards. Then the main bookshop supplies are in our little back porch off our kitchen. There one can buy Bibles, New Testaments, gospels, simple readers, hygiene books, wedding invitations, wedding certificates, stationery, ands an assortment of other Amharic and English books. Our attic contains the bulk supplies.We are the nearest place for 225 miles where people can buy even the smallest book. Bibles are our biggest sale. There's a lovely custom here that a bridegroom gives his bride a Bible on their wedding day so we always have many on hand. With each purchase we hand out a colourful tract with the prayer that the Lord will bless his word to unbelievers who might read it."

Selling from our back porch did have its moments, especially on wash day. We wanted to improve our facility so we could cater also for those in the town of Dilla, and urgently needed a cement block bookstore located by the roadside. The opportunities were limitless, but space was limited.

We asked supporters to contribute towards a new bookshop and were touched when sufficient money came in to erect the building on the roadside. This took place after we had left for New Zealand.

75 Prayer By The Red Sea

By this time we had been in Ethiopia for fifteen years, and many times the four children had begged to go for a holiday to the Red Sea. Finally we made the effort and decided to go in the Christmas holiday period of 1968. We met the children at school in Addis and took three days and three nights to make the trip up to Asmara, where Norene's uncle Allan Tucker and his wife Lilian, were serving with the Middle East General Mission.

On the way up north we stayed with missionaries, George and Dorothy Middleton, good friends of ours.

"Why don't you borrow our stainless steel spear, Bruce?" they suggested. "You and your boys are so keen on fishing and could make good use of it. The fish are plentiful in the Red Sea."

We hesitatingly accepted their offer.

First of all we celebrated a memorable Christmas with the Tucker family (Philip being the only one of their five children with them at the time.) After that we travelled down the windy road to the sea and pitched our tent right on the sand. There were no stretchers or extras. We just slept on top of our sleeping bags on the sand as the temperatures were warm.

With the tent up, we four "menfolk" were impatient to try out our borrowed spear.

"I'll give you your first lesson on how to spear a good fish," I told the boys. "You 'ladies' start the fire, heat up the frying pan and we'll be back in no time." (Pride sometimes cometh before a fall.)

As we ran along the shore, so excited to be by the salty sea, we found the receding tide had left large, deep puddles, some many metres across. In one of these pools we caught a glimpse of a huge fish which appeared to be stranded.

With a mighty effort I heaved the spear and with a thud it found its mark.

"I've got him, boys," I exulted.

At that moment, however, the fish, having been rudely awakened by this sharp barbed spear, started flapping with all its might, making its way towards the open sea. We were surprised at how fast it moved. Deeper and deeper it went into the water, until it gradually disappeared like a submarine, with the spear being the last part visible. Now there was no way we could reach it.

"Oh, no," groaned Steve, "it's a huge stingray. Now both our dinner and our spear have gone!"

As we four forlorn figures plodded back along the beach, there was little excitement in the air. What could we tell Norene and Becky?

"Open the baked beans," we suggested. "The fish is another story."

There was little chatter at the meal table that night.

As we were settling down to sleep we prayed together. Just as we said our "Amen" a little voice whispered, "Daddy, you forgot to ask God to bring back the spear!"

We had taught our children God answers prayer, but this came as quite a test. I prayed briefly again, reminding God we had just lost someone else's spear.

The next morning I got up early, which is not unusual for me. I thought the spear might have been washed up overnight by the incoming tide. But there was no sign of it.

After breakfast we had a short family devotion and the same little voice reminded me again to pray about the spear.

At about ten o'clock we were swimming and snorkelling in the clear warm tropical water. Did I say *we*? I wasn't exactly feeling like swimming under the circumstances, and so decided to watch the tent while the others swam.

Suddenly the cry went up, "Stingray, stingray!"

I rushed down the beach telling the family to get out of the water. Then Dave called out, "Dad, I think it's the one with the spear in its back!"

I had to think quickly, so grabbing a large fish hook we had brought for catching sharks, I attached it to a long pole. Because the spear had a handle, I was then able to slip the fish hook through it. With a mighty yank I pulled out the spear. The stingray gave a great leap and sped away, no doubt relieved to be free of that metal in its back.

As we thought about it, we realised stingrays would normally steer clear of noisy humans splashing around and swimming, but God had brought this one right to our feet. In fact, it was more than a kilometre away from where it had been speared.

As I walked up the beach holding the precious spear, a little girl ran after me and grabbed my hand.

"Daddy, God *does* answer prayer, doesn't he?" she said.

76 Barnabas

I admit we were reluctant to go to Dilla when first appointed, mainly because we felt inadequate to fulfil the tasks which had been assigned to us. As the months and years passed, however, we realised that during these four years there was no other place in Ethiopia or in New Zealand where we would rather have been. They had been the most rewarding years of our missionary journey up to this point in our lives. We had been privileged to experience church growth, the likes of which few will ever experience. The number of churches had doubled every two years, as had the number of believers. Evangelists had been sent out to at least three other tribal areas and many students had graduated from both the Dilla and the nearby Yirga Chaffee Bible Schools.

The effect the gospel was having on the whole community was unbelievable. The standard of housing was increasing dramatically, with even the unbelievers starting to change their ways. Education of one's children became the aim of every family in the area. The clinic and hospital had never been so busy. New methods of growing, harvesting and processing coffee were introduced, which meant everyone was a little better off.

But politically, things were starting to unravel. Haile Selassie, although still king, was an old man and everyone wondered when he would appoint his heir. Student unrest in Addis Ababa was blatantly obvious and yet nothing seemed to be done to ease the situation. In the province of Gedeo where we were, there was considerable unrest amongst the landless masses. The landlords demanded up to twenty-five percent of the coffee crop from those living on their land, and there was no recourse for arbitration. We constantly heard rumours of people buying guns and ammunition and wondered what might happen if law and order broke down.

Our Dilla "Barnabas" (Encourager) was a man named Morkati (pronounced Morketey) who was the president of the Kale Heywet Church in Dilla. A more godly and humble man I have never known. His testimony to the

Morkati (Barnabas) and fellow elder Gidechew

unsaved and his challenge and encouragement to the believers was unparalleled. Our four-year ministry in Dilla was greatly enhanced by our relationship with this man. He was such good company for me, and when it came time to say goodbye to each other we both wept, knowing we would probably not meet again on earth. He left us with the verse from Hebrews 6:10:

God is not unjust; he will not forget your work and the love you have shown him as you have helped his people and continue to do so.

Morkati maintained his outstanding testimony even after the Marxist regime took control of the country in 1974. When he died from cancer in 1983, even although large gatherings were forbidden, thousands of people fearlessly turned out to honour this great man of God.

As we prepared to leave we were humbled by the gifts showered upon us by individuals and by the church. When we objected they said, "If you had not come, we would never have heard the message of Jesus."

Of course they meant that if you *plural* had not come. There were doctors and nurses, builders and teachers, both elementary and in the Bible School, and all played a vital part in planting the church in Gedeo.

77 Stunned by a Question

Because the education programme at Bingham Academy was based on the American curriculum, there were some areas which made it difficult for the children from "down under" to adapt to once they reached secondary school level. That year we were the only New Zealand family with children in Bingham, out of a total of 170 students. Although the school tried to make their curriculum a little more acceptable, we had to make the difficult decision as to when it was the right time to leave Ethiopia and go home to New Zealand. Norene and I constantly prayed and discussed together our future as to where we would settle and what we would do. How much easier it would have been in some ways to remain in Ethiopia which had become our comfort zone. All our married life thus far had been spent there, but clearly we were being led back to New Zealand, at least for a time.

For three of our four years in Dilla I had been elected as SIM's district superintendent for the Arsi and Sidamo provinces. Twice a year this meant visiting all the SIM stations in the area and attending SIM Council meetings in Addis Ababa. I enjoyed taking our district needs and concerns to these meetings and returning again to the various mission stations to report on the decisions made. During those years SIM was expanding its ministries greatly and invariably there was insufficient staff to meet all the needs. Particularly was that true of our various hospitals. At that stage SIM had established and were administering five hospitals, two of which were in my area of responsibility, at Shashamane and Dilla. Both of these places were important to me and I would do my best at the six-monthly Council meetings to find the medical staff requested to operate these large institutions. But every district had its own needs and one had to be careful to see the total picture and act accordingly.

The General Director of SIM was Dr Raymond Davis, a man we had never met but nevertheless esteemed highly. As a mission we had always appointed godly leaders and men of outstanding faith. Dr Davis was one of them. Because Ethiopia was experiencing some major personnel problems, our SIM Ethiopia Council asked Dr Davis if he could come to advise us.

At last, I thought, I will have the opportunity of meeting him before returning to New Zealand.

A special Council meeting was called, and although it proved to be a difficult one, a conclusion was reached which was honouring to God. Being the youngest and least experienced Council member I had little to say, but was most impressed by the way Dr Davis chaired our meeting.

As we were leaving, Dr Davis took me aside, asking if we could chat for a few minutes.

About what? I wondered.

He had never met me and I was sure he didn't even know my name.

"Bruce, I understand you're going back to New Zealand soon because of your children's education," he said.

So he did know my name and he even knew which country we were from. He even knew we were on our way home.

"We are looking for a new SIM Home Director for New Zealand," he continued, "and would like you to consider taking on this responsibility."

I was stunned into silence, but my mind was churning out all the reasons why this was an impossible suggestion. My only response was,

"What about so-and-so? (naming another New Zealander.) Why wouldn't you choose him?"

Dr Davis simply answered,

"I want *you* and your wife to pray about this suggestion and let me know how you feel."

I returned to Dilla absolutely dumbfounded that Dr Davis would even make such a suggestion, and couldn't wait to hear Norene's reaction.

The same excuses came flooding back into my mind, as when I was first asked to teach in the Bible School in Dilla.

"After all, am I not an agriculturalist?"

We both felt the same. This position was way beyond our gifting and training.

In the trauma of packing up and leaving Ethiopia, we continued to pray about our future as Dr Davis had challenged us. But we left feeling confused.

Chapter Six

New Zealand

78 A Major Decision

Jack Nicholson, the first SIM New Zealand missionary to Nigeria, was about to retire, but in the meantime had been appointed acting director until a new SIM Director for New Zealand could be found. Obviously he had been in touch with Dr Davis and was privy to our conversation back in Addis Ababa. The Nicholsons met us at the airport, no doubt happy that their replacements had at last been found and would be taking up their duties shortly.

I'm sure they were quite upset when we told them we felt inadequate for the job and would be searching elsewhere for employment.

"You know I'm an outdoor sort of man and would really like to work on the land," I said to Jack.

He looked at me.

"I was raised on my father's farm in the district of Gore and wanted to stay on the farm," he said, "but God had other plans for me. My whole working life has been involved in Nigeria. How privileged we feel to have had that opportunity."

With that he left me with the challenge to "pray about it."

Norene and I were confused. We searched for other opportunities from one side of Auckland to the other. A friend offered his successful orchard to us with the agreement that we pay him as we became established. It was a tremendous opportunity, but still we had no peace in our hearts. We had made a commitment to the Lord that once our children were through their teenage years and training we would try to return to Ethiopia.

After some time we turned down our friend's offer to take over his property and told Jack we would do our best at the SIM office. Jack couldn't have been more helpful. We had settled in to a small rented place in Cook Street, Howick, and after a few months were led to a neat, but small, three-bedroomed home on a one-and-a-quarter acre section. (It had lots of scope for growing a large orchard, grazing a few sheep and even keeping some pigeons to remind our children of Ethiopia days). This was miraculous in that we were told about this suitable property at the eleventh hour, just as we were about to sign up for another house on a smaller property. SIM, family members and friends helped us with this purchase.

God provided for us in countless ways. For instance, our children all remember the morning we prayed for a refrigerator in our morning devotions.

Only a few minutes later Vic Cope of Howick Baptist arrived at our door.

"Bonds, I have ended up with two refrigerators," he said. "Would you be able to use one?"

Then later on Philip prayed fervently for a TV and one morning told us he had a dream that a TV had ended up down in the gully of our property and we just needed to bring it up the hill. A few days later a TV arrived at our front door and Philip was overjoyed. He excitedly ran to tell us, "We didn't even have to carry this one up the hill. It was right by the door!"

So God provided all we *needed* as well as some things we *wanted*. (We never did find out who gave us the second-hand TV.) A lot of our furniture was provided from the beach house which Norene's Dad had sold before we arrived home.

After we were settled in and the children were all in school, Jack took me around New Zealand, particularly the South Island, introducing me to many SIM supporters. He offered to stay in the office for a year and give me a further opportunity to learn the ropes. What a beneficial year it was, working with Jack alongside me.

A year after returning from Ethiopia I was appointed SIM New Zealand director for a five-year period. This was a difficult assignment for a family man with only an office secretary and no other full-time staff at the time. I was constantly away from home, travelling either within New Zealand or on overseas assignments. Norene was left with so much responsibility for the family.

Finances were difficult too. After paying our monthly mortgage we stumbled along from month to month with hardly enough to care for ourselves. Of course our garden and orchard helped. My lawyer brother had a small farm up the road, and seeing I was handy with a butcher's knife, we had the arrangement that I would slaughter one of his woolly animals once a month and we would share the meat. In different ways we were taken care of. Another dear friend gave us money for a freezer so we could make the most of any surplus from our garden

For Norene and me, feeding, clothing and educating a growing family with our meagre financial resources became almost impossible, until I decided to inform our international department that I would need to seek part-time employment to subsidise our income. Our cry for help was finally taken seriously, and our international treasurer, when visiting New Zealand from the USA later on, agreed to make some adjustment to our monthly allowance, thus enabling us to continue serving the mission full-time. Our two older boys (thirteen and twelve) were determined to help themselves and took on paper runs. This meant being up soon after 6am, six days a week, and delivering from their bicycles.

79 Those Wonderful Difficult Years

Although throughout the year I had to be away, we decided we must celebrate Christmas holidays as a family. On our previous furlough in 1965 we had been invited to take a missionary meeting in the home of Les and Joan Higham who were farming in South Head on the Kaipara Harbour. From then on we became lifelong friends. In 1971 the Highams invited us to camp on their property for our Christmas break.

That year we camped with just one other family and thoroughly enjoyed ourselves, even though our camping conditions were fairly primitive. For example there was no toilet, no running water, and of course no electricity. Nor were there any shops for about thirty kilometres. We thought we were back in Ethiopia! Always our first jobs were to dig a pit toilet and dig out a spring at the base of the cliff. Joan and Les and their family of four were wonderful hosts, sharing everything they had with their "townie" friends.

Those were relaxing holidays, although for Norene, the cook, that was a little dubious at times. Our days were filled with a huge assortment of activities, including flounder spearing, snapper fishing, mullet netting, possum and rabbit shooting, wild turkey hunting, hay making and swimming. Board games were fun on wet days and in the evenings. The Sunday morning singsongs and church services under the big pohutukawa tree on the beach will always remain in our memories. Mary Higham owned a pet deer which would often join us on the beach.

As the years passed, many more campers came and there were gradual improvements in the amenities. Eventually Noel and Janet Higham took over the ownership of the farm. Noel with his heavy machinery improved the size of the camping area and the access road. Flush toilets and hot showers followed, with a new and improved cook-house. Hundreds of shelter and ornamental trees were planted, making it one of the most attractive camping areas in the region.

We usually brought along extra friends and cousins to share the holiday with us. Of course having a large group of young people together was a sure recipe for mishaps. One night we were woken at midnight with the news that one of our boys had accidentally speared his brother's foot right through,while out floundering. Emergency help at midnight was 100 kilometres away.

Then there was the night when our trusty little dinghy mysteriously floated away on the midnight full tide. Of course no one was the last to use it and all insisted it had been properly anchored!

On yet another occasion the boys had borrowed a friend's boat for part of the holidays and that, too, disappeared. After several days of fruitless searching a fellow camper offered to fly his light aircraft around the harbour.

He finally spotted the boat camouflaged in the reeds, miles away across the other side of the harbour. Many hours (and dollars) later, the boat was returned to its owner.

As with every family, there were the encouraging school reports and the discouraging ones too.

During those years, though, we were so grateful to have a good church base at Howick Baptist for our young people. This was strategic in helping them during the difficult transition between life as it was in Ethiopia and life in New Zealand.

We were aware we didn't have all the answers in how to make a successful transition. The problems we had would prove that statement! But we did know the importance of establishing a solid Christian home and choosing an evangelical church with a vital youth group.

Yes, those five years were wonderful and difficult ones.

But from mid-1975 big changes were in store for us as a family.

Two beautiful babies outside our Shashamane home 1956
Stephen our first

A fond greeting for Philip

David, our future Vet., examining a hyena attack

Becky and Philip all dressed up for 'Aunty Jewel's' wedding 1967

Beautiful Bishoftu/Babogaya

The kitchen 'Girls' at Bishoftu/Babogaya 1987

Two little Ethiopian friends

Family group before we separated for '76 - '77 stint in Ethiopia, *L to R* David, Rebecca, Phil and Steve

Overview of Kuriftu.
From left around circular road: Container house, permanent house, shade plant houses. On hill, Beehives, Dairy unit, Poultry unit, *right foreground,* Assembly Hall/Church

Kuriftu Church completed

View of Kuriftu. On hill at left, our house, and on its right the Container house

David and Grace and three children with friends when they came to Kuriftu to help 1990

Releasing fish fingerlings into the Maazey Fish Pond

Balsa wood boats
crossing to Island

View from the
Sof Omar Cave
1964

All of us with
Aunty Doris cross-
ing river on way to
Goba airfield

Our oldest son, Steve, and Gail and three daughters visited Ethiopia in 1992

With our 12 grandchildren, Christmas 2004

Chapter Seven

MARXISM 1976 – 1977

80 The Red Terror

Although we came home to New Zealand in 1970, we were always aware of what was happening in our beloved country of Ethiopia.

Everything started to change in 1972 when the north-eastern province of Wollo suffered a catastrophic drought. By 1973 thousands of hungry people from Wollo were seen making their way to Addis Ababa to try to find food. About the middle of that year, a British television reporter, Jonathan Dimbleby, was permitted to come to Ethiopia to film the unfolding disaster of the results of the drought. His heart-rending pictures of starving, fly-covered children lying in the dust next to their dying mothers suddenly woke the world to action. Never before had such distressful pictures been seen on our TV screens. As a result, people from around the world gave millions of dollars to aid famine victims, including $100,000 from New Zealand. But for many it was too late and it was estimated that in that year more than 200,000 people died of starvation. Many more lost everything they possessed.

The question everyone was asking was, "Why was the world not alerted to this impending famine before such a terrible human tragedy took place? What was the Emperor, Haile Selassie, doing? Did he know about the impending drought?"

Selassie was an old man of 82 by now, and probably did not know the full extent of the famine until it was too late. At any rate this famine precipitated the events which were to follow. Early in 1974 an army revolt took place in the southern part of the country, followed by student and worker disturbances throughout the whole country. Rumours spread, and before long the masses were demanding that the Emperor abdicate.

Time magazine talked about the "bloodless coup." No shots were fired, yet a group of young army officers, took control. They began to systematically arrest many of the government officials, members of the royal family, and wealthy land owners. What a sad day it was when a group of soldiers went to the palace, arrested the Emperor, and took him away in a small Volkswagen. It was reported at the time that as the front seat of the Volkswagen was pushed back for him to get in, he simply asked, "What? Into this?"

We will always hold the Emperor in great esteem. He was a man who did more for the development of Ethiopia than any other.

However, it appeared to many thinking people that the Emperor had failed by not appointing a younger person as his successor many years before. Immediately after his arrest, the army officers leading the coup announced that Crown Prince Asfaw Wossen was to become King of Ethiopia. This was an appeasement to those faithful to the royal family. Few people believed it would happen, as the prince was living in England and was in poor health after suffering a stroke.

81 The Derg

The army announced it was establishing a provisional military government to be known as the *Derg*, which meant "committee." At first many people were happy with the change. Everywhere one could hear the revolution song, "Ethiopia Tikdem Yalla Minim Dem," which simply meant "Ethiopia first, without bloodshed."

But it wasn't to remain that way for long. First there was internal fighting among the army leaders of the coup. Mengistu, the strongman, was jealous of one of the other leaders, General Aman, who refused to endorse a plan to shoot in cold blood sixty high ranking prisoners who were being held in the dungeons of Menelik's old palace. So he ordered his troops to surround General Aman's home and arrest him. A terrible gun battle took place, and once the general was killed, Mengistu ordered the execution of the sixty political prisoners. They were then buried in a common grave along with the general.

Many were greatly distressed by this barbaric act and now knew for certain the type of man Mengistu was. We had personally met many of these men who had been shot. Some had become close friends as they had assisted us in establishing many of the SIM projects in Ethiopia. They were an unbelievable loss for Ethiopia. That event heralded the beginning of a blood bath which was aptly named the years of the Red Terror.

Students from universities and the senior secondary schools were forced to leave their education to become the vanguard of the revolution. After a brief period of Marxist indoctrination, they were sent throughout the country to explain and enforce the revolution to the peasants and to teach a nationwide literacy programme. All land was nationalised and given to the peasants to divide as they saw fit. All tractors and farm machinery were nationalised. All rented urban properties were also nationalised and people were permitted to own only the house they actually occupied. All businesses, including banks, flour mills and large shops were nationalised.

In order to control the activities of the rural people, "villagisation" was introduced. The peasants were forced to relocate from the traditional compounds they had inhabited for decades, if not centuries. Their houses had always been surrounded by their kitchen gardens and grain fields. But villagisation consisted of soul-less little grass-roofed or tin-roofed buildings set in two parallel lines with an open grassy roadway between the rows of houses. Many of the farmers were relocated miles away from their farms. The effort of carrying their wooden ploughs and driving their ploughing oxen to the fields, plus the weeding, protection and harvesting of their crops was enormous. This resulted in a sharp decline in the overall harvest of grain. Although many peasants sharply resisted this move, they were forced to leave. They were told to pull down their old houses and relocate them. This was easy to say, but almost impossible to implement. An old mud-walled tukul with a thatched roof simply could not be relocated, and little of the material was recyclable.

Hence hundreds of thousands of poor people suffered greatly with this crazy plan. Many had planted eucalyptus trees around their homes which they systematically harvested for firewood. These had to be cut down to provide enough poles to build the new houses. The countryside then suffered a further setback with deforestation. All this was in the cause of socialism. The "bloodless coup" had changed dramatically as every day many people were killed. A curfew was imposed at night and the police would force their way into homes, arresting or shooting any who they suspected of being anti-revolutionaries.

82 The Royal Family

Our dear friend Princess Tenagnework, with her daughters Ida, Sybil, Ruth and Sofia were all arrested with their royal cousins. Sybil (with whom we even now correspond) had to give up her six-month-old baby.

They were all held in a single room within the prison grounds for the next fifteen years. They had mattresses on the floor which they rolled up in the daytime. Later when we were back in Ethiopia we would send in tea, coffee, sugar and other food items with an Ethiopian friend who had permission to visit them. Outside was a tiny area where they could exercise. One day our "visitor" friend told us Princess Tenagnework was not able to make use of the exercise yard in the rainy season because she had no raincoat. Plastic raincoats were unobtainable in the shops, but both Norene and I had a light plastic raincoat which we always carried in our hand luggage. Norene's red one wasn't suitable in a communist regime, and so we sent in my grey one. As time went on the rules became a little more lenient and books were allowed in. The first book Princess Sybil requested was a Bible.

In August 1975 a report was published that the Emperor had died of natural causes. Nobody believed it. (Years later the Emperor's servant, Eshete, who was permitted to care for him in those sad days, told how one morning on entering the King's room, he found him dead. He remembered there was a strong smell of ether in the room. It is believed Mengistu had smothered him with a pillow.)

Haile Selassie, with the titles of "Elect of God," "King of Kings" and "The lion of the Tribe of Judah" was dead and not even permitted a public burial. No one knew where he had been buried.

Postscript. It would be twenty five years later, in November 2000, that a fitting funeral service would be held. The man who had been forced to dig the original grave, now himself a prisoner, revealed where the body lay. It was under the floor of Mengistu's office. The remains were removed, placed in a coffin, and buried in a tomb beside the Empress inside the Holy Trinity Cathedral. A large crowd gathered, including all the remaining members of the royal family who were living overseas. By this time the princesses had been out of prison for several years. Our dear friend Princess Tenagnework, the only survivor of the Emperor's children, was given as a memorial keepsake the Ethiopian flag which had draped the coffin.)

83 Please Come Back!

In 1975 Dr Ian Hay, our SIM General Director, asked me if I would make a visit to Ethiopia, Kenya, Nigeria, Niger and Benin, to visit our various community development programmes and bring to the General Council meetings suggestions for discussion re SIM's policy for helping meet human needs. This meant I would be away from home for more than two months.

The first country I visited was Ethiopia. There I discussed with Don Stilwell, who was in charge of our SIM development programme, various possibilities of how the mission could best help the national church during this difficult period of Marxism. After some days Don said to me:

"Yes, I agree wholeheartedly with your suggestions, Bruce, but who do we have here who could implement them?"

Then he looked at me.

"Would you and Norene be willing to return and help us?" he asked

His question was quite unexpected. We had been back in New Zealand for five years, with all the children enrolled in different educational activities, and I had just been reappointed for a further five years as Director for SIM New Zealand. We were reasonably settled, but continued to have a keen desire to be involved in Ethiopia. Many missionaries were being forced out of Ethiopia, and yet here was Don asking us if we would return. Norene was in New Zealand, keeping the home fires burning, but a day or two before I had left, kind friends from our church had decided they would raise the money to enable her to meet me in Kenya after three weeks. We would then travel for three weeks together in West Africa before she returned home and I went on to the General Council meetings in the USA.

I promised Don we would discuss this possibility together and let him know.

Norene and I had a great reunion in Kenya. Then I shared with her Don's challenge. Naturally as a mother she came up with all the practical reasons why it would be difficult. We were loath to break up our family circle again. The two older boys (nineteen and eighteen) would remain in New Zealand and the two younger children (fifteen and thirteen) would accompany us. Steve had just commenced a managerial course with Woolworths New Zealand and David was just finishing seventh form at secondary school and heading for veterinary training the next year. Becky and Phil were both at secondary school.

As we travelled together through West Africa, visiting all our New Zealand SIMers, we discussed over and over the pros and cons of such a decision. Before we parted again we agreed to share this challenge with our children and pray for some special signs from the Lord as to what we should do. (One of the first questions the kids asked was, "What would we do with the family dog?")

84 The Big Decision

After my long safari across Africa and attendance at the SIM General Council I was more than happy to be home again. But we were anxiously waiting to know what lay ahead for us. Our family, ever supportive, encouraged us to return. Steve said he wanted to experience his big OE and would probably work in Australia first. David pointed out that he had to leave home anyway to attend Massey University in Palmerston North. As for Becky and Philip, they were quite excited when they heard they would board at Bingham Academy and enrol at an American high school, Good Shepherd Academy, in Addis Ababa. When Phil, our sports lover, heard the school had a terrific sports programme, he was particularly encouraged.

Everything started to fall into place. Don and Ruby Coop, who had just arrived back from Ethiopia, agreed to take over my SIM role in New Zealand for a two year period. God led us to some practical promises from his Word. Our daily readings took us through the book of Job, and chapter five seemed to contain a particular message for us as a family and the encouragement we needed as parents. We were dreading the separation from our two older boys and perplexed about taking our two younger children into such a volatile situation. Speaking at our mission farewell, Norene spoke of "Six S's – Our Promises from God," found in Job 5:19-27:

✤ Safety in travel – "He will deliver you again and again, no evil can touch you."

✤ Serenity of mind – "No need to fear the future…"

✣ Spiritual enablement – "You shall laugh at war and famine."

✣ Sickness, freedom from – "You shall live a long life. You'll not be harvested before time."

✣ SIM staff and home in New Zealand – "Nothing shall be stolen from your home."

✣ Sons and daughter cared for – "Your sons shall become important men... Your descendents shall be as numerous as grass."

With the blessing from our home church, Howick Baptist and SIM, we committed ourselves to serve as the community development advisor for SIM in Ethiopia for the years 1976-77. Our Christmas camping holiday at Highams Beach was a happy one, but departure day in mid-January was almost upon us.

It is always hard for a parent to see their children suffering through separation. Especially hard at this time was to see our teenage sons feeling the parting so deeply. Unfortunately that is one experience in life which never gets easier with practice.

On arrival in Ethiopia we experienced first hand the trauma the people were facing as communism gripped the country with its terrifying tentacles. Norene particularly empathised with the women whose husbands and teenagers were being torn so brutally from their homes. She wrote the following, shortly after our arrival back:

A Country Beloved
Dear Lord, my heart is torn
For the women of this country
The sadness
The sorrow
The hopelessness
Which is theirs.
Lord, why should I be so favoured
To be born in my country surrounded by
The love,
The security,
The contentment,
Which is mine?
Yes, these women are torn by heartaches
Which a few years ago
Were unheard of—not dreamed of.
They lived in happy family circles
With their children at their knee
Now those same children are
Imprisoned,

Tortured,
Yea, even dead,
Because they rose up to disagree with this
Insidious,
Deadly,
Cruel,
Tool of Satan himself,
Communism.
Thank you, Lord, for
Bringing me to live here and
Observe,
Sympathise,
Agonise,
So that I may experience more deeply
How you, O Lord, suffered
To bring such to yourself.

85 An Amazing Journey

Soon after arriving in Addis in January, we met our good friend Malcolm Hunter.

"Bruce, welcome back!" he said. "You're just the one we need to visit Getemay Island in Lake Margureta."

While working at Dilla we had visited another island in Lake Margureta, namely Gedicho. Now Malcolm was telling us about some amazing changes taking place on a different island on the western side of the same lake. We heard that due to the change of policy of the new government, these island people were desperately short of food and needed our help. When Becky and Philip heard we had been asked to visit Getemay they pleaded with us to arrange the trip during their Easter school break.

Our Landrover was finally packed with drinking water, sleeping bags, food, fishing lines and hooks, plus a small gas burner and kerosene lamp. Two days later saw us at the lake's edge making the necessary contacts with those

Balsa boat

who had arrived to ferry us across to the island.

"Have the rafts arrived?" Philip asked anxiously.

"Yes," he was told, "they are down at the lake's edge being readied for our journey."

"But when can we leave?" asked Philip with more than a tinge of impatience.

It was now Friday afternoon. To his great disappointment, the boatmen said we couldn't leave before Saturday afternoon as they needed to attend the local Saturday market to buy supplies for their families on the island. We drove into the nearest town, Araba Minch, to find a bed for the night in a little hotel.

On our return on Saturday afternoon, we were told, "The wind is too strong to attempt a crossing. You'll need to spend the night right here, near the shore, so we can be ready once the wind drops."

Being hospitable folk, they offered us the best accommodation they could find in one of their little grass-roofed tukuls. In fact our host and hostess moved from their own simple little slat bed, made with sticks, offering it to Norene and me while Phil and Becky slept on the simple camp cots we had brought with us.

Shortly after our host and hostess were sound asleep on the dirt floor we realised we were in the company of thousands of bedbugs and fleas.

"Check my back," I pleaded with Norene. The little critters were having a feast. No way could we sleep there, and so we moved outside to "sleep" under the stars. But where *were* the stars? It had started raining.

Becky and Philip, who weren't too happy trying to sleep next to the cattle in the house, made their way to the Landrover and the parents searched out the most rain-proof tree available. We were just starting to doze before dawn when the rowers called:

Arriving at Getemay Island in our Balsa wood boat 1976

"The wind has dropped. We must go quickly."

Sleeping bags were quickly rolled up and our meagre supplies carried over the ploughed fields to the waiting rafts.

The four-hour trip to the island will never be forgotten. Like the papyrus boats of old, the water sloshed in and out of the balsa wood but its buoyancy kept us afloat, even if a little wet from the waist down. We moved along slowly with two punters who plonked two large balsa wood plugs into the water and pushed against them. But the pace was painfully slow. There was great excitement, though, as we frequently encountered herds of hippos and numerous crocs suddenly surfacing close to our craft.

"Boy, my cousins would be jealous if they could see me now!" Philip was heard to remark.

What a royal welcome awaited us as we arrived and were able to stretch our legs on the rocky shore. So many hugs all at once. We realised why the islanders were so excited to greet us, as some of the women had never seen white females before. They were fascinated, and most wanted turns to stroke Becky's soft golden hair. Our every move was watched.

86 Thirsty For More

After initial greetings we were ushered from the lake shore, up the hill

Meeting with a group of the Getemay Island folk. April 1976

into the large round grass-roofed church. The four of us were hoping to be offered food at this stage, but obviously had to ignore our hunger pangs a little longer. Everyone on the island gathered at the church that Sunday morning. Those who couldn't fit in, sat outside in the shadow of the church. We were puzzled to know how these new believers had such a large meeting place. Later we solved that mystery.

After the usual preliminaries I was asked to teach them more from the Bible about their newfound faith. Having spoken for about an hour I sat down exhausted. The people looked aghast.

"Please give us more than that!" the older men begged.

"We'll come back this afternoon," we offered, "but only if you bring us some refreshment in the meantime." So they brewed us some coffee and served it with salt and boiled sweet potatoes.

During our coffee break I asked:

"Can we hear the story of how you all came to trust in Jesus?"

What an amazing story it was. These folk had been under the power of the local witchdoctor who had instilled fear into every inhabitant and kept them poor by continually demanding gifts. Among other things he said he ruled the wind and the waves, so they had to appease him with a gift each time they crossed to the mainland.

In September 1975 he suddenly announced he was leaving. This was unbelievable, as he had exercised demonic power over them all for more than forty years.

"I have seen a vision," he then explained. "One day you will believe in a much stronger god than I serve."

With that he suddenly left the island with all his witchcraft paraphernalia.

The people were distraught. Finally some of the older men said:

"Why don't we call back Wolde Georgis?"

"But who is he?" some of the young men asked.

"He was the man who came teaching us a new religion forty years ago, but we wouldn't listen and chased him away," the older men said.

The Witch doctor who left the Getemay Island

Baptismal scene on Getemay Island 1976

They went on to tell us that forty years before, Wolde Georgis had lived on the island with his extended family. Due to a terrible fight with his brother, he returned to the mainland in order to purchase a gun so he could finally settle the score with his brother.

But God had other plans. Wolde met one of the first Christians in that area, and after hearing about God's forgiveness gladly accepted Jesus as his Saviour and hurriedly returned to the island to tell everyone his good news. That was when the local witch doctor stirred up opposition among the locals, threatening dire consequences if the people listened to this new message. He had Wolde removed from the island.

Forty years had now passed. In the meantime Wolde had gone to Bible School and had become a skilled evangelist. Asked to return, he was sceptical at first but then realised his people were now earnestly seeking to know the truth. So he had agreed to come. What a welcome he received this time round! After a period of teaching, all 268 adults with one accord professed salvation in Jesus Christ. Following that, a young evangelist and his wife were sent over from one of the mainland churches to continue teaching these new believers.

And what about the need for a church? Why not clean out the witch doctor's large house and dedicate that for worshipping the true God?

After our "brunch" break and recording the above story, we gathered together for another service. Even that didn't satisfy them. They still wanted more so Norene agreed to have a women's meeting early next morning.

In the meantime we set up housekeeping in the church itself. Becky and Philip rolled out their sleeping bags on top of reeds and cow hides on the mud floor and we parents had the luxury of our low camp stretchers. Our cooker sat on the floor, with Norene and Becky balanced on the three-legged stools to do their simple cooking, Ethiopian style. Becky fell in love with the children and felt deeply for them as they obviously did not have enough to eat.

There was absolutely no such thing as privacy. And no toilet. After dark was the best time for such things. What is more, the kids followed us wherever we went. The "ladies" had their "wash 'n wear" dresses and so found it easier and less embarrassing to go into the water for a wash, clothes and all. What a time saver! In no time they were dry all over. We only hoped the crocs weren't there waiting for a tasty meal.

The island, we discovered, was small in size, perhaps not more than 50 acres, rocky and hot. Vegetation was nil – not a crop or a garden to supplement the people's diet. Grain was scarce, as every bag had to be brought from the mainland market.

"But how do they pay for the grain?" you might ask.

All the men were weavers. This meant they would buy raw cotton from the mainland and the women would then spin it into thread. After this the men would weave it into cloth which they sold at the market back on the mainland. For decades they had existed quite well like this. That is until Marxism took control.

Petros's big one! on the Island

87 Peter the Fisherman

"The line went taut as Petros (Peter) gave a cry of delight.

"I've got one, I've got one!" he screamed.

From all over the island, people came running to see for themselves. Excitement rose as he pulled his new nylon line to the shore. Yes, it was true. He had actually caught a Nile perch. It hardly seemed possible that such a shiny, silver-coloured fish could live in those muddy brown waters of Lake Margureta.

We knew there were lots of fish in the lake, but there was no way the islanders could catch these without a supply of hooks and strong nylon line. We had come prepared. Just imagine a missionary teaching people how to catch huge fish! It was right up my alley, and Phil's too.

Early Monday morning all the men and boys gathered at the shore. First we gave out light nylon and small hooks and set the boys fishing for live bait-fish. In they came, thick and fast. Then we divided the men into twelve different groups, giving each group a long strong nylon line with a 50mm hook. All the men were to have turns trying to catch a fish. The live bait-fish were properly attached and then the lines stretched out in the water as far as they could go. When Petros cried out, "I've got one, I've got one!" and furiously started hauling in his line, everyone started to believe the stories they had heard about large fish in the lake.

Petros's fish was only ten to twelve kilos, but we knew larger ones would follow. And they did.

Just as the sun was setting, another excited young man hauled in the catch of the day. With a strong pole through its mouth and gills, it took two men to carry this 30-40 kilo monster up the bank. What a feast everyone enjoyed that night, including our own family as we had been short of food.

The rest of our time on the island was spent teaching the men and women from God's word and helping them hone their fishing skills. The fishing hooks were certainly put to maximum use, with many Nile perch and catfish being caught. But one day there was a wail of grief as one man lost his valuable and irreplaceable hook inside a large perch. Then a night or two later a hippo got tangled up in a line and took the whole thing with it. We left feeling rather disappointed that only ten hooks remained.

A week or two later I had to return to the general area, and there waving me down on the mainland road, was one of the islanders.

"A few days after you left we hauled in another monster perch," he told me, "and when we cut it open we found the missing hook inside its stomach. Then some days later, after crossing to the mainland, we found the line and hook which the hippo had dragged off, wound around the reeds just waiting to be retrieved. We returned it to the grateful owner."

So we knew, as they did, that God had enabled them to retrieve those two valuable hooks.

People have often asked why we just didn't buy enough hooks for every male adult. The year, 1976, was at the height of the Revolution and although we searched every source in the capital we could find only twelve hooks.

A few months later we were invited back to the island to attend a special occasion. A unique event was taking place on the shores of Getemay Island

– one hundred and fifty adults were deemed ready for baptism. What a great day of rejoicing that was! Elders from the Word of Life (KHC) church on the mainland had come over to examine each candidate to decide whether or not each one fully understood the decision they were making. Never before had we heard of or seen a whole tribe of people believing in God at one time.

As mentioned earlier, the Getemay Island people had been able to survive by weaving cotton blankets and taking them over to the market on the mainland to sell. Buyers from many places in Ethiopia would purchase them. But due to the Government's travel restrictions, sales had dropped and the Getemay people had no money for food. As conditions within the country worsened we realised that the long term solution for these people's survival was for them to have some suitable land on which to grow their own crops. Malcolm Hunter was SIM's district superintendent and together we applied to the local government for an area of uninhabited land close to the lake where the Getemay Island people could settle.

88 Resettled

Amazingly, the government officials were sympathetic to this request and in a short period of time land had been assigned enabling the entire population to move to the mainland in September 1976. In fact at that time the government still had their ferry running on the lake and agreed to transfer all the people, their goods and a few dozen goats and chickens to their new property. Some were reluctant to go, but the government gave them no alternative. All must move at the one time or no land would be given.

Of course it was chaotic to start with. The whole population of adults and children added up to 549 and they were being dumped onto their new land with no protection from the elements, no food supplies, and no agriculture tools for clearing the land. Eventually they did receive a supply of corn and *fafa* (a milk formula for young children), plus one hundred blankets to share between them. Initially SIM was able to supply them with hand tools to enable them to clear the land and build their own huts. We were able to obtain an ox for each family, making a team for two families. As far as we could ascertain, the forebears of the Getemay Island people had fled to the Island 60-80 years before in order to escape the slave-traders who raided the district at that time. Now they were back again in their traditional land of Weregayu.

Shortly after their transfer we made a visit to Weregayu and were amazed to see the progress the settlers had made. With some help from Gemu Christians they had built a large grass-roofed church which measured 52 feet in diameter, where the entire population could gather. They had also built 141 houses, sufficient for everyone. Admittedly, the houses were of poor quality and not completely watertight, but they would do until more time and better materials became available. We were delighted to see these new believers actively forging ahead to re-establish themselves in the new village. Already about a hundred acres of small scrub-like bushes and thorn trees had been cleared in readiness for ploughing and planting.

We made our final visit to Weregayu to visit our friends in 1977 with Grahame and Nola, my brother and his wife. It was another delightful experience, driving through their tall fields of corn to be welcomed like royalty. They escorted us into their church building and immediately washed our feet. I can assure you some of us needed more than our feet washed. Driving in the six kilometres from the main road we had encountered part of the track completely flooded and the only way we could proceed was for Norene, Grahame and Nola to walk in front of the Landrover, link arms and wade along to make sure there were no stumps or holes. It was like a lake of water. At one place Norene stepped into a hole, disappearing almost up to her armpits. Although not so funny for her, we couldn't help laughing as we saw my poor wife floundering around in the muddy brown water. That discovery, however, saved the Landrover from overturning.

During the night the rain poured down and the flood water swept right through our sleeping quarters in the church building, not to mention pouring through our poorly thatched grass roof. What a miserable wet night we spent together! Fancy our VIP visitors having to experience such hardship.

As we departed the next morning for the last time, the young men escorted us safely through the flooded areas – a bittersweet moment for us all. Then people came running from all directions, bringing us corn cobs as a thank offering for what we had done for them.

"But you need this food more than we do!" we objected.

"When we first trusted Jesus as our Saviour, we didn't know he would send his angels to help us," they replied.

"We are not angels!" we protested.

"But God sent you to help us in our time of need. Not only have our sins been forgiven, but our stomachs have been filled."

God had called us so clearly to return to Ethiopia. Had we come only to help these Getemay people, it would have all been worthwhile.

89 Tsetse Flies

On another occasion, soon after our arrival in Ethiopia in 1976, I found myself surveying the great Maazey Valley. Who could believe that such a fertile valley, some thousands of acres in extent, had not one living soul in it? Just a few kilometres away there was a vast population, many of whom were living in poverty. The reason? Tsetse flies.

These blowfly-sized creatures held complete sway in the valley of Dera Malo, nestled between two great mountain ranges. Malcolm Hunter had flown over and trekked through the valley, seeing its great potential. He was so excited about the possibilities, that five days after our arrival back in Ethiopia in the January, I was travelling with Malcolm to help evaluate the situation.

What scope! What an ideal location for a resettlement project. As far as the eye could see, there was this seemingly endless valley. The valley was well watered, with numerous streams flowing down from the mountains above. Wherever a stream flowed through the valley a strip of luxuriant forest trees grew, while the plains were covered with long elephant grass, growing to a height of two meters. Malcolm had even brought a team of workmen from Kamba, another SIM station, and they had started to clear a small airstrip for the MAF planes.

Two major hurdles needed to be overcome before the project became a reality – malaria and sleeping sickness. Malaria could be partially controlled by the taking of regular prophylactic medication and spraying inside the houses with DDT. But sleeping sickness, from the dreaded tsetse fly, was more difficult to control.

We soon experienced the bite of the tsetse fly ourselves. Any warm-blooded moving creature was fair game for it. With its powerful proboscis it would quickly penetrate the thickest clothing and start sucking up blood. A second or two later one would feel the bite, but by then the damage had been done. The tsetse fly's belly quickly became bloated with blood. What an efficient hypodermic syringe that proboscis proved to be! Fortunately not many humans were affected with sleeping sickness, but for domestic animals the death rate was high.

We knew that if we could obtain the funds, we could buy sufficient medication to inject the cattle, giving them protection for a month or two. The valley was 35 flying minutes away from the nearest airfield, 35 kilometres from the nearest dry weather road and 500 kilometres from government officers who controlled this area.

After some months the resettlement project was approved, which included the establishment of a medical clinic and the training of two cattle vaccinators. Saturday, 26 August 1976 was *S Day* (Settlers' Day.) Our aim was to resettle 450 poor families from the surrounding mountains – a total of 2,500 people. Each family would be given half a hectare for their personal use and a share in the community fields. SIM promised to provide one ox per family and the government agreed to give sufficient grain to each family until their first harvest. The mission was to provide a nurse to run the clinic. We were thrilled to hear our long-time friends, Eric and Ngaire Klein from Palmerston North, New Zealand, had agreed to come over and help us with our building and agricultural work.

Three weeks after *S Day*, September 18, Norene and I flew down with MAF for a few days to check on the progress of the project and offer encouragement and help. Kees from Holland was at that time the only SIM missionary there and he was involved in surveying half-hectare sites for those chosen to resettle at Maazey. A spare tent was available for us, but the heat and the flies were unbelievable.

90 Maazey From Norene's Perspective

On September 18 we flew over the mountains and down to the vast plain of the Maazey River Resettlement project. We travelled lightly, with a change of clothes and some food supplies which included fruit and vegetables from Addis. From the air we were thrilled to see the tent settlement which looked rather like a gypsy camp, with an airfield right beside it. It was extremely hot and we longed for a cold drink, but since there was no refrigerator we settled for a cup of tea. Someone had sent us some sticky fly rolls – the sort you hang from the ceiling and unroll. It was so hot the sticky substance melted and ran off the paper. Kees, a Dutch agriculturalist was the only missionary on site at that stage, but a few minutes later another small plane swooped in. Helen Johnstone, an Australian nurse, had arrived to start holding daily clinics in a tent under the most primitive of conditions.

We had a gas stove for cooking, a home-made "bench" and shelves, plus a few odd dishes. The margarine was almost liquid from the heat. There were some huge cans of dried milk, and some oranges from Addis. Nearing completion was a little shed which would serve as a kitchen. This had a mud floor and tin roof and was much cooler than a tent. There would be a small makeshift clinic under the same roof, and we expected to move in to these new buildings in a day or two.

Trial vegetable plots were organised as little food could be purchased locally. There were some small potatoes and tomatoes, a few eggs, sweet potatoes and the occasional chicken. We had some canned food, plenty of flour for making bread, a gas stove which worked well, plus a few gifts of food from grateful patients. One day I helped the nurse by holding a torch or flashlight in the tent as she performed simple surgery. We slept in sleeping bags on air mattresses, but one air mattress was always flat by morning and so we took turns with that one!

The scenery was glorious, with majestic mountains surrounding the vast valley and bright colours dashed across the sky at sunset, as in a child's painting. We had our daily bath and washed our clothes in a nearby fast-flowing river. "Wash and wear" clothes were handy in that heat as at Getemay Island.

Insects were a problem, and we were bitten all over by tsetse flies. (Thank goodness they only cause sickness in animals.) Flies swarmed by the

The 'Gypsy' Camp at the Maazey Resettlement Project

thousand, there were sand fleas under our toe-nails, and plenty of snakes. The toilet was my greatest challenge. It was just a hole in the ground with no seat.

Bruce continues:

Two days after our arrival at the camp we were startled to hear the following message on the SIM radio transmission:

"Attention all SIM personnel. This is an urgent message. The government has grounded all light planes until further notice."

Surely it couldn't be true? We had so many other plans. We began to think of our options. We were 135 sweltering kilometres from the nearest eastern SIM mission station. There was not even a track to follow and eight rainy-season rivers flowed between us and the station. We could head to the north to our SIM station at Chencha, but that meant climbing over a 10,000 foot pass, which seemed unwise in view of Norene's heart problem. Or we could stay in the valley until the flying ban was lifted.

We chose the latter option even although we had only one change of clothes each. We felt badly for our two teenagers who were boarding in Addis. They'd be concerned about us and anxiously awaiting our return, and so we sent them a radio message about the delay.

We also felt guilty, draining our two fellow missionaries of their meagre supply of food. After all, we were only meant to be there for a few days. But they insisted we share with them.

"The Lord will provide," they said. And he did.

We had various other commitments during the next few weeks, including a speaking engagement at a conference in Kenya. All that had to be cancelled via the radio transmission, as we daily waited for progress. Not that it was difficult to fill in our time with so many activities taking place. During those uncertain days we read Psalm 34 (Living Bible) over and over:

"Put God to the test... He freed me from all my fears... The good man does not escape all troubles – he has them too. But the Lord helps him in each and every one. God even protects from accident."

Each day we expected to hear the no-flying ban had been lifted. But that wasn't to be for many months.

91 Relief Arrives – But at a Cost

After about a month, SIM administration in Addis asked a fellow missionary to drive our Landrover into Maazey. We were most apprehensive as the so-called "track" had not been used for three years and was overgrown with elephant grass. Even so the radio message arrived, telling us our vehicle was on its way, accompanied by a second one. The men would also bring in urgently needed supplies.

Some three days later the vehicles arrived at the isolated and primitive settlement. What a sorry sight our Landrover was! The four fenders were all smashed in to some extent, the front-wheel drive broken, and much of the chassis was bent. I could have cried, for it was a vehicle World Vision had loaned to us for our time in Ethiopia. But we had to realise these two inexperienced drivers had offered to drive the vehicles over unknown and unformed tracks.

The question now was, whether our vehicle could be driven back. Fortunately the winch on the front of the car had not been damaged and the back wheel drive was still working, and so after a few minor repairs we decided to give it a go. We left early in the morning and managed to winch ourselves out of some of the more difficult rivers. In one place we slid into a bad hole and our vehicle slowly tipped over onto its side. We crawled out the top, and then with our trusty winch and an extra long length of steel cable, managed to anchor the wire rope around a distant tree, pulling ourselves out without inflicting any more damage on the vehicle or ourselves. The tsetse flies had a feast, as it was too hot to travel with the windows closed and they simply swarmed into the vehicle, particularly when we were near the rivers. Each time we had to negotiate a particularly difficult spot we stopped and asked for the Lord's help, thanking him once we were through. The return trip took two thirteen-hour days, with a night in an Ethiopian house. How grateful we were to make it safely home.

Fortunately at that time in Addis Ababa there was a large foreign company which assembled Landrovers and so they were able to supply new fenders, straighten out the chassis and generally repair the vehicle.

The Maazey project continued to prosper. Everything was coming together nicely. Helen, the nurse, was ably providing medical care for all the patients and distributing their weekly prophylactic pills for malaria. The two cattle vaccinators received their training from a government programme and were successfully keeping the settlers' animals free of sleeping sickness. The local Word of Life church sent us a literacy teacher who quickly established daily classes and before long was reporting good progress. We had brought down a variety of vegetable seeds so the settlers could establish their own productive gardens, and plants matured incredibly fast. Soon there seemed to be enough tomatoes to feed an army, but the people had no way of sending them out of the valley. Within a year they were picking ripe pawpaws. Bananas and pineapples also grew like weeds.

A man from California offered to send me some sweet orange tree seed which he claimed would come true-to-type from seed. I ordered a whole kilo of seed, intending to give some to all the settlers. However, when the seed arrived in Addis Ababa, an over-enthusiastic quarantine officer fumigated the lot against disease to the extent that the germination was ruined and only a few seeds survived. How we nurtured those few sweet orange tree seedlings, planting them out with much care.

Twelve years later when I went back I was amazed to see grove after grove of heavily-bearing sweet orange trees. Unfortunately, long before the fruit was properly coloured and ripe it was picked from the trees and sold in the local markets. Those sweet orange trees are a source of income to hundreds of families in that valley today.

92 A Fishy Story

Knowing these poor people in the Maazey Valley could rarely afford to buy meat, we decided to introduce an aquaculture project and needed to find a suitable site. This project proved challenging, for there was no similar project in Ethiopia which we could follow. However, during our prolonged stay at Maazey we established a good location where it was possible to run water from the river by gravitation to fill the ponds. With wheelbarrows, shovels and picks the settlers gradually carved out a fish pond 1,000 square metres in size.

We made two aborted attempts to fly in fingerlings that year. Finally by the following February, on our third attempt after MAF had been given permission to fly again, we were able to net all the fingerlings we required and fly them in from Addis Ababa.

I'm sure we made history that day. Apart from the pilot and myself, the inside of the Cessna was crammed full of tilapia fingerlings. These were packed in large plastic bags of water, pumped full of oxygen and placed inside four-gallon kerosene tins. *(See coloured photo)*

The flight went without a hitch and when we landed there was great excitement for the settlers. The tins of fish were eagerly carried to the pond and the fingerlings released with very few losses. But we hadn't counted on predators. Quickly all sorts of birds decided they liked the taste of fish too, and so we appointed a day guard to keep our feathered friends away.

The Kleins arrived in Ethiopia on December 20 and were raring to get started on their new assignment. In a miraculous way Steve and Dave, our two oldest sons, had gathered together enough money to visit us for the Christmas holidays. (See chapter 105 for more on this family visit.) I felt more confident making the trip in a fully reconditioned Landrover and had a great crew to help with the driving. Often I would hear remarks like this coming from Eric:

"People at home just wouldn't believe that a four-wheel drive could keep on going on a track like this."

The wet season had passed, the rivers had dropped, and so the two-day journey was much less stressful. The hardest part was leaving Eric and Ngaire in such an isolated spot, without any knowledge of the culture or language. They did have Kees and Helen to help them, but it was tough. They adapted well, and within a few days Ngaire was turning out bread baked in Eric's innovative home-made outside oven.

Despite the primitive conditions under which all of them were working, wonderful things were taking place in the hearts and lives of our new settlers. Many were responding to the gospel message which was faithfully being taught by our national evangelist. Now the new believers had been able to build their own church. Even some of the people who lived in the surrounding mountains were coming down to worship with the new settlers.

But conditions within the country were deteriorating, and after some months MAF decided to fly all its planes down to Kenya before they were nationalised. With the departure of MAF and the isolated situation of our missionary staff at Maazey, SIM decided to withdraw the missionaries from the area. That was a sad day for those of us who had invested much effort into making this project a success.

We continued to keep in daily contact with our Ethiopian national personnel at Maazey via our SIM two-way radio network. One morning the man in charge of the fish-pond project sent me the following urgent message:

"The alligators are coming into the fish pond and eating all our fish! What shall we do?"

To start with I knew he meant "crocodiles." But no crocodiles had ever been seen in the local river where we all washed and swam. Could it be a Nile monitor? At any rate we sent back the following message:

"Drain most of the water from the pond and try to kill the villain!"

The settlers, expecting great excitement, surrounded the pond with their clubs and spears, waiting for the water level to go down. With only 300mm of water left, up jumped a crocodile and fled to the far bank, only to be confronted by many clubs and spears. It made a dash for the other side, but again met fierce resistance. Trapped, it didn't know which way to turn. Finally some brave men went into the pond and finished it off.

At the time of my next visit I found only part of the jawbone with the row of teeth to confirm the story. This I brought back to New Zealand to remind us of the thief who stole so many of our precious fingerlings. The crocodile was not large, as crocs go. He was only two meters long, but he was fat and sleek. When his belly was slit open, out poured many of our healthy fish. I was told later that once the water level was lowered and the fingerlings could be seen more easily, some had grown to 150mm (six inches) within six months of being introduced. At that rate of growth they would begin harvesting within the next six months. Also it was noticed they were starting to breed, as there were lots of small fingerlings in the pond. No wonder the tilapia in Borneo is called the "mad fish." It grows like mad, eats like mad and breeds like mad.

Norene wrote a little ditty about this episode.

Maazey Monster

Urgent message by radio sched:
"Alligators eating our fish", it said.
"What shall we do?" the question went
"Empty the pool," reply was sent.
Pool was reduced to water and mud,
But no sign of the beast - no splash, no thud.
The villagers then were quite disappointed,
When one brave soul used a stick real pointed.
With a massive splash the beast took fright,
From bank to bank, to a corner tight.
In no time he was battered to death,
A Loch Ness monster or whatever your guess.
His tummy was cut and duly dissected,
Then countless fish were quickly inspected.
Sad to say much of the fish population
Had suffered by means of this nasty creation.
But lots of fish had been produced
And now two ponds we'll introduce.
So one good thing came out of this incident:
They've accepted the project without precedent!

93 A Miraculous Escape

At last we were nearing home. Philip (14) and I had been revisiting our Maazey resettlement project and had spent the last night of our 1,000 kilometre trip at a small hotel in Wando Genet. As mentioned previously, we loved going there. The place had special memories for us as we had been responsible for supervising the building of the hot pools for Princess Tenagnework. Now the complex had been nationalised and was open to the public. The rooms were comparatively expensive, but to have a swim in the hot mineral pools at the end of a tiring day was just paradise for us. The following morning, after a quick breakfast, we reported in to SIM on our two way car radio on their morning schedule. We said we expected to be back in Addis Ababa about 2pm and asked that Norene and Becky be notified of this.

Everything had become unsettled in Ethiopia, but daily we were conscious of the Lord's protection and care. We arrived at Shashamane, which was familiar to us because of the ten years we had spent at the nearby leprosarium. Passing through the town we noticed a lot of unusual activity, with soldiers running everywhere waving their guns.

"I think we'd better get out of this town as quickly as possible," I told Phil. "I don't like the look of all this activity."

At the far side of the town we were stopped by a crude road block – just a few tree branches thrown across the road. We would have skirted around them, but for the presence of some soldiers who told us emphatically to stop. When asked the reason they told us they didn't know, but these were their orders. It was nine in the morning. Another missionary family and some of our Ethiopian friends were travelling behind us and before long we were all ordered out of our cars and told to hide in the ditch beside the road.

Soon after that shooting started in the town and we realised a battle was taking place. We prayed for protection, particularly for the boys. Army vehicles sped past carrying the wounded to the SIM hospital some eleven kilometres out of town. About three hours later we were ordered back into our vehicle and told to drive back into town. Grisly sights awaited us, which we will never forget. Bands of Arsi men were chanting their war cries and holding their guns and spears aloft with the victims' clothes displayed on the tips of their spears. Some were dragging the torsos of mutilated bodies along the road. We had to drive through many such bands, not knowing if they would turn on us at any moment.

As we all assembled at the hotel, we found a large number of nationals and foreigners all terrified by the day's events. We were just in time to buy the last soft drink and miraculously were able to phone Norene in Addis to ask her to alert people by telephone to pray for all of us who were stranded in Shashamane. We told her we thought the local bank had been robbed and that the army and local Arsi were searching for the robbers. As the shooting and chanting intensified, we realised we were all in danger as there was complete anarchy in the town, with thousands of armed men out of control. I had a strong feeling we should return to the spot where we had been stopped in the morning and beg to be permitted to proceed. Another carload of SIM missionaries had now joined us, and so we travelled in convoy, moving slowly through the menacing crowd until we reached the original road block. Hundreds of armed men were there, and there was no way we could get through.

Suddenly a man in civilian clothes approached our vehicle, pointing his gun at us. My heart seemed to miss several beats. Was this the end? As he came closer he motioned me to unwind my window.

"Mr Bond, what are you doing here?" he blurted out.

I recognised him as a friend I had known twenty years before, and his name flashed into my mind. (This was a miracle as I was not blessed with a good memory for names.)

"Ato Ephraim!" I answered. "Please help us!"

He lowered his gun and explained the bank had been robbed and they were guarding the road lest any of the robbers try to escape.

"I am in charge of the local militia," he added, "and will escort you safely through this mob of people."

True to his word, he walked in front of our vehicle and waved off any who tried to molest us until we reached the original road block, which he then ordered to be opened. There was some argument with the guards, but after showing our travel documents we were free to leave that terrible scene. Just as we were about to leave, a bus coming the other way was stopped. The guards swarmed into it, dragging out innocent victims, some of whom were executed on the spot. The whole scene was developing into a tribal vendetta and there was nothing anybody could do about it.

No wonder we stopped down the road and gave thanks together to God for our miraculous escape.

Postscript. It was now 1993, sixteen years later. The Marxist government had been overthrown and once again Ethiopia was beginning to enjoy a time of peace and freedom. I was now SIM Director for Ethiopia and a great number of foreigners and nationals would come to my office for many different reasons.

One day an elderly, white-haired Ethiopian gentleman came to see me, but Sylvia, my secretary, did not catch his name.

"Don't you recognise me?" he said after some polite greetings.

I had to confess that I didn't. He laughed.

"I'm Ato Ephraim, the person who saved your life sixteen years ago," he said.

Of course I knew him. How could I ever forget that incident?

In the meantime he had aged and his dark hair had turned completely white. As he smiled and talked to me, the image of Ato Ephraim approaching our Landrover with a loaded gun pointed at us came flooding back.

"Because you don't understand the Arsi language," he went on, "you were not aware that some of the local Arsi men at the roadblock recognised you. 'That's Mr Bond, the man who stole all our money from the crops he grew at the leprosarium,' they said. 'Let's kill him now!"

Ato Ephraim told me it was only because of his position in the militia that he was able to protect our lives.

We wept and hugged each other and I realised God had allowed him to thwart the evil intentions of men that day.

94 Planting an Orchard

Chencha was in the highlands of Ethiopia (over 8,000 feet or 2,460 m) and part of the Gamo Gofa region. With the rapid spread of Marxism, the church elders in Chencha had the foresight to ask for suggestions as to how they could help their people become more self-sufficient and better prepared to face the future. We made five return trips to Chencha (about 1100 kilometers each trip) between January and September 1976 to talk with the elders and try to determine how we could help. The church had bought an area of land adjacent to the SIM compound, which they agreed could be used for development projects. There were three projects which we thought would be helpful to the area – a dairy cow breeding project, a reforestation project and an orchard project.

Planting an Orchard

We decided to focus on the orchard project first. We prepared a budget and a project proposal, which the Canadian government agreed to fund. The aim of the project was to enable every farmer living in the highlands of Gamo Gofa to procure and plant at least one apple and one plum tree in his own garden. The highlands were densely populated and extra land was not available to them. But within the confines of their own gardens, which are normally fenced and well-protected from animals, space could be found to plant a couple of fruit trees.

Was this just a dream or would it one day become a reality? The early missionaries to Chencha had planted fruit trees in their own backyard, but they had all been forced to leave a couple of years before. We wondered if some of these trees were still living. We were encouraged to find several trees, both plums and pears, and although somewhat neglected, they were surviving and productive.

Everything came together quickly. Our budget proposal was accepted and a suitable site, about one hectare in size, was available in the church property. Even the Ministry of Agriculture gave permission for us to have, free of charge, 200 fruit trees from a newly established plant nursery some 400 kilometres away. These included apples, pears, peaches and plums. Six trees of every variety from their nursery were given to us.

Phil (13), our youngest son, was a tremendous help as he was able to accompany me during his various holidays from school. We transported and planted the trees together in the high-altitude orchard. Once the trees were planted, the church elders built a strong bamboo fence around them and we looked forward to seeing which varieties would best suit the region.

Our next challenge was to establish a little fruit-tree nursery. We needed to determine which of the root stock was most suitable for our high altitude region and to start a training programme in methods of propagation. A New Zealander, Janet Winch, who was well trained in horticulture and had the right skills for this task, applied to SIM and was shortly on the job in Chencha. Everything was progressing well as far as the orchard was concerned.

95 Suffering For Christ

Sadly, we would not be able to visit to Chencha again for many years. Politically dark clouds were gathering as Marxism was starting to take full effect. Christians were being persecuted, and everyone was suffering.

"The Bible is an imperialist book," chanted the communist cadres. "Down with it! Destroy it!"

Churches were being closed and their buildings and properties seized. Many leaders, young and old, were already in prison. The communists often targeted young choir members, both men and women, and beat them. Most mission compounds had by now been nationalised and their property seized, with the missionaries being forced to leave the country. The remaining thirty-five SIM missionaries were treated with suspicion.

In Chencha where the orchard had been planted, the final straw came in December 1978 when sixteen of the main church elders were imprisoned in the local jail and their church property appropriated. All the physical suffering the men, their wives and families suffered in those dark days will only be fully known when we get to heaven. It was only after their release from prison, two years later, that we heard the miraculous story of how God had protected them when they were all poisoned with Malathion.

The president of the Gamo Gofa churches, Ato Tesfaye Tole who lived in Chencha, told us the following stories:

"One day," he said, "Our guards ordered us to dig a deep hole in the prison grounds, which took us ten days. Rumours quickly spread to our families and friends that we were digging our own graves, and many people prayed that the wicked plans of men would be thwarted."

The Muslim governor of the region, Ali Musa, was a notoriously wicked man who openly avowed to eliminate all Christians. He had ordered the large hole dug in the prison yard in order to bury these Christian men alive at a public gathering. He himself made a special trip up to the mountainous region of Chencha to personally oversee this plan, boasting to everyone that this day was the last one for the Christian leaders.

Just before the appointed public burial, he was invited by a friend in the Ministry of Agriculture to view a new irrigation project which had just been completed. This included a large catchment pond for collecting rain water. For some reason he ordered a co-worker into the water to prove how deep the pond was. The man swam out to the middle and drowned. Ali Musa, upset by this tragic turn of events, jumped into his vehicle and with his large retinue of officials and police, headed back to Araba Minch to bury his colleague. A few days later an order came from the central government in Addis Ababa that it was illegal for anyone to be executed without a proper trial. Thus the Christian elders were spared from death.

After a few days, word came that Ali Musa was to be transferred to the Bale region, and the prison guards ordered the Christians to fill in their own empty grave. Of course his transfer to Bale meant he would continue his nefarious deeds elsewhere. On his way to Bale he stopped off at Shasamane and many people who were condemned as enemies of the government were rounded up and thrown into a deep pit which had been dug by a bulldozer, and then covered with earth. This wicked man was responsible for the death of hundreds of people wherever he went, thus gaining promotion and favour with the leaders of the Derg. However in May 1991, when the Derg was overthrown, before he could be arrested he ended his own life with a single bullet.

96 Bond Red

It was not until 1988 that I was able to make a return trip to Chencha.

The road up the mountain had not improved since my last visit in 1977, the country was still in the grip of a Marxist government, but things were beginning to change and we as Westerners were welcomed in some parts of the country. The church elders had been released from prison, and even some of the church buildings and land had been returned. We wondered what had happened to the orchard.

It was completely gone. The fence, too, had long gone and no doubt had been put to good use for many a cooking fire.

Had all our work and effort been in vain? It appeared that way, until somebody told us the following story:

Back in 1979, when the church property with the newly-planted orchard was nationalised, the bamboo fence was torn down and all the neighbourhood cattle had free grazing. A couple of neighbours, recognising that the trees which the foreigners had planted might become valuable, went at night and dug out several apple trees, planting them in their own backyards. In the following years two of the varieties grew well and started to produce heavy crops.

These two neighbours eventually became Christians, and feeling guilty about what they had done, wanted to make restitution to the church. Of course they couldn't dig the trees out, but they offered to make their trees available for propagation purposes for the reestablishment of an orchard. The church leaders were delighted and established a plant nursery for that original stock. Contact was made with Tear Fund UK who sent out good root stock and helped provide the expertise to establish the nursery.

So after eleven years, here I was revisiting Chencha where I was delighted to view rows and rows of budded apple trees ready for distribution in the next rainy season.

Today the trees are bearing an abundance of red apples which are being transported and sold in the Addis Ababa market. Everyone in the area is catching on and wanting to plant a tree or two in their own backyard. A friend of ours, Tony Rinaudo who now works with World Vision, Australia, visited Chencha in 2001.

"Bruce, you'll be interested in this," he told me. "The nursery is now propagating ten thousand budded apple trees each year for distribution in the highlands. Furthermore, when I asked the name of the variety of red apple they were growing the people said, 'We don't know the actual variety so we've named it *Bond Red*.' Now it's known all over Ethiopia by that name!"

Malcolm Hunter, whom we have mentioned several times in these chapters, has always taken a keen interest in the work and ministry of the Gamo Gofa churches. In 2003 he was visiting in Chencha.

"Bruce, in my opinion, of all the community development work you were involved in, this project has had the most significant impact," he told us later. "Not only has it been able to lift the living standard of the people due to the sale of apples, but it has had a direct influence in helping to spread the gospel in Ethiopia."

Surprised, we asked him what he meant.

"Christians in Gamo Gofa are all subsistence farmers," he replied, "with little money to support their many missionaries. Now with the proceeds of the abundant apple crops, thousands more dollars are being given to support the national evangelists and so increase the ministry of spreading the gospel."

All this resulted from a simple orchard being planted years before!

97 Reforestation

We are told that only two percent of the natural forests of Ethiopia remain today. It was tragic to witness during our time in Ethiopia the disappearance of the great Podocarpus forests of the south which grew so luxuriantly on the eastern slopes of the Rift Valley. They were a natural treasure.

Thousands of truckloads of logs were shipped out from the Arsi Region between 1955 and 1980 to Addis Ababa to be milled. Little effort was ever made to replant these areas, and today one is hard pressed to see any of the virgin forest that existed in Arsi only a few years ago.

With tree seedlings for Reafforestation Project

I remember some of my Arsi friends inviting me to their annual hunt in the vast Podocarpus forests. Hundreds of Arsi men gathered, each carrying one or two long spears. They divided into two groups. Our group spread out along the banks of a small river, while the second group went miles upstream, driving dozens of wild animals as they advanced towards the first group. As the two groups merged, there was tremendous excitement as spears were flung in all directions at the fleeing animals. Many animals were harvested and somehow the meat was evenly divided, for everyone returned home with some fresh meat that day.

Today that forest has gone, as have those exciting annual hunts. All that remains are the stories the old men pass on to the younger generation.

The floor of the Rift Valley covers hundreds of thousands of hectares which were originally covered with one of many species of acacia sometimes referred to as the "thorn tree." This tree is suited to the long dry seasons, when there may not be any rain for six months or more. But within a week or two of the first rains, the trees break out in a canopy of green leaves and fragrant white flowers. By the time the rainy season is over the trees have produced an abundant harvest of seedpods, which the nomadic pastoralists greatly value for their grazing stock. The trees also provide erosion control in the dry sandy conditions experienced during the dry season. And because the trees are slow-growing, their wood is hard and makes excellent firewood and charcoal.

Unfortunately, with the population explosion taking place in Ethiopia and the lack of cheap alternative fuels, these acacia trees are being decimated at an alarming rate. All along the main south road, hundreds of people can be found selling sacks of charcoal and piles of firewood to merchants who in turn sell it in the capital city, Addis Ababa. Where trees once grew, fields of corn now grow. Unfortunately the area does not have a regular rainfall as in the highlands, and in marginal years drought and famine do occur. In many areas we have been saddened to see on market days, hundreds of donkey loads of dry cow manure being taken to the market for sale as fuel. In other words the lack of available firewood has forced the people into selling their valuable organic matter as fuel, instead of returning it to the soil.

In our community development programme much emphasis was placed on helping different communities to re-establish some of the forests which had been destroyed. We quickly discovered that when planting bare-rooted tree-seedlings, a high percentage died within the first year. We switched to planting all our seedlings in plastic tubes, about 100mm to 150mm long. When the rains came the plastic tubes would be slit open and the seedlings planted out without disturbing their root system at all. This method is labour intensive, but productive in establishing young trees in a hot climate. Many of the plantations established in 1976 and 1977 have now been harvested.

We were also able to plant out some of the indigenous species, like the local cedar tree (*Juniperus procera*) and the korso tree (*Hagenia abyssinica*), both of which grow in the highlands. The korso is a red wood and good for building and making furniture.

98 Of Honey and Hives

For months we had looked forward to sharing in a special seminar organised by Paul Balisky. Because of the onslaught of communism in Ethiopia, Paul, together with the officials of the 'Word of Life' church had requested a community development seminar in Jimma. Their aim was to better prepare church leaders and evangelists for what lay ahead, for it was becoming increasingly difficult for evangelists and even pastors to continue their spiritual ministry without involvement in the community in some practical ways.

For many months before the seminar, Paul had asked if we could work together on a twelve-week course which would be intensely practical and yet strongly biblical. In the morning we would teach biblical subjects, and in the afternoon practical ones. The course was to be held in the rainy season and would involve church leaders and evangelists from all over Ethiopia.

The most suitable place for this seminar was in Jimma, where SIM had established a theological training facility known as Grace Bible Institute in 1964. For three of the twelve weeks I was to teach various practical subjects such as apiculture (bee keeping), aquaculture (fish farming), rabbit farming and rat control. One of the biblical subjects I taught in the mornings was the relationship between the Great Commission and the Great Commandment, based on John Stott's book, *Christian Mission in the Modern World* (IVP, 1975).

Honey production played an important role in the life of many Ethiopians. Their own beekeeping methods, however, did not produce a great harvest of honey – hence our decision to include this subject.

Traditionally a beehive was made from a hollowed out log which was then suspended high in the branches of a tree. Agile men climbed the tree, securing their hives with ropes or leather straps, and then waited for natural swarming to take place. After the rainy season some clever men would smear their bodies with a bee repellent and then bravely climb the trees at night. Armed with smoking cow dung to anaesthetise the bees and keep them from stinging too much, they lowered the hives to the men who were waiting to harvest the honeycomb. One end of the hive was opened and the honeycomb and brood scooped into a container. Finally the hive was re-hoisted into the branches and securely tied. By the time this manoeuvre was over, the bees were in a state of agitation, ready to sting anything that moved. Many bees were killed and the hive almost completely destroyed, but the end result might amount to only four kilos of mixed-up brood and honeycomb. Our challenge was, how could we do better, given that no modern bee equipment was available in Ethiopia?

It was time to introduce the "Kenya Top Bar Hive." This required no movable frames or foundation wax. The end view of the hive was elliptical in shape, with the length of the hive almost one meter. Inside, instead of the standard honey frames, bars or pieces of bamboo were used to support the combs of honey which the bees attached to the bars. Sometimes the bees could be encouraged to build their honeycombs on these bamboo strips by coating them with liquid wax. The tremendous advantage was that once there was honey in the hive, the lid could be opened and the bars containing the honeycombs taken out without unduly disturbing the whole hive. Because the African bees were vicious, it was advantageous to always work them in the darkness of the night and then keep animals and people away for the next day or two.

Jimma, where our community development seminars were being held, was a large city in the southwestern part of Ethiopia, where limited quantities of cedar planks were available. During the woodwork classes in the afternoon, the students were all able to make their own "Kenya Top Bar Hives." This was great fun but no doubt there was some scepticism about whether or not they would actually work.

During our lessons on beekeeping we taught some of the mysteries of the bee world and all the students were extremely interested. As a demonstration we hung up one of our newly-made bee-hives in the tree immediately outside our classroom. Some of the cynical students suggested:

"Mr Bond, if you really want to attract a swarm of bees in this country, you'll need to hang the hive high up in the branches of a large tree."

"No," I said, "if the conditions are right the bees will go anywhere to make their home."

Norene and I were able to stay only three weeks in Jimma at that stage, and so had to leave the other teachers to carry on with their different classes.

No sooner had we arrived back in the city of Addis Ababa, when a radio message was sent to us:

"Yesterday afternoon while the students were in the classroom, there was a great humming when a large swarm of bees swept down from the sky and entered your demonstration beehive. Furthermore, because it is right outside the door of the classroom, the bees are viciously attacking the students as they pass. What shall we do?"

This was a practical demonstration that these Kenya Top Bar beehives really worked, wherever they were suspended. But the safety of the students was paramount, and so we suggested that at night, when all the bees had entered the hive, they moved the hive a few metres until it was well away from the classroom entrance.

When we returned for the second seminar we now had a working hive at the back of our classroom, which enabled us to show in a practical way how bees worked. I explained:

"The bees always raise their brood in the middle of the box and on either end store the provisions for raising their brood. This includes pollen and honey. If we lift the lid off our beehive, we should be able to take the outside combs without disturbing the brood in the middle. Remember the brood and the honeycombs were attached to simple strips of bamboo."

There was great excitement among the students when we agreed to lift the lid off the hive and peep inside.

One evening we all dressed as best we could to withstand the onslaught of the bees, and with copious smoke approached the hive. There was a great hum as we opened the lid, and bees came attacking in all directions. But we held our ground and slowly removed the outside combs of honey in the dark. Quickly replacing the lid, we rushed inside to nurse our stings and remove the bees which were still caught up in our clothing. But what a reward! Fresh and pure liquid honey! We quickly divided the honeycomb, so that all could share in the bountiful harvest – and that after only a few weeks. In our haste to rob the hive we had taken some brood, and so I wondered what we would do with that.

"That's the most delicious part, Mr Bond," they said as they quickly divided it amongst themselves for a succulent morsel.

99 Of Fish and Rats

We then went on to teach aquaculture. This was entirely foreign to almost all the students as the nearest ocean from Jimma was hundreds of kilometres away and the fresh water lakes were few and far between. But heavy rains in the highlands meant there was a good potential for aquaculture and that proved to be the most productive method of producing protein. Freshwater fish farming was successful in many countries of the world, but in Ethiopia it was completely untried. We had approached the representatives of the Ministry of Agriculture and Fisheries to find out about their plans and were given full cooperation and help in our proposed venture.

Already we had an aquaculture project going in our Maazey resettlement programme, and by now knew of the possibilities elsewhere, providing conditions remained stable. We taught the practicalities of where to site a fish pond (i.e. near a suitable river or depression which could be filled either with rain or river water), how deep to dig the pond, and how to stock it with suitable fish fingerlings.

This was all theoretical, as many in our group had never seen a fish, let alone eaten one, and they needed to be convinced it was a worthwhile venture. Norene came up with the idea of buying tilapia fish from the Addis Ababa market and giving a demonstration of how to cook them. We managed to persuade someone in Addis Ababa to buy one fish for each student and send them to Jimma, 350 kilometres to the southwest.

Excitement was high when the fish arrived. There were many comments made and questions asked.

"Look at its big eyes!" someone said. "How come they're still open? Is it really dead?"

Others asked how the fish was killed and whether the scales were eaten.

We explained the different methods of preparing the fish for cooking, but in order to be as simple as possible, we decided to scale and gut the fish and then fry them whole in a pan over an open fire, just adding a little local oil and salt. We warned about the dangers of eating the bones, and hesitatingly everyone started trying it.

What a fantastic time of laughter and fun as we all feasted on fish and locally-made bread. The end result was a pile of neatly picked-over bones and the commendation that fish was an excellent and tasty food.

One afternoon, after finishing our classes on honey production and fish farming, I announced to the students that our next subject would be rat control. As we were walking home, we happened to overhear a conversation going on between two of the students.

"Two weeks ago Mr Bond taught us about beekeeping and we ate some of the honey," one of them said. "This week he has taught us about fish farming and we ate some of the fish. But wait. Next week he's going to teach us about rat control!"

100 "The Mad Dog"

Our part in the seminar seemed to finish quickly and on a Saturday morning we planned to drive back to Addis Ababa. Things were becoming increasingly difficult for all concerned, both nationals and foreigners. Next door to the SIM compound in Jimma the MAF (Missionary Aviation Fellowship) compound was situated, where several foreign families lived. Realising their flying days in Ethiopia were numbered they began to make plans to send equipment and personnel out of Ethiopia before everything was nationalised. On hearing we were leaving for Addis Ababa with an empty Landrover, they asked if we could help them out. Each family was keen to send a suitcase of their most precious belongings to Addis. They knew it would be difficult to take them through the local airport, as luggage was searched thoroughly and even books and photographs were often confiscated. Norene and I agreed rather reluctantly to take their suitcases, knowing the danger of being searched at the various road blocks along the way. But things were deteriorating quickly and we realised it was perhaps the last chance these families had to save a few of their family treasures. They promised to pray through the period of time we would be travelling to Addis Ababa. Paul and Lila also sent one small trunk of treasures with us to Addis Ababa.

The local curfew lifted at 6am, and so we drove out of the compound on the dot. We were not looking forward to meeting "the mad dog" again.

When travelling down to Jimma, just a few weeks before, we had had a nasty shock at a roadblock on the outskirts of town. As we travelled along we had passed a small, innocuous-looking shack on the side of the dusty gravel road. Once past it, I glanced into the rear view mirror. I was terrified to see a man jump to his feet and aim his rifle at our departing vehicle. In a split second I realised we had passed through a roadblock without stopping.

I jammed on the brakes and reversed at high speed back to the shack. The guard was ropable, and ready to shoot us. We were "foreign pigs" and "CIA agents," flouting the law by failing to stop at a government road block. Perhaps the locals knew of its existence, but we certainly didn't. There was no sign or indication that this was a compulsory stop. We have rarely seen or heard a man act the way that man did that afternoon. After searching us and our vehicle, he cooled down enough to let us pass.

"Thank you Lord," we whispered.

We nicknamed him "the mad dog."

Now at 6am we had to meet this road barrier guard again. Hence our request for prayer for God's protection when we thought of our precious cargo in the back. To our amazement the door of his little shack was tightly closed. As we approached we slipped the car into neutral and silently descended the slight decline, keeping our eye on the rear mirror in case of any sudden action. Our "friend" must have still been in a deep sleep.

"Thank you, Lord, for the first miracle of the day," we gratefully whispered.

One down and many more to go. This was scary stuff.

"Lord, keep us calm," we prayed.

The next noteworthy roadblock was at the Gibey River. This turned out to be a simple one. No way could we cross that bridge without stopping, for there was a barrier across the road. We stopped, bought some local pineapples, showed our travel documents, joked in our best Amharic, and then were free to cross the bridge. The friendly guards did not even go to the back of the Landrover to check our baggage!

101 Saved By A Typewriter

"Spies! CIA agents! Look at their typewriter. Let's arrest them!"

We had passed through many roadblocks that day and in no instance were asked to open our rear door. Finally we reached Wolkete, where we were stopped on entering the town. After questioning us and viewing our work permits, the officials allowed us to proceed. We then stopped to buy ourselves a cold drink in a small hotel in the town. Feeling relieved we had passed through the worst of the roadblocks, we were surprised to find a second crude roadblock at the end of the town. Ironically this was manned by muscular women guards armed with Russian rifles.

Our hearts missed a beat. These women were fearsome. Commanding us to stop, one of the guards stepped round to the passenger side, and flinging open Norene's door tried to pull her out. I quickly grabbed the door and slammed it shut, knowing how cruel and ruthless some of these women could be, even in their body search. Of course that provoked further trouble and shouting, and soon we were surrounded by a great crowd of guards and onlookers.

At that moment one of the guards spied something on the middle seat which we had covered with a towel. Leaning over me she yanked off the towel, revealing our old typewriter.

"Ah!" she gloated. "These foreigners have a typewriter. They must be CIA agents!"

To them this was the crowning evidence. We argued that we were teachers. How could we teach without a typewriter?

"Then where is your receipt?" they demanded. "Where is your permission to carry a typewriter?"

All the time we stuck to using English, thinking it might help us in this situation. However, as they argued our fate, we listened in on their conversation in Amharic. They were convinced we were American spies, but where to incarcerate us posed a little problem. Apparently they thought their prison facilities unsuitable for foreigners.

About this time a nicely-spoken young man approached us.

"These are bad people," he said in English. "Don't you have any documentation to prove that you are permitted to teach and own a typewriter?"

"Well, no," we answered. "We do have our work permits, but they have nothing to do with permission to carry a typewriter."

"Don't you have any other official papers?" he continued.

Then I remembered. Tucked in our glovebox was an official-looking document to say we were permitted to travel around even on the "car-less" day. (Because fuel was tightly rationed, all cars had been assigned certain days in the week when they were not permitted to be on the road. But because of our community development work, we were exempt and had been given an official letter stamped by different authorities.)

I hurriedly found the letter and thrust it into the hands of this young man who seemed relieved. He ran up to the arguing mob.

"We can't arrest these people, or we'll be in serious trouble," he said. "See, they have this official letter."

Amazingly, many of these guards were illiterate. One was even viewing the document upside down. They had been thrust into guard duty and didn't have a clue what they were supposed to be doing. But they took our letter and pretending to read it, decided it must have something important to say. Returning it to us, they commanded us to go.

Who, we wondered, was that young man?

As we sped onward to Addis, we realised yet another miracle. During that half-hour delay, not one person even attempted to open the back door of our vehicle A simple old typewriter had been the means of blinding their eyes to those precious belongings.

It had been quite a day. The "Mad Dog" was sound asleep. The guards at all the other roadblocks were courteous and helpful. And here the determined women were frustrated by the intervention of a "guardian angel." What a relief to hand over those precious possessions to the SIM and MAF colleagues in Addis Ababa.

Once again we called to mind the verses God gave us as we were leaving New Zealand:

"He will deliver you again and again, so that no evil can touch you." Job 5:19

Postscript: After the second community development course at Jimma, the Baliskys continued on with their teaching ministry at Grace Bible Institute despite the deteriorating situation. But it was to be shortlived. On 23 March 1978 Paul and Lila travelled to Addis Ababa to bring their three boys back from boarding school for the Easter break. When they returned to Jimma they found their house was sealed by the authorities, forbidding them to enter. Five days later, about three thousand people surged onto the SIM compound, bearing banners and chanting slogans such as:

"Missionaries go home. Close GBI forever!"

Then part of the crowd yelled, "This is the new compound for our political school!"

"We have found it! We have found it!" reiterated the rest of the crowd.

The next day the missionaries were given an official notice. They had twenty-four hours to leave the compound and the district.

In 1992 Dr Mulatu Baffa, the general secretary of the Word Of Life churches, flew with me back to Jimma to meet the government officials who officially handed back both the old SIM and the MAF compounds to the KHC (Word of Life) churches. This was a victory. After being evicted twelve years before, the church was now permitted to return. Of course several of the buildings had been damaged, but it was nothing a skilled carpentry crew and some money could not repair.

God fulfilled another of his promises: *And I will restore to you the years that the locusts have eaten.* (Joel 2:25 AV)

102 Unsettled Times

We often felt frustrated because it was difficult for the folk at home to know the true situation in Ethiopia during those years of the Red Terror. There was no email, and so everything had to be sent home by letters. We never knew whether or not our letters would be opened and read, as there was definitely some censorship going on. At one stage Norene worked out a code for our two sons and close family members when she wanted to write something sensitive. We were often reminded that the Ethiopian government had a massive number of people involved in espionage work.

For a few months we rented an apartment in a government housing block. Some of the Ethiopian people in that block we came to know well, but others would have nothing to do with us. The occupants of one apartment downstairs always kept their doors closed, but as we were passing one day, somebody opened the door just at that moment and we glimpsed a whole array of weapons in the room. Another day a couple of men from that apartment climbed into their Landrover clutching automatic rifles. Were they security men or counter-revolutionaries? We dared not ask.

Every building in Addis Ababa was being systematically searched for hidden arms and any so-called "counter-revolutionaries." Everybody had to carry an identification card issued by the local *kebele* or authority. If anyone was caught without identification, or lived in a different area and didn't have a plausible reason for being there, they were arrested or could be executed on the spot. It was a reign of fear and terror. Without any warning, an area of the city would suddenly be surrounded by troops with all escape routes cut off. Then, while several armed men surrounded a house, others would enter and search it from one end to the other, leaving no stone unturned. They marched in sometimes with their dirty boots, leaving the occupants terrorised as one never knew what item they would consider to be "counter-revolutionary."

Sometimes even teenagers would be shot right in front of their parents, should they be accused of being against the *Derg*. Certainly any firearm, binoculars or even a typewriter was enough evidence to judge a person guilty of crime. To hear shots being fired during these searches in the neighbourhood only heightened the fear of what these ruthless guards might do once they reached your own home. We heard of one mother whose three sons were shot, and the guards turned round and asked her to pay for the bullets they used.

We knew our own house would be searched one day and we tried to prepare accordingly by getting rid of as many suspect things as we could. I was also concerned that they might do the search when I was away on one of my trips and Norene would be on her own. Sunday proved to be the day the guards chose to seal off our area. We had both gone away on Saturday night, so missed the drama of our house search, but our neighbour gave us details of those frightening minutes. Telephone connections were cut and nobody was allowed to leave their house.

After armed guards had been stationed around our apartment block, they started searching room by room. Then they came to our closed door on the second floor, with no one to open the door. Normally they would break open the door or seal the unit so it could not be opened. Our neighbours told us they pleaded on our behalf.

"There are foreigners living in there," they told the guards. "They are helping the poor in Ethiopia, and they don't have much in their house."

With that the guards moved on, and that night when we returned to our unit our neighbours shared their experiences and told us the good news that our unit had not been entered, nor our door sealed.

Nevertheless, thousands of Ethiopians lost their lives during the years of the Red Terror. Despite the curfew every night, we would constantly be woken by the noise of gunfire in different parts of the city. In the morning dead bodies could be seen lying on the footpaths, with notes pinned onto their clothes telling the reason for their death. On some mornings our own teenagers saw some rather horrific sights on their way to high school across town.

My task as community development advisor to the Kale Heywet (Word of Life) Church often involved travelling to various districts. In fact I clocked up more than 30,000 kilometres in the Landrover and countless kilometres by air during 1976-77. This put me at greater risk than those who resided in the location.

103 "Please Come Home!"

At this stage we received two significant letters from New Zealand friends whom we greatly honoured and respected. Both letters had been copied to our SIM general director, Dr Ian Hay.

The first letter was from Dr Blaiklock, Professor of Classics at Auckland University. He had never written before, and so we wondered why he was writing now. We were soon to find out. He pleaded with us to come home immediately, as he felt we were putting ourselves at unnecessary risk and causing stress for our two teenage boys and other family members. He admitted that the murder of his brother-in-law, Cliff Mitchell, by the Arsis twenty-two years before had coloured his thinking and given him reason to write as he did. What should we do?

While we were pondering Dr Blaiklock's plea, another letter arrived from a man whose books and messages had been a blessing to us. J.O. Sanders was the past general director of the Overseas Missionary Fellowship. He, too, pleaded with us to return to New Zealand.

We felt privileged that both of these men would write and ask us to come home. But what a dilemma it placed us in. Were we being unwise in staying on? Was it just bravado? Neither the mission nor the church we were working with was forcing us to stay there.

Our dear friend Dr Mulatu Baffa, with whom we had worked at the Shashamane leprosarium when we were first married, had recently suffered at the hands of some disgruntled employees. As he was going to work one morning, about fifty men suddenly surrounded him, stripping him of his jacket, shoes, watch and wedding ring. Then he was forced to walk on the hot asphalt road with his followers taunting him as he went. Unfortunately his tormentors were daily exhorted by the propaganda broadcast over the government radio. The "broad masses" were told to rise up and overthrow the "enemy."

After some time his captors grew tired of their sport and locked Mulatu up in their local prison, intending to harm him later that night. At the same time Christian friends and family spent time praying for his protection from these evil men. Late that night God sent some real friends who were able to negotiate his release, and he escaped with only badly blistered feet.

We ourselves had been invited back to Shashamane (where we had worked from 1954 to 1964) for a visit. The night before we were due to go we received an anonymous phone call in which we were warned, "Please do not come to Shashamane. There are some evil men, waiting to harm you."

End of conversation.

So why not just pack up and go home? We prayed much about this matter, and one day our daily reading was from Acts 18:9-10.

"One night the Lord spoke to Paul in a vision, 'Do not be afraid; keep on speaking, do not be silent, for I am with you. No one is going to attack and harm you, because I have many people in this city. So Paul stayed for a year and a half, teaching them the word of God."

The date scheduled for our departure was still a year and a half away, and on reading the above we believed it was God's plan for us to remain in Ethiopia.

Shortly after making this decision we received a copy of a letter written to Dr Blaiklock and Mr J.O. Sanders from our SIM General Director, Ian Hay. In this letter Ian thanked the two gentlemen for their concern for the Bond family but said, "I believe that those closest to the action have the best understanding of their situation and am happy to leave Bruce and Norene to use their own judgement as to whether or not they return."

We did stay the next eighteen months, trusting God to see us through the various experiences he would allow in our lives. We knew that as Christians we could not expect to be protected from all suffering, and we often witnessed the Ethiopian church members suffering greatly for their faith. But it was a privilege for us to be alongside them through their dark days.

They had nowhere to run.

104 Knocked Out

In the November of that year I was slated to attend the international Council meetings which were to be held in Switzerland. A few days after I had left, Philip had a bad accident at Bingham Academy where he and Becky were boarding.

He and some other boys were asked to roll some sports equipment (pipes which held the volleyball nets) down a hill to the gym. The pipes had been anchored in used car tyres and then set in concrete. As Phil rolled one of them down the hill it gained momentum and at the bottom suddenly sprang up and smacked him on the side of the head with full force. Somehow he was able to run up a ramp to the dorm, find his bed and lie on it before losing consciousness.

The school nurse phoned Norene at our apartment some kilometres away and told her to come quickly as Phil had had a serious accident. All the way out she wondered if she would find her son alive or not, as the nurse didn't give many details. Becky and the other teenagers all hovered around her, offering her cups of tea as she sat for hours by his bed praying for God's intervention. She hesitated to phone me in Switzerland as she didn't want to cause disruption to our important meetings. An SIM doctor in the city was able to attend Phil, and seeing there was a curfew at night he spent the first night at the school. He warned Norene that when Phil did finally regain consciousness he might not respond to her at first. After a long eighteen hours, he suddenly woke up.

"What happened?" he asked.

He didn't remember a thing about the accident. Only after that did Norene phone to tell me about the accident and to assure me I didn't need to return home early.

Norene wrote about this experience:

Accidents happen to young and old
But Bingham the record seems to hold.
This time Phil Bond was the sorry victim,
"Who did you say was the one who hit him?"
It wasn't Peter, Thomas or Mike,
'Twas a great big heavy old two-inch pipe.
The volleyball net was attached up higher
To a pipe set in cement in a great big tyre.
Our Phil was rolling this heavy thing back
To the gym with a friend, Dale Adams, in fact.
Right then the pipe hit the gym upright
And swung up in the air with all of its might.
With a great big thud it hit Phil's head;
Some heard the crack and thought he was dead.
For eighteen hours he suffered concussion,
While the teenage girls around him were gushin'
Drs Scheel and Bowers, Nurse Jean, the Maxsons
All helped so much by their comfort and actions.
Much prayer went up for his full restoration,
God answered our prayers --give him adoration.

Norene wrote:

"After that difficult experience Bruce was impatient to fly home to Addis. He was due on his birthday, and so we made a nice cake and the three of us went to the airport. Phil had recovered by then, although he did experience a couple of more bouts of concussion later on. We waited and waited until the last passenger arrived out of the terminal, but there was no Bruce. All day long there was no message, and we were concerned. In those days in Ethiopia no passenger manifest was ever made public, and so we had no way of finding out when he was travelling.

Finally he arrived the next day, and we heard the story. He and other passengers had been dumped from the plane in Lagos, Nigeria, for no reason at all. The officials then took his passport and sent him to a rather dodgy little hotel. When he returned to the airport the following day, there was no sign of his passport. This was a scary situation! After a long time of searching, someone spotted it under a table leg in the office.

The passport had been used to stabilise the table!

105 Family Reunion

At one stage during 1976, the six of us were living in four different countries – Ethiopia, England, Australia and New Zealand. But we all wanted to be together – if at all possible – during the Christmas period. Becky had been in England for three months for extra tuition, and her airfares had been provided for us. Stephen was in Australia, working hard in the open-cast mines north of Perth. He was determined to earn enough money to come and visit us. In fact because David was a student and not earning money, Steve offered to help him with his fare. So we decided that despite the uncertain conditions in Ethiopia, we would make this a great family time.

Ethiopia was our second home, of course, and although our older boys had been out of the country for more than six years, it was still very much home to them too.

What a joy it was to welcome David on 12 December. His exciting news was that he had done well enough in his first year of the veterinary degree course to be accepted into the second year of the six-year training. How proud we were that he had worked so hard at his studies, having experienced some lonely times.

Steve arrived on 20 December and we realised that was another miracle. Having worked for sometime in the Brisbane area, he had decided to try for a job over in Perth and had travelled on a motorcycle across the widest part of Australia. That was a scary and dangerous experience and he wonders now how he braved it. His bike broke down in the wilderness and another motorcyclist eventually towed him at high speed to the next major town for repairs. He had come off the bike as he was being towed, suffering significant injuries. He has said since, "I would never want my mother to see the state of my helmet after that accident. God certainly protected me."

In Perth two ex-SIM missionary families, the Locks and the Nevilles, were kind to him and as a result well-paying work opened up for him in the open cast mines to the north.

After the boys' arrival we drove Eric and Ngaire Klein into Maazey where they were to work. En route we called in at Lake Shalla to show our visitors the variety of bird life there. Pelicans and flamingos were particularly plentiful. Some of the local boys offered to cast their nets, for a price, to catch some tilapia for us. They were successful and so we enjoyed a fish fry for our evening meal.

The visit to see the birds was meant to be a quick detour, but three hours later we were still trying to winch ourselves out of some scary sinking sand. We almost despaired of ever getting the vehicle out. Just after we finally succeeded, the winch broke.

106 Trip "Down Country"

We quote from Norene's letter home:

On Christmas Eve we made our way out to Bishoftu, the SIM rest and conference centre, where we spent an enjoyable Christmas together. It was great to have a special Christmas dinner prepared for us all, and how we enjoyed those couple of days relaxing, swimming and playing tennis. God had been gracious to allow us such a great family reunion.

For the following two weeks we all squeezed into our Landrover like sardines, with sleeping bags, tents, clothes, food, drinking water and petrol cans all tied on the roof rack. We knew we would be able to buy little food along the way, and so I had prepared ahead of time as best I could. The boys had brought some instant foods to help too. We combined work with pleasure, as Bruce visited many of the community development projects along the way. We travelled many miles over varying types of roads and tracks, and cooked our own bread and meals as we went, sometimes on an open fire, sometimes on our little gas burner. We erected our tents in various safe locations – beside a lake, inside an unfinished mud house, and of course under the stars. We heard the lions roar in the night (rather scary in a tent) and saw numerous antelope, baboons, monkeys, hyenas and birds of all descriptions A magnificent leopard put on a great show for us one night as it sat preening itself in front of our car lights for a good five minutes. (Who wouldn't be a missionary kid?)

Setting off on our 'down country' adventure as a family (Christmas 1976)

Our first stop after leaving Bishoftu was Lake Langano, where SIM had set up a camping ministry and conference centre. As no conference was being held at the time, we were able to use the camp kitchen for our cooking and eating. Our young people pitched their tents right at the lake's edge, as there were other missionaries camping nearby.

One night we lit a cheerful log fire on the beach. Another night we had one in the camp lounge. What fun it was to sing and harmonise the Scripture in Song choruses after such a long absence from each other. Steve had borrowed a trumpet from Bingham Academy and enjoyed being able to play again. Our cup of joy almost overflowed simply from being reunited as a family. Our boys relived their childhood experiences as they watched the colobus (black and white) monkeys leaping from tree to tree in the forested area of Langano. We were amused to hear the boys walking down the dark, shadowy track through the forest to the beach at night. They sang loudly and shouted, no doubt trying to scare away the hyenas.

Our next stop was up the mountains to the unoccupied SIM station of Chencha. Along the way we called in to Lake Chamo to see the crocodiles and hippos, and so it was getting dark as we ascended the rocky, steep, mountain road to Chencha. On arrival at 10pm we moved into an empty house, set out our sleeping bags and used the wood stove for our cooking. Bruce was able to check on the orchard he had planted previously and show the boys around before we set off the next day for Maazey, across the mountain range. We climbed even higher than Chencha to 11,000 feet (3,384m) and then gradually dropped to 4,000 feet (1,230m) at Maazey.

The first stretch of the road was wet and slippery and we wondered if we would need to abandon the trip altogether. But gradually it dried up and we proceeded. The road was narrow and some of the sheer drops to the floor of the valley would have been 500m or more. Several times it seemed as though the other vehicle travelling with us could have easily tipped over the cliff.

Once at Maazey we received a royal welcome from Eric and Ngaire Klein who had been preparing for our coming. But there was hardly time to rest before we had to set off up the mountain to attend a wedding. We were told it was "a little uphill" and would take about two hours. But it rained on the way up, soaking us, and the hike took more than three hours.

The ceremony went well, after which the relatives of the bride offered us a big, round, empty mud hut for our bedroom that night. Along with other visitors, we all decided to put our sleeping bags around in a circle, with our feet all facing the large centre pole like spokes in a wheel. Lots of delicious injerra and watt made up for all the hardships we thought we'd endured from the long day. Even when we were settling down for the night, our hosts called out:

"Don't go to sleep yet, there's another meal coming!"

After more rain overnight, we literally slipped down the mountain on the muddy tracks until we reached the Maazey Project where we set up camp again. It was hot during the day and we couldn't buy much food locally except for a few bananas and a live chicken. The latter we cooked slowly on an outside fire in a large milk can, with some packets of dried vegetables.

Our boys joke about which one of them always ended up in the middle sleeping bag when the lions roared at night. We even saw a lion's skin in one of the settlers' houses. Only a few days before, a buffalo and a lion had fought each other to death. The settlers had thereupon butchered the buffalo and skinned the lion.

Back in Addis Becky and Phil started a new term in school and David took off once again for New Zealand. How sad we were to say goodbye, and yet grateful that this miracle trip had even taken place in such unsettled times. We often lost count of the roadblocks along the way.

107 Steve's Experiences

After David returned to New Zealand Steve stayed on and the following is his own account of a working trip in the south.

It all started on 24 January 1977 at 9am when Tom Fellows, Mrs Jean Hunter, her daughter Moira and I set off from SIM headquarters in a diesel Landrover bound for Chencha and eventually Kucha. Once out of Addis it was soon apparent our vehicle was seriously lacking in power. It had picked up that annoying habit known as "hunting" which gives one the impression of riding a particularly lively bucking bronco at a rodeo. We travelled all day and finally turned off the main road for the two and a half hour crawl up the famed Chencha "road." The first half of the road, as well as being steep, was full of great boulders and ruts.

Finally a tired foursome rolled into Chencha at 7:30pm. To add insult to injury it started to rain, and so we had some idea of what the road would be like the next morning. We took the same route as we had done as a family a few weeks before, climbing to 11,000 feet and then descending to 4,000 feet. This would not be the place to learn to drive, because as yet cars do not have wings. It must be some of the most spectacular scenery in Ethiopia and I enjoyed the trip as much as it was possible to do so. We finally bucked our way into Maazey, expecting to drop off Jean and Moira and pick up two nurses who were supposed to fly in and accompany Tom and me into Kucha, further south.

True to tradition, however, the flight had not eventuated, and so it was left to Tom and me to drive the four hours up another mountain range, pick them up, and return (hopefully) to Maazey the same night.

They told us the only time the road into Kamba was impassable was when it rained, and so just as we were bouncing along quite nicely, the rain poured down. After being pulled out of a few holes, and some slipping and sliding sideways, we finally arrived at the mission station, to the delight and greetings of the two nurses, two adult dogs and an array of small pups. (Both dogs had given birth together.) A welcome bed was waiting for us, as there was no way we could think of returning that night. Breakfast next morning was at 5:30 and we were then slithering down the mountain on our way back to Maazey, where we arrived six hours later. A quick drink, more gas, and we four young people were off to Kucha with an interpreter for yet another language group.

As we were crossing one of the many rivers our vehicle died, and as it was diesel Tom and I knew little about how it worked. We decided this was it, and resigned ourselves to spending the night by the river, providing endless entertainment for the tsetse flies. Just when the coffee started brewing the motor started up again, and so we all jumped in and made it to the point where we were to meet some evangelists with mules.

From there on Steve had a trying trip as he and Tom worked on an airstrip in Kucha. He had problems with migraine headaches and no medication on hand. He put it all down to experience, however, in the great land of Ethiopia.

When he arrived back in Addis Ababa he was downtown one day when a nasty character, assuming he was a rich foreigner, took a knife to him and demanded he take him to a restaurant and buy him a meal. Steve somehow managed to escape and didn't stop running until he arrived back at our SIM headquarters. Most Ethiopians are gracious people, but in every society there are the "down and outs" who take advantage.

Steve left us for England soon after that, and after working there for a while made his way back to New Zealand. During that trip he had some trying times when he ran completely out of money and felt all alone in the world. He decided against informing Dave he was coming home to New Zealand, and one afternoon surprised him, after travelling eight hours to Palmerston North by motorbike, by sitting in his brother's room when he came in from lectures. Family members kindly offered him a home until we returned from Ethiopia.

108 Country of the Nile

An unexpected challenge came to us in March 1977 when our SIM Sudan Director, Loren Knox, wrote to us asking if we would come to the Sudan for a month to help him with a community development project in the southern area. They were beginning to experience a little more freedom for missionary activity since the missionaries had all been expelled in 1962.

After the highlands of Ethiopia, the temperatures in the Sudan were *hot*.

Loren organised all the travel permits and provided our transport—a four-wheel drive pick-up. Our load consisted of four drums of petrol, kerosene for cooking and lamps, a box of spare parts for the vehicle, 100 litres of drinking water and two Sudanese guides.

There were only tracks in the sandy soil, but choosing which track to take was a problem. With no road signs, even our guides often became lost. Our guides' names were Paul and Timothy, and so we were in good company. The tracks became rough and tough on both machinery and body. Our drums of petrol were so dirty and contaminated that we were forced to stop in the desert to clear out our carburettor more times than we could count.

Most nights we spent in so-called "rest houses." Such as they were, they were available for all genuine tourists with correct documents. The four of us often had to sleep in one room, and were provided with beds, mattresses, sheets and a pillow. We often noticed as we were leaving that the caretaker would come in and fold up the sheets for the next guests. We figured that was one way of conserving water! At one mission station, at the back of the house and sitting in isolated splendour, was the "throne" with a nice green seat. The walls and roof had long been blown away by the fierce winds. That one must definitely be used after dark, we decided, and wondered how many more kinds of toilets we would find on our trips.

Eventually we were able to visit most of the old SIM mission stations which had been abandoned fifteen years before, and although only the skeletons of the buildings remained, the few believers we were able to contact had remained strong in their faith. They were excited to think the missionaries might be able to return.

After travelling under these conditions for more than three weeks we arrived back in Khartoum, out of petrol, out of drinking water, out of food, and many kilos lighter ourselves. But we felt a burden to help the southern Sudanese people.

We quickly confirmed what others had said, and wrote up a long list of recommendations for SIM and the SIC local church. We believed the southern Sudan could be the future bread basket of Africa, just awaiting development. Unfortunately conditions did not improve at that time, and as of 2005 the people are still waiting for lasting peace.

109 Thoughts Towards Home

Norene writes:

As our two-year term in Ethiopia was about to conclude, our thoughts turned towards our little home in Howick. During those two years we had lived an active, busy and somewhat scary life as Bruce or both of us had been away on trips a good part of the time, and living in a communist state was not the most relaxing experience. We had lived in seven different locations within Addis Ababa – twice at the SIM headquarters in small rooms, and then to an apartment in the basement of a KHC church in the centre of town. After a short time there we moved to a youth centre where we lived with young people from Ethiopia and other nationalities who were all serving the Lord in KHC ministries. From there we moved to a spacious city apartment which was adequate when our whole family were together during the Christmas break.

Finally we moved to a house on the SIM printing press compound, where we enjoyed the company of other missionaries. We expected this to be our safest location, but one night when all the other missionaries were away and Becky and I were alone in the house, shooting broke out around our compound. Bruce and Phil had been away for a few days and we hadn't expected them home until the next day. How grateful were we to see them drive in shortly after the shooting ceased, just as bodies were being carried away from our compound fence. God was good to care for us that night, as there was no vehicle on hand either.

So after all this I was feeling rather like a mother hen, wanting to find a safe place for my brood for a while. We were especially sad to miss Steve's twenty-first birthday and knew that David would be looking forward to our arrival home for his Christmas break from University. Don and Ruby Coop had been living in our home and were preparing to move out to their own home.

After a great welcome from family and friends we settled in and became involved again in SIM, with Bruce as director and myself as prayer secretary. In our church, Howick Baptist, Bruce became an elder and I loved to teach Bible class and lead a women's group. Again we enjoyed being able to welcome many young people into our home.

A little more than two years later we were preparing for the first two weddings in the family, and grandchildren started arriving in 1982 (with the first two only four days apart.) Two more weddings followed in 1985, and we were soon experiencing the empty nest syndrome.

We had always told God that we didn't feel our years of service in Ethiopia were completely past. In fact we'd often said that when all our children were either married or off our hands, we would be willing to return to the land and the people we loved.

We had thought that finding God's will for our lives would become easier, the older we grew. It was not so. As we drew near to the eighth year after arriving home from our 1976-1977 stint, we pondered and prayed to know what we were meant to do for the remaining years of our active service.

Chapter Eight

Bishoftu / Babogaya 1987-1988

110 Should We or Shouldn't We?

My third five-year term as New Zealand SIM director was almost completed. During those fifteen years (two of which were spent back in Ethiopia 1976-77) SIM had experienced several ups and downs as far as the recruitment of missionaries was concerned. But now we were in a time of growth and progress. Our move from a three-room rented office at the top of Queen Street in the city to a spacious new office complex in the suburbs was a miracle. This had been my dream for several years, and we had been able to procure a suitable property in the centre of Howick on which to build. We even had a sea view. I was grateful to have Murray Dunn as my right-hand man during the saga of erecting a new building, and we had practical help from missionary-minded handymen from various parts of New Zealand. When the new building was dedicated, we were grateful God had enabled us to open it debt-free.

Four years earlier SIM had merged with Andes Evangelical Mission working in South America. Now five career couples were in the process of applying for Africa and South America. We had also been able to recruit a well-trained staff, after working for many years with a minimal number. In one way it seemed a great time to continue in this role. Yet as we weighed up everything, the green light to return to Ethiopia was shining brightly in our hearts.

Norene writes:

"The passages which spoke to us during these days of searching for God's will were from the story of the children of Israel, as God led them through the wilderness. By day God led them with a pillar of cloud, and by night with a pillar of fire. Their marches and halts were all controlled by him. We sensed God was moving us on also, and we had to trust him. He assured us that both in the sunshine (the cloud by day) and in the darkness (the pillar of fire) he would be with us. Sometimes the children of Israel might have felt it was an inappropriate time to see the cloud starting to move. In some ways we felt like that.

One day we read: "Let us be sure that neither the warmth of the campfire nor the attractiveness of the site retain us."

Murray Dunn had been my deputy for some time and he and Pam were well able to step into our shoes and continue our New Zealand ministry. From enquiries made in Ethiopia it seemed there was a needy position we could fill.

The Marxist Government was still in control and it was difficult for missionaries to be granted a work permit. Most missionaries had been forced out of Ethiopia but SIM still maintained a small presence with thirty five foreigners. Miraculously the rest and conference centre at Bishoftu was still under SIM control and even although the use by foreigners of the facilities had greatly dwindled, now an expanding ministry to nationals was opening up. Church leaders whose churches had long been closed and who were forbidden to gather together even in small groups were able to come to Bishoftu to meet for planning seminars and fellowship. In fact hardly a week went by without one of these gatherings being held.

The missionaries running this facility, Howard and Ruth Borlase, had not been home for seven years, as they didn't want the conference centre to be closed down because of lack of replacement staff. Once our availability was known to the SIM Ethiopia director, Dr Bruce Adams, he suggested we might be able to replace the Borlases. He said he would be willing to work hard in procuring a work permit for us.

We waited and waited. Murray officially took over my position as New Zealand director on 30 October 1986. After five months we were rewarded with the good news our work permit was granted. When the Borlases heard we were actually coming, they wrote as follows:

"Fabulous! Only a few more days or weeks before we'll be drinking tea together again. Are we thrilled! I believe we told you the way Ruth and I have been praying for several years that the Lord would raise up a 'mature' couple, with a genuine heart for Ethiopians, to take over this unique ministry. In his laying of this burden upon your hearts, we feel the Lord has answered in the ultimate and also in the realm of the impossible. I would not have thought you folk could be released from your responsibilities there in New Zealand, and I'd have worried that you guys ('Guys' meaning Grandparents Utterly Young), when you took a hard look at the possibilities, would get cold feet. And who could blame you, with hearth and home and grandkids all established? To swap that for a shack on an African hillside seems ridiculous... unless, unless... one has personally savoured the peace and joy of being in the centre of God's will. His compensations are fabulous."

Howard and Ruth went on to say, "You'll be serving so many meals (17,000 in a year) that it might pay for you to pack a wheel barrow and a shovel. During the last six months we have hosted fifteen large conferences, representing twenty-one different organisations."

We were convinced we were heading in the right direction and each day looked forward to hearing good news.

As we moved out of our home, Norene wrote the following:

DEPARTURE DAY
I always put off dismantling the Christmas tree,
It seems to make me depressed. Today it was worse.
It wasn't only the tree, the lights and the manger scene,
It seemed we were dismantling just everything.
As I took down the last few strands of tinsel
I heard the dialling of the phone and my husband's voice,
"From tomorrow on could you kindly disconnect the phone."
Next call, "Could you please read our power metre and send the bill"
Another call again, "Please note our change of address."
Yes, it was 20 January, 1987. Departure Day for us.
A few hours later Son number one arrived.
Our piano, freezer and stereo went his way.
Son number two came next and out went all the beds
All being drenched in the pouring rain (Or were they tears?)
Son number three drove in to help move more treasures,
Whilst Daughter had already left for south with her 'inheritance.'
The tenants walked in and we showed them around.
My heart was sad. I remembered the manger scene under the tree.
Dear Jesus, you understand how I feel today.
You left your home with your Father in heaven
And came as a babe to this sinful and lonely old world.
Can I not leave my temporary, earthly home here
To return to a desperately needy land?
Oh God, your Word says that no man leaves houses or lands,
Children or grandchildren for your sake and the Gospel's
Without all these being restored to him a hundredfold.
What will we do with a hundred homes, Lord?
Perhaps this means we will bring You to a hundred homes
In our adopted country more than half a world away.

We then rented a small apartment in Howick and waited. And waited.

Finally word came through in early March, five months later, that our work permit had been granted. How we thanked God that the green light was again shining brightly. Now there was no turning back. We were grateful for all the people who had prayed and worked on our behalf.

But what a traumatic time saying goodbye to family and friends. March 14, 1987, saw a crowd of more than seventy gathered at the airport as we finally took off again for Ethiopia. By that time our four young people had been married and we had six beautiful grandchildren, all under five. What a wrench to leave them all behind!

Once settled in the plane we wept as we pondered again the implications of leaving. We had asked the mission if we could come home briefly every two years, and this eased the parting a little. The Word of God reassured us from Revelation 3:8:

See I have placed before you an open door that no one can shut. I know that you have little strength, yet you have kept my word and have not denied my name.

Since both of us were getting on towards sixty at that stage, this was an appropriate promise for us.

111 Devastating News

We arrived in Singapore, just the two of us. This was the first time in our missionary journeys as a married couple that we had travelled without any family with us. Things weren't going well. First of all we searched for our baggage and you've guessed it. It was back in Sydney.

On our second day in Singapore the phone rang in our hotel room. To our delight we heard our son, David's voice. What news did he have for us?

"I'm sorry to be the one to bring sad news to you, Mum," he said. "Your Dad passed away this evening."

All we could think of was how well Norene's Dad had looked at the airport, although he was obviously sad to say goodbye to us both.

Norene had said to him, "Now you be here when we come back in two years' time, Dad." Evidently he had been working that day in his garden when he felt some pain and died from an aneurism before any medical help arrived. He was eighty-three years old.

What should we do? We thought of all the ways Norene's Dad had helped us during our missionary career. Each time we had left for Ethiopia, he had always been such a help in supplying our needs. As mentioned previously, he had sent the necessary money for me to fly to Aden to meet Norene when she first arrived. For years he had ably illustrated our newsletters, and been much part of our ministry. (Note his illustrations in this book.)

We agonised over what to do. We didn't have the money to return home for the funeral, and might have lost the opportunity to enter Ethiopia if we delayed. Norene's Dad's wife assured us she and the family would understand if we couldn't return. Although it was a difficult decision to make, we decided we must continue our travels.

So on we went towards Africa. Our first stopover was in Nairobi, Kenya, where we were met by two special Kiwi SIM missionaries, Bev Fruish and Anne Power. It is always great to be met by friends when travelling in a foreign country. They helped us gain our equilibrium and comforted Norene in the loss of her father.

Before we left New Zealand we had promised we would visit our SIM missionaries Max and Anne Cope and Steve Thompson, working in northeast Kenya amongst the Somali people, and had asked the SIM administration in Nairobi to arrange suitable transport for us. Unfortunately the administrator, wanting us to experience "real" Kenyan travel, had booked us on the "Garissa Express," rather than on a one-hour flight on Kenya Airways. It wasn't that we hadn't travelled many hours on Ethiopian buses over the years, but we felt our time was at a premium. A little way along the journey we renamed the bus the "Garissa Boneshaker." The shock absorbers must have given out years ago, and for fifteen hours we endured a tortuous journey in the ramshackle old noisy bus. All that on the day of Norene's father's funeral. Needless to say she ended up with a thumping migraine-type headache hours before we reached Wajir. It was one day we will never forget.

At last we made it to a hot, dry and sandy Wajir where we were met by Max and Anne Cope from our home church in Howick and Steve Thompson (who, incidentally, was born of missionary parents in Egypt on the same day as our Stephen in Ethiopia.) With relief we alighted from the bus and made our way through deep sand to the mission station. We were impressed by the ministry of these three New Zealanders who were working in a difficult location among the largely unresponsive Somali people. Talk about faithful service! Surely this was it.

Max and Steve were busy in various agricultural irrigation programmes, while Anne was involved in making friends with the Somali women. She and Max even lived in the same compound as some of them, and Anne drew her water from the community well by bucket and rope. We couldn't stay long in Wajir as we were needed in Ethiopia as soon as possible. Fortunately, though, we were able to organise our own return trip, and so booked on Kenya Airways to Nairobi. What a relief!

112 Howard and Ruth Borlase

A remarkable couple, Howard and Ruth had arrived in west Africa in 1936 and finally retired in 1991, fifty-five years later. As a young married couple they were assigned to a new mission station in northern Nigeria, a Muslim area, one hundred miles away from their nearest fellow missionary. After eight years of learning the local language and becoming friends with many important people Howard was asked to move to east Africa to become the field director of Anglo Egyptian Sudan (as the Sudan was known then.).

After five years there they were asked to move again, this time to Ethiopia, in administration, to help in the reestablishment of the work after the Italian army had been defeated and Haile Selassie had returned.

Not too many years later they were assigned to their fourth country, Somalia, to head up the work there. Finally, when all the SIM missionaries were expelled from that country, they returned to Ethiopia. We felt inadequate to follow in their shoes when we took over the ministry at Babogaya. The Lord never gave them any children of their own and so they had an amazing ministry to young people wherever they ministered.

Almost nine years had passed since we had left Ethiopia. Would we remember the language? We were never experts, but we did have a good working knowledge of the spoken language before we left. What about now? Our Ethiopian friends greeted us just like brothers and sisters, hugging and kissing us with tears of joy. They wanted to express their appreciation that we had come back to Ethiopia in their time of great need. Somewhere from inside our brains, our internal computer switched on and we were hearing and speaking our Ethiopian tongue again. Now we felt we were really home.

Our first ten days were spent in Addis Ababa, attending to all the formalities that foreigners are subject to, plus seeking to obtain a valid driving licence and clearing our unaccompanied luggage from customs. Unfortunately we were not successful in either of the last two tasks, but we were free to travel down to Babogaya to begin an intensive period of orientation with Howard and Ruth. This was great fun. The host and hostess seemed to be "all things to all people" and we needed to learn from the Borlases just what our roles would be. *(See coloured photo of beautiful Bishoftu)*

113 Bishoftu / Babogaya

Norene writes:

"In earlier years in Ethiopia, I had always considered the role of hostess at Bishoftu as the last one I would ever accept. But God had so clearly put into our hearts to offer for this position that I had to put my confidence in him to enable me to perform well. We had six weeks overlap with Howard and Ruth, although we expected a much shorter time. They seemed loath to leave after so long there. The hostess's job started the night before when menus were worked out and the required food for up to thirty or forty people was taken out of freezer or pantry in preparation for the following day. Little cards in the Amharic language would be put on the wall, detailing the menu for each of the three meals. Then the following morning we needed to be up by six to see the night guards before they went home. Devotions with the workers was at 7am.

As the nearest main shopping centre was 50 kilometres away in Addis

Ababa, the most important part of the job was to make sure the necessary supplies were on hand for at least a week in advance. The hostess had to be more of an organiser than a doer. All the bread and buns were made in the kitchen on either the large wood stove or the smaller gas ones. As time went on we decided to include Ethiopian food, injerra and watt, in our menu. This proved a popular decision. Some of the staff each day would be involved in the normal duties of cleaning the guest rooms. The bookings for individuals and conferences and the charges were my responsibility. I left the other book-keeping to Bruce, such as the complicated system of the workers' wages and taxes.

Besides this I taught Bible and sewing to the women and girls. My involvement with the many poor women in our district was enervating, for I felt sympathy for the mothers who had little to offer their children. I think this emotional strain wore me down more than the physical work. We both enjoyed conversation round the meal table with Ethiopians and missionaries alike.

We were grateful for the valuable help given for several months by Bruce and Joan Crawford of SIM Howick. Being an extremely practical couple, who had a great respect and love for the Ethiopian people, we found their involvement with us a tremendous blessing when our workload was heavy.

As host, Bruce was responsible for a whole string of practical work to keep everything running smoothly, including:

- Electrical work (there was no electrician available)
- Plumbing, including keeping our three-phase electric water pump going when often only one or two phases reached the pump.
- Carpentry, meaning minor repairs. Fortunately a well-stocked workshop was on the property.
- Shopping. Yes, to keep the guest house going he had to make a 100-kilometre round trip once a week, challenged by traffic, animals, thieves and a shortage of everything.

Bruce writes:

I cultivated my own little circle of guards who some called "street beggars." Whether I was parking outside a butcher, a baker or a candle stick maker, they would come running and fiercely ward off any thieves who tried to touch my vehicle. Of course I rewarded them and we became good mates, having some interesting conversations together.

Then, as Norene mentioned above, I paid the wages, paid the taxes for the employees, and balanced the books.

The garden/orchard responsibilities were so enjoyable for me, for a good staff made me feel like the lord of the manor, just supervising what needed to be done.

Jesus said in the gospels, "The poor are always with you," and this was certainly true at our gate. We were able to help many with their daily bread.

One of the advantages of living at Babogaya was being able to enjoy the birds. Birds of all types and varieties would pay us a visit in the course of a year. Howard had built a bird bath right outside our front door and in the course of one day hundreds of birds would come for a drink or their daily bath, although some were too shy to come so close to the house. We particularly enjoyed seeing the European roller, a migratory bird which flew down to Ethiopia to escape the harsh European winter. It had mainly pale blue plumage with a chestnut back. In flight it had vivid blue wings.

But not all species of birds were enjoyable. There was the sneaky mouse bird, surely the most destructive bird ever created. It had the same colouring as an ordinary garden sparrow, but a slightly larger body with a long powerful tail and strong legs. It ran up and down branches like a mouse or rat. But could it eat! It seemed to devour everything in the vegetable garden. Then, when one's vegetable garden was gone, it started on the fruit – mangoes, bananas, guavas, pineapples, and its favourite, cherimoya or custard apple. We mentioned we had trouble with this bird in earlier years. Much of our gardener's time was spent on bird duty, chasing the mouse birds away.

Little did we know we would soon have news from home which would sadden us both. First Bruce's oldest brother, Doug, died suddenly of a heart attack and we longed to be with his wife Elsa, and the whole family. But of course that was not possible financially. Our close Ethiopian friends were sympathetic towards us during that sad time. Also we heard that one of our dear little granddaughters, three-year-old Megan, who had been born with a hole in her heart, was slated for open heart surgery. We found those days stressful, as we longed to support Steve and Gail through this time. But we could pray. Finally we heard that all was well and Megan (and her parents) were recovering.

114 The Underground Church

We weren't at Babogaya many days before a group of local church elders arrived one evening with a tasty and spicy meal of the local food, injerra and watt. As we shared the meal with these men they told us of their love and gratitude for all the Borlases had done for them and expressed their desire for a similar working relationship with us both. We were impressed by the calibre of these men, all of whom were members of the Ethiopian Air Force. All had received specialist training overseas and spoke English fluently. Not only were their gifts obvious, but they had a deep desire to serve the Lord. We were delighted at the prospect of working with such men in the next few years. They told us about the early history of their church in Debre Zeit and the important role the SIM staff had played.

The elders' story:

September 10th, 1974, saw the birth of the first KHC church in the Debre Zeit district. We decided to meet in the little grass-roofed tukul down by the lake's edge on the SIM compound where we would be free from the observation of officialdom. At the first service there were nine of us present, plus the SIM couple in charge of Bishoftu Guest House, Birdell and Lois Emmel. That day six of the nine of us believed. With the agreement of the local farmers' association we obtained a small section of land outside the SIM compound and with the missionaries' help we built a small tin-roofed building which served as a venue for church services on Sundays and as an elementary school during the week.

Numbers coming to the services started to grow and many of the local farmers' children were making good progress in their learning. A young man, Ato Belaye Wondafrash, one of our first believers, who wanted to serve the Lord as an evangelist/teacher, was sent to the SIM Bible School in Saja to prepare for service within Debre Zeit. Sadly, after his first year of study the government closed down that Bible school. Belaye returned home to become a faithful and fruitful evangelist, and he is still in this ministry today.

Opposition increased by the day as the local radio station beamed a continual barrage of propaganda against missions and evangelical Christians. Everyone was urged to be vigilant, and in particular the communist youth movement was encouraged to take the appropriate action against the 'imperialists and their lackeys,' meaning evangelical believers.

One Sunday during the morning worship they surrounded the building and pelted the windows and roof with stones. Then they forced their way into the service. The men and boys were beaten up and imprisoned, and the women were incarcerated for the rest of the day. All the Bibles and hymn books were confiscated and destroyed, and all benches and chairs stolen, including the pulpit.

Eventually the building was completely demolished, leaving only the concrete floor intact. After a week or two the men were released and commanded to have nothing more to do with this false religion. Some found the pressure too great and turned their backs on their new-found faith, while others were strengthened by this experience and could not be silenced.

Some time later, the leader of the communist youth movement was passing near to where the church building had previously stood. With devilish glee he had helped destroy the building. Now, as he passed by, he suddenly became demon-possessed and violent. His friends, concerned that he would harm himself or others, tied him up with leather straps. In a loud voice he called out, 'Call Ato Belaye! Call Ato Belaye!'

On arriving, Belaye immediately realised this pathetic figure thrashing around on the ground was indeed demon possessed and needed to be delivered. He prayed for him in the name of the Lord Jesus, commanding these evil spirits to leave him. The evil spirits cried out and begged to go back to live in one of the nearby lakes where thousands of people made an annual pilgrimage to worship Satan. After a violent struggle the evil spirits left. Negussie, after being untied, fell at Belaye's feet and cried out, "How can I be saved?" Belaye led him to the Lord.

Now the persecutor became the persecuted, like Paul in the New Testament. He suffered terribly, was imprisoned and severely beaten. But he never wavered and eventually led many others to the Lord.

Although persecution, imprisonment and threats continued, we decided to meet secretly on Sunday nights in one of our houses. We have been doing this for the last few years."

Bruce continues:

Norene and I were excited when we heard about the underground church and asked if by attending on a Sunday night we would draw too much attention to their secret meeting. They recommended we wait until after dark.

We attended the following Sunday night. The house we approached

Bruce with faithful evangelist Belaye. 2003

appeared to be in darkness and a knock at the front door brought no response. Eventually someone appeared from out of the blackness and led us around to the back door which was ajar. We stumbled inside until our eyes adjusted to the darkness. How amazed we were to find the front room packed with people sitting on the floor, listening intently to the whispered preaching of the Word of God. The pulpit was a simple child's highchair. Once the preaching was over, little groups of twos and threes disappeared into the darkness of the night. How deeply moved we were by the fearless courage these people showed as they gathered for worship under these circumstances.

We were invited to join the elders' meetings, which for security's sake were held at the SIM compound. We gradually came to grips with the aims and aspirations of these believers, and sought to help them in every way we could. They had so much zeal to serve the Lord, despite the dangers and restrictions that were placed upon them. In our first year at Babogaya forty-five new believers were added to the underground church.

The increase meant they could no longer meet all together, as there just wasn't enough room. So they decided to divide into several smaller groups and meet in different parts of town. A mini revival was taking place! Some young people who had claimed to be communists and had welcomed the change of government at the start of the revolution had become disillusioned with the godless Marxist philosophy and had sought out believers to find the secret of their happiness. Many demon-possessed people were healed and became strong believers. The underground church was alive and thriving, and we were excited to be a part of it.

Despite the restrictions, the elders were still keen to reach out into the district. One day I hiked with the elders up a nearby hill, a volcanic cinder cone which commanded a panoramic view of the surrounding countryside. As our eyes gradually became accustomed to the glare, we were able to count twenty-five different villages which had been formed under the "villagisation" scheme. Each village had at least two thousand people, and some had many more. This meant that within the radius of a few kilometres more than fifty thousand people lived. Although this appeared to be one of the most densely populated areas in Ethiopia, the elders said it was just the tip of the iceberg, for there were hundreds and perhaps thousands of villages beyond those we could see. They also knew that none of them had ever heard the message of salvation. What a challenge!

115 Community Service

We had no sooner settled into the ministry at Babogaya when we had a visit from the chief administrator of our local district (the equivalent of a local mayor in our New Zealand culture). He was also a part-time lecturer in the local veterinary college. We became close friends and were able to work together on various projects within the local district.

"I know you've come to Ethiopia to work at the SIM guest house," he told us on his first visit, "but we expect you to help in our district as well."

Talk about community service! It was compulsory service. However I was more than happy to do something to help. After all the negative propaganda, it would be a positive move to demonstrate that we wanted to help their country. Several suggestions were made, but finally we agreed I would establish a tree-planting project on the steep dry banks of the crater lake opposite to the SIM guest house. This was quite a challenge, as the area assigned to us was stony and dry with all the top soil having been washed away.

We hired a project manager, one of the believers, and about twenty needy workers, both men and women. Some of the area was covered with the cactus plant, commonly called the prickly pear, which provided good food for camels but not for cattle. It was also home to many species of snakes. Before we started, and even in the presence of the administrator, we met together on the site and asked for God's protection and blessing.

The big question was, what species of tree would we plant? We could have chosen eucalyptus which grew well in most parts of Ethiopia. But this was a hostile environment, in which little would grow except maybe an indigenous species such the wanza (*cordia abiscinica*). Its timber was highly prized for furniture making, window and door frames. Buying seedlings was out of the question as nobody had ever attempted to raise them before. But there was one mature tree growing on our own SIM compound, the seed of which we gathered and planted in individual plastic tubes about fifteen centimetres (six inches) deep. We prepared ten thousand of these tubes, filling them with soil and planting a seed in the top. To our delight they started to germinate and were carefully watered each day. In the meantime the crew set to work on the site, cutting out all the prickly pear and killing dozens of snakes. Because the run-off was significant, being a fairly steep slope, we dug ditches parallel to the water's edge, every few meters up the slope of the crater, in order to retain any moisture when it rained. We paid our workers with cooking oil and grain.

Finally the day came when the seedlings were about thirty centimetres (twelve inches) high and big enough to plant out. Although the rainy season had not arrived, we decided it was better to water the plants until the rains came and hopefully they would be well established before the next dry season. (We had six dry months in the year.) With ten thousand seedlings and no road access to our site, we simply loaded them into our dinghy in boxes and I rowed them across the lake. We didn't want to risk any accidents with non-swimmers on the deep crater lake, and so I took on the task of transferring the seedlings.

Then we simply cut the plastic tubing off, leaving a perfect plug with roots undamaged, and planted the seedlings, making sure they were well watered. No wonder we had almost one hundred percent success. That year the rains didn't come as early as expected, and so the workers had to water from the lake with buckets once a week.

By the end of the first rainy season the seedlings had successfully taken off and I took a photo of Norene beside them with some already taller than her.

Two years later when we had to leave Babogaya, the project suffered badly from a lack of supervision. Nevertheless the district administrator was appreciative and brought many an official out to see the project as an object lesson of what could be done even in a hostile environment. Had we not fenced the whole project with a six-strand barbed-wire fence, the seedlings would have been eaten off in a few months as hundreds of cattle each day were brought to the lake's edge for a drink. We did leave an access to the water, though, for both people and cattle.

116 A Dream or Vision

In Acts 2:17 we read, "Your men shall see visions and your old men dream dreams." This was quoted from the prophecy of Joel but I was hardly a young visionary now. In fact most would have said I was getting "past it." In any case, whether it was a vision or a dream, we know it was God who nudged us through a series of events which led to the opening of Kuriftu Children's Centre. Let me take you back to the beginning.

We were meeting regularly with the Debre Zeit KHC elders, discussing and praying about many issues. These men were an inspiration to both of us. We prayed regularly for the persecutors of the believers, that their eyes would be blinded to the work of the growing church and would not hinder it.

For some time now the Marxist government had been trying to make provision for growing numbers of orphaned children – a direct result of the war in the northern provinces of Eritrea and Tigre. Several times government officials had asked the general secretary of the KHC in Addis Ababa, Dr Mulatu Baffa, if the organisation would start a project to care for such children. It was a real conundrum, in that on the one hand almost all of the KHC churches had been closed and many leaders beaten, imprisoned and even killed. Yet on the other hand the church officials were constantly being requested to provide aid of one type or another. Not only in Addis Ababa but also in Debre Zeit, the elders were still being recognised and were receiving similar requests.

During an afternoon walk I had an urge to see what was just round the next corner, as all of us do. I was being followed by a retinue of fuzzy-haired children who always accompanied me on such occasions. Over the next hill we went, and there it was. Unbelievable! Another circular lake, almost the same size as Lake Babogaya on which we lived. It was so beautiful and yet not a house was in sight. Adjoining the lake was a bridge of land then a dry crater.

Immediately the thought came to me, is this our promised land?

I trekked around the lake and was amazed at the fertility of the black, rich cotton soil. It was totally different from where the rest home was situated. I hurried home excitedly to share with Norene what I had discovered, "just over the hill." The next afternoon I headed into the township of Debre Zeit to share my discovery with my special air force friends as they returned from work. They were free to come and see for themselves. As we trekked over that last little ridge, there was an overwhelming sense of God's approval as we viewed the two craters, one with water and the other dry. My three friends Girima, Teshoma and Solomon, being men of faith, immediately paused to pray for God to reveal his will clearly regarding this property. (Little did we know that this site was already under consideration for a commercial project.)

About this time I was called to the administrator's office for an urgent meeting. Not knowing the reason for it, whether good or bad, I decided to take some of the church elders with me for moral support and to give them visibility. His request?

"Mr Bond, please can you help some of the starving people in the district? The rains have not come as expected this year and many are in desperate need. What can you do to help?"

Amazing! To think that although most Western missionaries had been 'sent packing,' the church building had been destroyed and the local believers were suffering terrible persecution, now we were being asked to help in the district. What an opportunity to show Christ's love and compassion!

Diplomatically we promised to call the church and mission authorities in Addis Ababa to see if they had any donated surplus grain and oil in store. Dr Mulatu (general secretary of the KHC) agreed to come and meet the officials himself. At our next combined meeting, to our delight he indicated KHC had a few tons of surplus grain which they would be willing to donate to the district. Furthermore, he was able to donate five hundred blankets to be given to the poorest of the poor in the district. The government officials were absolutely delighted, thanking us over and over again.

117 Venue for a Centre

Dr Mulatu, diplomat that he was, reminded the officials that even although evangelical Christians were being vilified, it was always their intention to help their own country wherever possible. He told us that the Children's Commissioner had made a request to KHC to try to find suitable land to open a children's centre or orphanage. He said for some time they had been searching unsuccessfully for land in Addis Ababa and wondered if there might be a suitable site in this district for such a project.

"Yes, we have just the place for you," said Ato Aberra without hesitation.

The two evangelical churches in the district had been closed for more than ten years, and yet here we were being offered land for a children's centre.

"Could we see the site?" Dr Mulatu asked.

"Why not?" replied Ato Aberra.

With that we all marched out of his office and into the available transport to view the site he was offering us.

My heart skipped a beat as I realised we were heading in the direction of the place we had already seen and claimed for God's work. As we trekked up and over the last little ridge, there before us lay the expansive vista of the twin craters. In all there were more than forty hectares (one hundred acres.)

"How about this?" Aberra asked proudly.

I shuffled to the edge of the crowd and silently thanked God for this miraculous answer to the prayers of the local believers. I marvelled at his sovereignty as I realised we were being offered this million-dollar site, absolutely free, by a representative of the Marxist government.

Ah, I thought, I've proved it again. Many of these government officials are not committed Marxists. The vast majority still believe in God, but in order to retain their positions they keep quiet about their religious beliefs.

Dr Mulatu thanked our host and asked if he might bring the Children's Commissioner to have his permission and approval of this site. This man was much respected in government circles as he was a progressive, a man of action. A few days later Dr Mulatu arrived with the Commissioner, who was impressed first of all when he saw what SIM had already achieved at the picturesque rest and conference centre of Babogaya.

"If I had known such a place existed so close to Addis Ababa, I would have had this Babogaya centre appropriated for government's use!" he joked.

I knew there was an element of truth in what he said. As a mission we had been protected from the Government's avaricious eyes.

We quickly toured the proposed site at Kuriftu and waited for this man's reaction.

"Far too small!" he replied. "Unless you add this further section of land (pointing to some land east of the crater) I won't agree."

I was shocked. How could KHC manage such a large area of land?

"The policy of the Ethiopian government today," he went on, "is to provide homes for these orphan children, where they will not only receive a primary and secondary school education, but also vocational training. They need to be taught some practical skills to prepare them for adulthood."

I was elated after his visit and shared with Norene that I felt we had the skills and gifts to get this project up and running and should offer our services to work full-time with the Kale Heywet Church. Although we were happy in the ministry at the guest house, we felt this Kuriftu project was a unique ministry to be involved in from the beginning. We therefore proceeded to ask permission from SIM to be seconded to KHC.

SIM Administration agreed to our secondment, as did KHC.

Some years before this I had read about the concept of an integrated aqua-agriculture project which was successfully being practised in different parts of the world. Here in Kuriftu, it seemed to me, we had an ideal situation to make this concept possible. The upper area of land overlooking the craters was reasonably flat and was ideal for the building of the children's homes and the facilities to care for up to 200 children. On the other hand, the areas around the lake and the dry crater could be developed into our aqua-agriculture project. We decided to draw up extensive plans of what we would like to achieve in the next ten-year period.

Our next big job was to prepare project proposals for all the different areas where financial aid would be required. This included homes for the children, a water reticulation system, bringing electricity onto the compound and roading around the project, a poultry project, a small dairy unit, a small apiculture project (honey-bees), a large orchard, a two-hectare aqua-farming project and a silviculture (tree planting) project. Once these proposals were drawn up and approved by the KHC board, they were distributed to different donors around the world for their consideration.

In the meantime Norene and I would continue our ministry at Babogaya until such time as the finance would become available to begin the project. A replacement would be needed for the guest house, but we expected to finish our two-year term there as promised, while continuing to prepare for the Kuriftu project.

118 Get Down From That Windmill!

While all this was taking place in the area of Kuriftu, exciting things were beginning to happen in our underground church. We were praying with the elders for two hundred believers to be added to the fellowship that year. It was now 1988, and many were becoming disillusioned with the empty claims of communism and seeking to know the truth about God. The threats to believers were decreasing and young people, particularly, were coming to Christ.

At the same time Norene, who had always suffered from a heart defect, was starting to have frequent chest pains. Tests showed she might have had a heart attack at some stage, and so the medical personnel ordered complete bed rest. We were fortunate to have an SIM doctor in Addis Ababa and he agreed to travel out to see her. He ordered certain medication, but said that if there was no improvement we should plan to return to New Zealand.

Surely not! we reasoned. We still had about three months left of our term, and were heading up all the preparations for this unique children's project. Now we were being told we might have to go home immediately. How confused we felt! Why would God allow this to happen to us just now?

We will never forget our KHC church elders, cycling or walking the five kilometres from the town of Debre Zeit to visit Norene. Kneeling at her bedside, with tears streaming down their faces, they prayed for her healing. Yet despite the medication and the prayers of our many friends, Norene's symptoms did not improve.

That afternoon will always remain in my memory. I was up the windmill! Yes, right on top, standing on a platform by the sails, determined to get it working again to draw water from the lake. Either because of the altitude or because I was scared stiff, I was feeling a bit dizzy and had tied myself on. Suddenly I had an overwhelming sense of God saying to me,

"Get down from that windmill at once and go and tell Norene, 'We're going home.'"

I untied myself, gathered my tools together, and trudged up the steep hill to our little cottage. With tears streaming down my face I said, "We're going home!"

We both wept, as we were sure we were ready to embark on the most important ministry of our whole lives and now we were about to leave. Surely God knew our heart's desire to serve him. Perhaps we wouldn't be able to return here at all. Surely he could have healed, but he hadn't.

In this devastating decision we needed our "spider webs" to be united and strong in the step we were taking.

Later on we read the following commentary in regard to Paul's thorn in the flesh:

"Tiresome though it was, Paul's thorn in the flesh had served to keep this great man of God humble and dependent. Many of us have had persistent physical problems and all know what it is to ask God for something and not get it. When this happens it is not because we lack faith, but because God wants us to experience his power in our weakness and not through his removing it. Think of a time when God did not answer prayer and ask him what you were meant to learn from that."

Norene was too weak to do much of the packing up, and so it was considered best for her to go immediately to Addis Ababa, where she would have better medical care, while I packed our goods. So we bundled her into the Combi van and headed for Addis. But when we drove into the town of Debre Zeit, the believers were waiting for us. They wouldn't consider allowing us to go on the further hour's journey before we went into one of their homes to pray again for Norene's healing.

We were both moved to tears again as we left the group.

The following day I had to go back to put our things in order, as we had no idea if we would ever be able to return. At the same time I had to obtain all the necessary documentation to allow us to leave the country. We had been granted our work permit from the local regional town of Nazareth and were told we would have to return there to obtain our necessary clearance. This was another hour south. We needed police clearance, income tax clearance, electricity clearance (stating we had paid our electricity bills), water (that we had paid our water account), and telephone clearance (even although we didn't have a telephone.) Each of these five offices required a letter of application written in the Oromo language, together with the required fee. All of this had the potential to drag on for days and even weeks if the department boss was not there to sign the appropriate release form. What should I do?

Enter my friend, our local administrator, who himself was concerned on hearing about Norene's sickness.

"Don't worry, I'll go with you," he said. "I know how to handle these men and I can write all your applications in the Oromo language."

We set off the next morning and headed for the police station.

"I'll take care of everything," he told me.

Without my appearing once in any office, he visited them all. Then, after lunch together, we revisited the five offices to collect the signed letters. How grateful I felt for this miracle. Just how much he had to pay (or bribe) I'll never know, as he would not allow me to give him one cent in return. As we travelled back we talked about Christian things and I sensed he was a secret sympathiser.

After hurriedly packing, I was back in Addis. A few days later we were issued with our exit visa and a seat on the plane for Singapore.

119 Singapore Saga

Unfortunately the supply of medication prescribed for Norene by the doctors had run out in Ethiopia and new supplies from overseas did not arrive before we left. It was arranged that a Singaporean doctor, a friend of the mission, would meet us at the airport with a new supply. All went as arranged and she handed us the medication, instructing us on the dosage.

After resting for a day Norene felt a little stronger, and not wanting to arrive home without any little gifts for the grandchildren, begged me to take her to a nearby mall for a short time.

What an amazing place for a grandmother to shop! When it came to paying the bill we realised I didn't have enough local currency, and so I ran around the corner to an exchange bureau. As I was finalising the exchange, a local Singaporean came running up to me.

"Come quickly!" he shouted. "Your wife has collapsed!"

I rushed back to find a huge crowd gathered around Norene, who was completely unconscious on the floor. Panic! What should I do?

"Please call an ambulance," I pleaded.

In no time Norene was being carried down the escalators and into a waiting ambulance, with a frantic husband at her side. With siren screaming, we wound our way through the heavy traffic and into the general hospital. She was rushed into emergency, while I was caught up at reception answering pages of questions.

Finally the moment of truth. They needed a huge amount of money from me as a deposit, because we were foreigners and they didn't know the extent of Norene's problems. There was no such thing as travel insurance in Ethiopia, and we barely had enough money to buy a few gifts for the family, let alone pay a hospital bill. I was threatened with all sorts of consequences if I didn't pay up.

Finally I was able to phone the SIM Singaporean office and a truce was reached, allowing me to visit Norene. She was still woozy, but conscious. I sat with her until late into the night, arriving back at the hotel in the early hours of the morning.

We worked it out together that because she had been without the medication for a few days, the large dose the Singaporean doctor prescribed must have been too high. I was devastated, not knowing the extent of Norene's problems, and fell to my knees, pleading with God to restore her to health.

The next morning at the breakfast table I met a close friend from New Zealand who told me he was leaving that morning. He asked about Norene and I told him what had happened the previous night. As I handed in my room key at reception, I was given an envelope. Opening the same I found it was stuffed with Singaporean notes, sufficient to pay all our hospital charges. My New Zealand friend (a member of another mission) just wrote a brief note, stating it was a gift to help with any extra expenses we might accrue in Singapore. (I had not told him about our financial dilemma the night before.)

We were encouraged to know God had his hand upon us in this confusing situation. Norene was somewhat better when I saw her, and after various tests the doctors felt we could continue our journey after a day or two. We arrived home to a sympathetic and loving reception from family and friends.

Our arrival at this time of the year was quite unexpected, but even so our artistic and resourceful grandchildren met us at the airport with hand-made banners and little ditties. (One banner read, "Welcome Home, Pops and Grops.")

Over the years we have kept all the touching letters we received from our grandchildren. Sometimes they would write and say, "I love you *this* much" and then draw a child with arms wide open. Or they would write, "The only days I love you are the ones that end in *y*." And so on. They seemed to have such affection for us, and we knew God was making up to us for all the separations.

Until our own home was available, our family members took pity on us, welcoming us into their own homes. We needed rest and quiet for some time, as we went about having all the necessary medical checks. God ministered to us through others as they showed us love and concern.

But what of our future?

A bundle of granddaughters!

Chapter Nine

Kuriftu Children's Centre 1989-91

120 Cosy Container

It was hard to believe that six months had passed since that day in Singapore when I found Norene unconscious on the shop floor and when the medical prognosis for her return to Ethiopia was not encouraging. Her ECG, which had come up abnormal in Ethiopia, and an angiogram confirmed she had had some sort of heart problem either from birth or as a result of a slight heart attack. The busy and stressful life at Bishoftu had also taken its toll.

After six months at home, the cardiologist said that he didn't honestly know how Norene had made such a quick recovery. Of course *we* all knew. There were so many in New Zealand and Ethiopia praying for her.

By March 1989, with a medical clearance, we were able to leave for Ethiopia. It was truly a miraculous day, when we considered our sad departure just six months before. But our grandchildren were a little older now and found our leaving traumatic. Ryan and Erika were both six, Laura was almost five, Megan four, Winsome three and Justine two.

Once or twice when we were due to leave again for Ethiopia, they would put on a little concert to farewell us. The tears would certainly flow at such a time. One time the six grandchildren sang something like this to us:

Now it's time for us to say goodbye for just a while
And until we meet again may God's love make you smile.
I will pray for you and keep you in my heart.
And we'll always be friends: Jesus, you and me.
He ties our hearts together and friends we'll always be.
Now when you see the sun you'll know I see the same one too.
And when you see the stars they'll say hello from me to you.
And we'll be friends forever, Jesus, you and me.
He ties our hearts together and friends we'll always be.

When we looked at the sun and the stars in Ethiopia we would remember the words of this song.

What a heart-warming reunion at the airport in Addis! Our national friends rejoiced with us and sensed God had answered prayer in returning us to them. Bunches of flowers were pressed into our hands and then we were whisked up town to enjoy a welcome feast of injerra and watt, followed by the unique and strong Ethiopian coffee.

During our time in New Zealand, KHC (Word of Life church) had been officially given the land for the Kuriftu children's project with a ten-year contract signed by the government. A perimeter fence had been started on the 150-acre property, to avoid any future problems. Tanalised posts were not available and as untanalised timber lasted only a year or two from the ravages of termites, it was decided to make concrete posts on site. That in itself was a huge job as the fence posts had to be two metres high for security reasons.

On our arrival back we wondered just where we would live, as there was not one building on the new property. SIM came to the rescue by offering us a one-room chalet at the SIM guest house where we had lived and worked before. This was some four or five kilometres from Kuriftu, thus enabling us to commute each day to oversee the project. But we needed to live on site, and finally it was agreed that a twenty-foot shipping container would meet our needs until a more permanent home could be built. A door and a couple of windows were cut into its metal sides and we had it lined with chip-board to give better protection from the boiling heat of the mid-day sun.

The KHC executive appointed a board of seven men who would be responsible for the overall running of the project. I was appointed project coordinator, but once the project was established my position was to change to that of advisor.

The local government administrator presented us with a list of six hundred names of the poorest of people, whom he suggested we employ. But how could we help so many? We decided on a compromise by employing two hundred people each week on a rotating basis. We had no cash to pay them, even though the daily wage at that time was still only $1(NZ). Instead we paid them with wheat and oil gifted to us from overseas. If they needed cash they were free to sell their wheat and oil at any time. We appointed supervisors, whom we spent much time teaching and training, to be in charge of the various work crews.

The rim of the crater was quite steep and there was no road in through the huge rock face. The cattle had made a walking track down to the lake shore for water, but we needed to take vehicles in there. With modern heavy machinery this would have presented no problem, but we were living in a war situation and only manpower was in plentiful supply.

But make progress we must. We supplied a large number of stone chisels and hammers to a team of men who set about chipping and splitting the rock until a reasonable track was formed down into the crater. Thus our vehicle, provided by KHC, was the first ever to drive into the crater.

A few weeks later a truck brought down our "container home." We had decided from the beginning that if we were ever to live at Kuriftu, it would be down on the ridge between the crater lake and the dry crater This we called our "million dollar building site." We levelled it off as best we could before hiring a truck to deliver our container.

There was no such thing as a hoist to lift the container off, but fortunately we found a crane driver who was willing to come after hours to help us. There was great excitement as the crane lifted our "house" onto its prepared site. We had taken three months to organise and establish our temporary home and we, too, were excited. Not that we had any mod cons such as electricity, running water or even a toilet. But the panoramic view from our perch, some twenty meters above the lake, was breathtaking.

Norene remarked, "When I made the promise on our wedding day, 'Where you go, I will go,' I didn't ever imagine I would be living in a twenty-foot container, in a dry crater, with few facilities and not a neighbour in sight!"

121 Kuriftu at Last

On the first Sunday morning at Kuriftu I woke up and peered out of our little window. Below us at the lake's edge was a fantastic array of water-loving birds enjoying their morning bath. I was so excited that I copied into my diary a list of the birds which had arrived during the night to welcome us. There were ten different species: five pelicans, twenty-four white-necked cormorants, four long-tailed cormorants, two yellow-billed storks, a grey heron, two Egyptian geese, a hammerkop, a yellow-billed egret, a little egret, and many sacred ibis. Where on earth could one see such a vista, apart from our little Kuriftu hideaway?

"Thank you, God!" I exclaimed.

We had previously decided it would be wise, while we had the use of the government crane, to bring another twenty-foot container into the crater, to be used as a small kitchen and storage shed. In placing it parallel to the first container we left a gap of about six metres, and then built a simple corrugated-iron roof over both containers forming a pleasant breezeway. This served as our reception and lounge area. Being cool in

Birkey the House 'Mother' with first three orphans

the hot season and fairly dry during the rainy season, it proved convenient when we were visited by people from various government departments, diplomats, nationals and foreigners from many organisations. They all found it interesting to view the new project and the progress we were making. In fact Norene and I recorded more than a thousand guests during those first few months, most of whom came into our "lounge" for coffee and refreshments. We both decided we must be running a café. I certainly was becoming a tour conductor.

Our lounge also had another useful purpose, which we had not originally counted on. When the wet season started in July, the rains came pelting down. Were we grateful for our iron container which we could retreat to! But what about our two hundred workers scattered around the compound? There were no trees as yet. When they saw and heard an approaching storm, they would flee for the only shelter in the crater, our containers. Just imagine two hundred bodies jammed into an area of six metres by six metres, with the rain lashing in from one open side! We quickly devised a system of plastic covers which we could roll down like blinds prior to a tropical storm. Often some of the young people would end up in our bedroom area, so then it was "cosy" fellowship.

Amidst all of the activity we constantly had to remind ourselves that we were Christ's ambassadors, and as such we were there not only to care for the orphan and feed the hungry, but also to share the gospel with those who worked for us. Regular morning devotions gave us and other believers the opportunity to teach.

Ones and twos began turning to Christ, and our special friend and faithful evangelist, Ato Belaye, started holding new believers' classes Many gladly gave up some of their lunch hour to attend these. In fact we couldn't believe how thirsty people were to hear more about the gospel. For fourteen long years all had been forced to chant the Marxist mantra, "There is no God!" Some had accepted such teaching, but most were sceptical. Now for the first time these young people were hearing the truth about Jesus. In fact in that first twelve months, one hundred and fifty became believers and started to grow in their faith. We often said they were like ripe fruit just waiting to be picked.

Our friends from New Zealand, Gordon and Aynsley Mackie, were making a long safari across Africa, visiting their missionary friends including us. The few older believers, who were acting as church elders, asked if during the Mackies' visit we would organise our first-ever conference. We held the meetings in our container lounge over a couple of days, when Gordon spoke from the Old Testament book of Habakkuk. What a challenge and encouragement those meetings were to us all.

Only those who worked for us were allowed to attend, as fourteen years previously the Marxist government had forbidden all public religious gatherings in our town.

There was no law forbidding foreigners to worship, however, and so on Sunday mornings Norene and I would take our two folding chairs down to the lake's edge and have our own little service. We felt so privileged to worship God in such an idyllic setting, and our prayer was that one day freedom of worship would again be permitted so that others could join us. Sunday morning was our quietest time of the whole week, and normally we told our guards not to permit visitors to come until the afternoon.

One Sunday morning after enjoying a leisurely time of worship, we decided it would be a great moment to have a swim together without a great crowd of onlookers. We had no sooner changed and jumped into the lake when we spied a vehicle wending its way down the crater "road" towards our home. We immediately recognised it as belonging to the Children's Commissioner, the man who was responsible for approving the project and signing over the land.

The guard at the main gate had been given instructions not to permit visitors on Sunday mornings. But what could he do when such an important guest arrived unannounced? How embarrassed we felt, greeting him with towels swathed around our swimsuits? However, Norene quickly changed and rustled up some food on the gas stove in our tiny make-shift kitchen. We sat down to a tasty meal and a good chat. Although he always maintained his stern exterior and Marxist stance, the man seemed to love to visit often and view the progress we were making.

Because of the enormity of the project we realised that if we were going to accept children within the year we would need to recruit extra help. The national board appointed Ato Girima Abebe, of the air force, to be our project coordinator. Later on when he left the air force and began to work for us full-time, he was a tremendous help to me and we developed a strong friendship.

122 Building Plans

For six months we lived in our small "container house" while our three-bedroom home was being built further up the hill, overlooking the lake. We still had our million dollar view, and a spacious verandah on the lakeside proved to be helpful for entertaining our many visitors. How thrilled we were to move into that new dwelling just around the time of my sixtieth birthday, when a surprise birthday party was arranged by our Ethiopian friends. Also about that time our first precious little orphans, three from one family, arrived and were settled in to our container house with a kindly mother figure in Birke who had been one of our faithful outside workers. She proved herself admirably in this task and stayed with the project for many years, giving stability in the home. Other staff members served for various lengths of time.

The year 1990 involved an ambitious building programme in which we aimed to build four large children's homes, a medical clinic and an assembly hall.

It seemed like a huge undertaking for one year, particularly in a Marxist country which was at war and where building supplies were almost non-existent. As we discussed and prayed about these objectives we were challenged by the prophet Nehemiah who, when he heard the adverse report of what had happened to the walls and the gates of Jerusalem, announced:

"The God of heaven will give us success!" (Nehemiah 2:20).

As a team we too claimed this promise as a reminder that our faith and trust was in God alone.

The building of the children's homes was paramount. We made a start on building two large homes with local cement blocks and then received an offer from Les Willliams of SIM USA to help raise the money for two pre-fab homes.

The medical clinic did not go ahead quickly, as permission from the Ministry of Health to build and operate a clinic was not readily given. It took more than twelve months of negotiations before formalities were completed, and so unfortunately there was no medical help available on the compound when the first children began to arrive.

123 Offers Of Help

It was the end of 1989 when we received a letter from a friend in New Zealand, Ken McIntosh, who mentioned that he had read our newsletter about the work at Kuriftu. He asked if we could possibly make use of one of his pre-fab buildings for our assembly hall. His price of $US90,000, including the shipping, could not be matched in Ethiopia even if the materials had been available. This would be a beautiful building (32 metres by 15 metres) made with laminated wooden beams and a coloured corrugated iron roof. In fact it would be the first building of this type ever to be built in Ethiopia. Were we excited! As mentioned earlier, one hundred and fifty people had confessed their faith in Jesus during 1989. What could we expect in 1990?

At that time we were planning on caring for two hundred children, and so figured that with our children, staff and day workers we would need a building that would seat at least five hundred. We had to call it an assembly hall, but knew we would eventually use it as our church if the Marxist laws ever relaxed.

One Sunday after a Bible study in one of the elder's homes, I shared Ken's letter and asked for their comments. Their response was electric! We placed the letter on a little coffee table in the middle of the room and knelt around it to pray. We knew that if it was God's will for us to proceed, then he would help us to raise the huge amount of money. We reminded ourselves that Ethiopia was at that time listed as having the lowest GNP (Gross National Product) of any nation in the world. When we finished praying, we came to a unanimous decision to accept Ken's offer, to enable the work to begin even although we had nothing to give at this stage. We negotiated a plan of bi-monthly progress payments, and started working hard to raise the necessary finance.

First we prepared and printed a little brochure telling about the work at Kuriftu and the need we had for this assembly hall. We agreed to send a copy to our friends both in Ethiopia and overseas. A few weeks later we gathered with a great pile of stamped, addressed envelopes ready to send out. But first we all knelt and prayed that God would use the information and meet our urgent financial needs. We claimed again our motto, *The God of heaven will give us success.*

For Ken, too, this must have been a real step of faith, undertaking to build and ship such a huge building without the usual financial guarantees.

Our local believers were also excited about the prospect of an assembly hall, and gave generously from the little they had. Every two months we promised to make an interim payment of $US20,000 towards the cost of the hall. The elders set a goal of raising 100,000 Ethiopian birr ($NZ25,000) from local believers and other interested people. Our treasurer gave us a progress report each week.

Two weeks before our third interim payment was due, we just didn't have the money to meet our obligations. We shared the problem with the believers and they agreed they would fast from food and even water during the day for three days during the next week and spend their lunch break in prayer. They would eat only in the evenings. Despite this sacrifice, nothing further was received during the week. What should we do?

Over the weekend two visitors from the United States and Canada came to visit our special friends Dr and Mrs Robert Thompson, who were spending a few weeks with us teaching the new believers. (The Thompsons had been our co-workers in Shashamane in the early days of our career.) They asked their two friends if they would like to see how an elders' meeting was conducted in the underground church. The visitors attended somewhat reluctantly, but were warmly welcomed and before long felt at home.

We quietly interpreted for them so they could follow the discussions. The treasurer gave a report on the lack of money to meet our third interim payment to New Zealand for our assembly hall. He mentioned the three days of prayer and fasting the believers had just undertaken, but as far as he knew, nothing extra had been received. Hearing that, one of our guests stood to his feet and said something like this:

"I am a business man, living on the west coast of America, and have been a Christian for some years now. Never before in my life have I been in a meeting like this and felt the Spirit of God speaking to me so clearly. Tonight, in God's presence, I want to pledge to give you $US20,000 for this project and I promise as soon as I get home to send a cheque."

Everyone started weeping as we realised how God was answering our prayers. What a tremendous encouragement this would be for all those who had fasted and prayed during those days. It was certainly an emotional moment as different elders, with tears streaming down their faces, gave thanks to God for his miraculous intervention.

But that was not all. After we had settled down, our Canadian visitor rose and said:

"I, too, have never experienced God moving in my life as I have tonight. Although I have a much smaller business than my friend, I promise with God's help to speak with some of my friends and together we will send you $US10,000 within the next few months."

The meeting concluded with a chorus of praise to God.

Both men honoured those pledges, and even though we had some more anxious moments near the end of our project we never missed a payment. In the end we were even able to order from McIntosh Laminates enough solid wooden pews to seat five hundred people.

124 Testing the Waters

About this time the Marxist government was beginning to be a little more lenient on evangelical Christians and therefore we decided to test the waters by commencing a morning service at Kuriftu. We borrowed an old army tent which was full of holes and announced to our believers we were going to have a morning service the next Sunday. We had no idea what sort of response we would have from the believers, nor did we know what the government officials might do once they found out. At last they could sing to their hearts' content and hopefully no one would interfere. Halfway through the service, from where I was sitting I spotted a number of officials standing on the rim of the crater peering down on us. I half expected police to follow. A scary moment indeed! But nothing happened that Sunday or during the next week. And so we carried on.

The tent became too small as more and more people joined us. In other ways it wasn't satisfactory either. During the rainy season the water would pour through the many holes and umbrellas would shoot up. But they only diverted the rain from the umbrella's owner to the poor souls sitting around. In fact it was like a circus, trying to dodge the drips. But nothing now could deter the believers from enjoying the privilege of corporate worship.

Never a Sunday went past without an appeal being made for people to come to Christ. It was now July 1990, and several hundred were coming to the morning worship service, whereas twelve months earlier Norene and I had been sitting alone on our camp chairs at the lake's edge on Sunday mornings. God's Spirit was being poured out in a way never before experienced. Many sick people were healed and evil spirits cast out just as in the Acts of the Apostles. We began to realise how perfect God's timing was in providing our assembly hall.

125 Assembly Hall

Excitement was building by the time the two containers arrived in the crater. The first was one metre by twelve metres (40 feet) and the second three metres by six metres (20 feet). At the same time short-termers Jim and Mary Peterson (USA), arrived and in no time had chosen a team of Ethiopians to make a start on the floor of the Assembly Hall. In an incredible way, every last item needed to erect that building was in those containers. Every nail, every bolt, every piece of wood, every sheet of iron, almost all the cement, every glass window, every shutter, every length of reinforcing rod, every tin of paint, and every tool required. There was even a beautiful cross to erect on the outside of the building. All of this had been carefully counted and meticulously overseen by Grant McIntosh, Ken's son and our nephew-in law.

Jim and Mary Peterson worked tirelessly and had a winsome witness to those who worked with them. In answer to our call for master builders, Frank and Peter Carter with Roger Nicholls – all friends from New Zealand – came to finish the project at considerable expense. How grateful we were to all of them.

God undertook in miraculous ways. Time and time again we came upon obstacles which we ourselves could not solve. But then God intervened. Jim Peterson wanted to pour the concrete floor in preparation for our new Assembly Hall. This was a big area, and as there was no "ready mix" available in Ethiopia at the time, every barrowload of concrete had to be mixed by hand. We had obtained plenty of bags of cement (some from New Zealand and some from Ethiopia) and plenty of sand, but absolutely no crushed stone. We tried everywhere, but it was not available. (All such building material, we were informed, was needed for the "essential work" of the war effort.)

One afternoon a massive air force twenty-ton truck came lumbering down our track, heading straight towards our building site. The driver backed up and started tipping a huge load of crushed stone onto our site. We were flabbergasted, as we had not paid a single cent. In a halfhearted way we tried to tell the driver he was at the wrong building site, but he wouldn't listen and drove off. As a result there was sufficient material to finish pouring our concrete floor. From that day to this we have no idea who authorised that free truckload of stone. (Can angels drive trucks?)

A few weeks later a high-ranking military officer came to visit the Kuriftu project. As usual we showed him around, ending up at the nearly-finished assembly hall. He was impressed with everything and asked me the purpose of this beautiful building.

"It will be our assembly hall," I replied.

The officer turned to me.

"You can't fool me!" he said. "This is going to be your church, isn't it?"

(Remember, we were still under a Marxist government and there was no permission for public worship.)

"Yes, that is true," I admitted, "but it will be used as an assembly hall too."

We never found out the real purpose of his visit, but we did know the officials were well aware of what we were hoping to achieve.

126 Aqua / Agriculture Project

As we considered the development of the integrated aqua /agriculture section of this whole project, we had three aims in view:

First, to give meaningful employment to the older children, helping them to learn new and profitable methods of using the land; secondly, to help provide basic food supplies for the use of the children's homes, namely fruit and vegetables, eggs and meat, milk and butter, fish, honey and firewood; and thirdly, to develop a model farm for the surrounding farmers so that they could learn different ways of diversifying their income and of profitably using the land.

Because it was an integrated project, we needed to ensure every aspect fitted into the whole plan. We started off by planting trees on the steep, dry slopes of the sides of the crater, as we needed both a good supply of firewood and source of nectar. We chose mainly *grevillea robusta* and *eucalyptus ficifolia*, plus several indigenous acacia varieties – a total of twenty-four thousand seedlings. Then we planted twelve hundred different varieties of tropical fruit trees and established a large vegetable garden. At the lowest point in the dry crater we started digging some fish ponds. Above the fish ponds a small twenty-cow dairy unit and a poultry unit were built. Some of the effluent from the dairy shed was sent down concrete channels to supply the necessary nutrients to increase the plankton in the fish ponds, which in turn the fish would eat. The poultry manure was used to fertilise the vegetable gardens.

Les Williams recruited Raymond and Frances Sperry, retired poultry farmers from Pennsylvania, to come and establish our first poultry unit. They brought a container packed full of 180 different items, including wheel-barrows, two pre-fab poultry sheds (8m x 20m), reinforcing rods and bags of cement. In fact they arrived with everything needed to establish a 500 laying poultry unit. And they aptly named their container, *God is love*.

The dairy unit and the fish ponds were built under the supervision of our family members. David, Grace and their family of three came for a six-month stint during the last half of 1990. How we loved having the family with us during those months. Ryan was almost eight years old, Laura six and Sophie two. (Jordan joined the family after their return to New Zealand.) Dave, a veterinarian, knew how to go about building an appropriate dairy unit. The animals were to be tethered inside, and their daily rations of food brought to them. The dairy was thirty-one metres by nine metres, and built with eucalyptus poles, open sides and a high roof. It was cool even in the heat of the day.

We grew all sorts of supplementary food such as elephant grass, lucerne, vetches and peas. On completing the building Dave was able to buy eleven young Friesian/cross heifers plus a few in-calf cows. He needed to test the animals for TB before they were brought onto our compound, since bovine tuberculosis is endemic in Ethiopia. In one government herd of milking cows which he tested, more than fifty percent returned a positive test. No wonder we insisted that all fresh milk be boiled before drinking. Before the family left Kuriftu, the dairy was producing on average thirty litres of milk per day and increasing all the time.

127 Of Fish and Bees

The construction and stocking of the fish ponds was supervised by our youngest son, Phil, earlier in 1990. With his love for fishing and his expertise in aquaculture, he eventually had the ponds formed, and filled with water and tilapia fingerlings. Unfortunately, because of the volcanic soil and lack of clay in the district, it proved difficult to seal the ponds satisfactorily. But after consultation with a world renowned aquaculturalist from the USA, he learned how to cope with this situation. We were told that before filling the ponds the bottom and the sides needed to be coated with a thick layer of cow manure, which then needed to be tramped in, and the ponds slowly filled with water. He suggested we add as much green algae (as found on stagnant water) as possible. When the green algae slowly settles onto the cow manure, a chemical reaction takes place in which an impervious layer develops. It took some months for the process to establish a good seal, but it sounded simple and it certainly was. More than that, it was affordable.

Phil with our two adopted grand children Paulos (L) and Mitiku. Fish pond in background

Of course critics came along and said the ponds should all be sealed with plastic liners, but such things were not available and would have been way beyond our budget. Furthermore, we were demonstrating how even the poorest of farmers could set up a small aquaculture project if they had an adequate water supply. It has been proven that even with a small pond, six metres by four metres, two edible fish can be harvested each month, giving a family a source of protein they could never obtain from that small area of land. Fortunately the lake at Kuriftu had a good supply of tilapia fingerlings, and Phil was able to net sufficient numbers to stock the ponds at a rate of one fingerling to a square meter of water.

As mentioned before, tilapia are farmed in many parts of the world and are often referred to as the *mad* fish. Our biggest problem after a few months was how to control the number in the ponds, as they quickly matured and bred. Several helpful suggestions were made, either to introduce a predator species to keep the number of fingerlings down, or to learn how to sex the fish and farm only one gender.

The apiary was established in the far corner of the property, to keep the bees as far away as possible from animals and people. Ethiopian bees, like most bees in Africa, are aggressive and need careful handling. We decided to build a small apiary of mud bricks to house the beehives. Inside, on a shelf running around the building, we placed twelve new "top-bar mud beehives" which we connected to the outside of the building by means of twelve 25mm plastic pipes. The bees landed on a little shelf outside the building and then ran into their hives through the plastic pipes which protruded slightly from the mud wall.

This worked beautifully and we were well pleased, until our beekeeper reported a problem. This landing strip outside the building formed a perfect location for the local lizards to sit in the sun, licking up the nectar-laden bees as they returned from their field trips. Talk about cast iron stomachs! Those lizards were not fazed by the dozens of stings they must have endured in a day. Bee numbers were rapidly being depleted, and so we set about a lizard extermination programme, which was easier said than done.

But our top-bar hives proved their worth and we were able to take up to fifteen kilos of honey per hive, as compared to four kilos from the local hives. The robbing of the hives had to be done on a dark night, and the following day no animal or person was able to approach within a hundred metres of the hive without suffering the consequences. Honey is an important ingredient in Ethiopian cuisine, but it is hard to find and expensive. Which is why thieves jumped over our high barbed-wire fence one night and stole one of our precious bee-hives. I wonder how many stings they suffered before arriving home? As our nectar-bearing trees grew, so our honey production increased.

128 Garden Of Eden

In viewing the project from the rim of the crater, one could echo the words of Ecclesiastes 3:10 – "God has made everything beautiful in its time."

We were amazed by the number of Ethiopian visitors who came to see the project and would say something like, "When I came over the rim of the crater and viewed the project I thought I was in heaven."

Surely this extinct crater did come to life. In fact some named it the Garden of Eden.

As we read Ezekiel 36: 34-35 we thought God must have been talking about Kuriftu:

The desolate land will be cultivated instead of lying desolate in the sight of all who pass through it. They will say, 'This land that was laid waste has become like the Garden of Eden.

Then in Isaiah 41:19-20 we read:

I will put in the desert the cedar and the acacia, the myrtle and the olive. I will set pines in the wasteland, the fir and the cypress together, so that people may see and know, may consider and understand, that the hand of the Lord has done this, that the Holy

Some of our Kuriftu children

One of Israel has created it.

As the thousands of tree seedlings grew to maturity this Scripture seemed to be fulfilled before our eyes.

Much of Norene's responsibility at Kuriftu was to entertain a host of guests, both Ethiopian and foreign. Apart from day guests we had many short-termers living on our compound for months at a time. She chose some Ethiopian girls who were gifted in various kinds of handicrafts to work in our lounge day by day. They made articles to sell as souvenirs, with the income going towards our new church building. Many pretty embroidered aprons and cloths found their way overseas as missionaries purchased them as gifts for supporters and friends. The girls whom she chose to do this work fast became friends and several married Christian young men who were also working at Kuriftu.

Norene also took an interest in the orphan children and their needs. At one stage we desperately wanted to improve their play area and wrote to a contact in New Zealand, asking if there was any way a "McDonald-type" playground could be sent over in a container. We were disappointed that for various reasons this idea never came to fruition. The children made their own fun, though, like tying old vehicle tyres to a tree and having hours of fun swinging on these. They all attended local schools and most did well in their studies.

How we loved having three of our grandchildren at Kuriftu for six months! Their mother, Grace, taught the older two by correspondence, but

With the Kuriftu teenage young men from the children's centre. 1996

the life experiences they picked up from living in such a different culture could not have been learned from books. Years later they still talk about their experiences in Ethiopia.

One event they will never forget was when their Uncle Phil brought home a baby deer he had bought on the side of the road. The three children took turns to feed it with a bottle until it was big enough to eat grass. Teeny lived with us for seven months, often coming inside and slipping and sliding across the wooden floors. She even learned where we kept a large tin of "famine biscuits."

Our Grandchildren Ryan, Laura and Sophie with our pet Deer. 1990

129 Bible School

It was during those difficult days of 1990, as the number of evangelical Christians was increasing so rapidly, that we agreed it was time to start an evening Bible School. You might say common sense should have dictated otherwise. Surely we should have waited until Marxism had been overthrown. But no, the elders believed they should go ahead in faith.

The local KHC church had no buildings of their own, but they were able to rent a house in the town of Debre Zeit. The desks we needed for the students simply weren't available at the time, so only chairs were supplied. The thirst for learning was so great that church leaders from all denominations came to learn as much as they could. I was able to teach one or two subjects each week, as was John Dakin from New Zealand. John and Margaret Dakin had taken over the guest house ministry at Babogaya and John was an asset to the Bible School. Most of the teachers were mature Christian men who came from Addis Ababa to help us establish the school.

Now fourteen years later (in 2005) the Bible School continues to grow, with a full-time Ethiopian director and hundreds of students who have completed a two- or three-year study.

130 Extinct Crater Comes To Life

On September 21 1991 the Kuriftu children's centre was officially opened. Yes, Kuriftu, an extinct crater, had come to life. Not that it blew its top again, but this was the place where evil spirits were once worshipped, and where even hyenas had taken up residence in a cave on the side of the crater. (Interestingly, those hyenas left the crater immediately our project started.) What a transformation had taken place as we had prepared homes for these eighty-three children. (We had planned for two hundred, but in the end the government slated only eighty-three for our centre.)

Three hundred guests from near and far arrived to share in the opening celebrations. There were government officials, church officials, mission representatives and donor representatives. Ken McIntosh, managing director of McIntosh Timber Laminates Ltd which had supplied all the material for the Kuriftu church, was present and was asked to speak. It was a joy also to welcome again our youngest son Phil, who was sent over to represent and bring greetings from, our home church, Howick Baptist. Government and church officials spoke, and I concluded with a summary of how the Lord had brought this great project into being.

Ken McIntosh left, Teshome Haile, Phil Bond and Sylvia Yandall (my secretary).

Flower gardens had been meticulously prepared, with the words *Welcome To Kuriftu Children's Centre* and *God Is Love* portrayed in different colour combinations. Church choir members, dressed in new robes, delighted the crowds with their lively singing. The workers had prepared a massive spread of the highly spiced national food which was served first to our three hundred guests and then to all the workers who had made Kuriftu what it was by their diligent work over the past three years. Ato Girima Abebe, the administrator of the children's centre had worked hard to bring this programme together, and much of the success of the day was due to his organisation.

131 A Service To Remember

Postscript: A few years after Norene and I had moved to Addis Ababa for the Mission directorship, one Sunday we decided to make an unannounced visit to Kuriftu. Our hearts tingled with joy as we slipped into the back seat of the spacious and beautiful church building. Our thoughts travelled back to when the project first started, five years before, when on Sunday mornings we would take our folding chairs down to the lake and have our own little worship service. Now here we were, sharing with more than five hundred people. True, even before Kuriftu came into existence, there were Christians in town who worshipped at night in little underground groups, but corporate worship was not permitted. We thanked God that those repressive days were over and many more were now coming to know Jesus as their Saviour. We reminded ourselves of that verse in Ecclesiastes 11:1 – *Cast your bread upon the waters, for after many days you will find it again.* Surely this was coming true of Kuriftu.

The new assembly hall / church building was refreshingly cool, despite the fierce heat outside and the hundreds of people packed inside. We thought of Ken McIntosh who had carefully designed the building and of Grant his son who had meticulously put it all together when packing the containers. We thought of our overseas carpenters who came to build the church, Jim and Mary Peterson, Frank and Peter Carter, and Roger Nicholls. We thought of all the donors, those living in Ethiopia and those from overseas. All of them would have been thrilled to be sitting with us that Sunday morning to see the results of their labour. And then I thought of the believers who had been faithful right through the project. Many had given sacrificially and had prayed and fasted until the building was completed.

After the preaching that Sunday morning there was a children's dedication service, when thirty-three couples came forward to have their children blessed. This opportunity had not been available until now. The pastor spotted me sitting at the back and called me up to pray for the children and their parents. What a thrill!

But there was more to follow. (There are no short services in Ethiopia.) We were then led down to the lakeside where fifty people were baptised, all of whom were our special friends. We were especially delighted to find that two of the fifty were our own "boys," Paulos and Mitiku, two needy boys whom we had more or less adopted in the early days. They had been with us since day one.

Finally, those who were newly baptised, along with all the other believers, were invited back to the church to celebrate the Lord's Supper. I was told there were 362 who shared in communion.

After the service we were invited to eat with the orphan children, all eighty-three of them. They were adorable kids of all ages, well looked-after and receiving a great education. Some of the older ones had already become Christians, and in fact five had been baptised that morning. One of the boys, Abraham, told us how he came to be at the children's centre.

"My parents were believers," he said, "when during the communist regime they and their four children were taken forcefully to work in Gambela on a state farm, growing sorghum and rice. There were many problems. The food was different and all of us suffered with malaria. My father died of chloroquine-resistant malaria. Many others died too, and so they buried several at a time.

"Everyone lived in a big *das* or open building. At the end of the same year my mother became sick and died. I was only twelve, with an older brother and two younger sisters. Without our parents we had no one to care for us.

"My brother and I set off for Addis Ababa, thinking we would find work. We tried to join the army, but were deemed too young and too short. Then the officials sent us to the Red Cross for help. The ambulance men were kind to us, offered us some tea and bread, and gave us an acceptance letter for the government orphanage. But there was no room. Yet we knew God was helping us all the way through those difficult days.

"I had been praying all along that God would take us to a Christian orphanage. Before my father died he made me promise never to leave God's way, even if difficulties came. Finally the government officials said to us, 'We have found a space for all of you at Kuriftu children's centre.' We were able to locate our sisters back in Gambela and the four of us came to Kuriftu. How grateful we are for this wonderful centre where we are taught about the God our parents loved and worshipped."

When Norene and I heard that testimony, we paused to thank God that he had guided us to dream of finding land for a children's centre. Thank you, Lord, I said in my heart, that we listened to your urging.

Now, in 2005, we hear that both Abraham and his older brother Belaye have had tertiary training and are both holding down good jobs.

132 A Missionary Mother's Ministry

The following is a shortened account of a heart-to-heart talk Norene gave to SIM missionary mothers in Addis Ababa at their request:

Making disciples in a country like Ethiopia can be a sacrificial task, involving high commitment to people, especially in terms of time. It is interesting to note that Christ spent only a third of his time in what we might call "religious activity." The rest of his time was spent in ordinary activities and relationships with people. This should be a comfort to us as married women, so we don't have to feel like a half-baked mother or an ineffective missionary all the time.

I so often find that mothers face a conflict or sense of guilt some of the time they are out here, because they sense they are not spending enough time "in the work." Perhaps it is even more likely to happen now that many of you are home-schooling your children. Those of us who sent our children to boarding school had more time during the term, when at least some of our children were away at school. I don't mind admitting I found it a tremendous struggle to send our five- and six-year-olds off to boarding school. No other experiences out here compared to that real ache around the heart.

During our ten years at the Shashamane leprosarium we had the great advantage of having been married right on the compound and our four children having been born during those years. One was actually born in our own home there. We tried to identify with the local women as we visited them when they gave birth to their children. (Nowadays many of you go to the homeland for the births of your babies.) The day we returned to Shashamane after the birth of our first child, the Arsi women flocked to our home to view this new little wonder – a white baby! We served coffee to all and stopped counting at one hundred.

There are several important matters to consider regarding having help in the home out here. First, some may protest that they can't afford to have home help, but surely this is not true. For example, I worked it out that our missionary allowance is twenty-five times the amount we pay our worker at present.

Secondly, house mothers have a unique opportunity to train those who work in the home. We can teach them to be a good parent, a true believer, a useful citizen and sometimes a capable leader. We have been able to influence Arsi , Amhara, Kambattan and Gurage young people.

Thirdly, the helper in the house can learn much about relationships between husband and wife, how they relate to each other, how they both cope with stress, how they welcome nationals into their home, and their love for God.

A missionary mother needs to cope with many new situations in her life, such as shortages of water and/or electricity, and having to boil the drinking water and to wash all raw food thoroughly. There's sickness, bugs, bargaining, and making meals interesting with little to work with at times. Sometimes the poverty and the beggars can get her down. One big stress can be trying to find time to have her own time of Bible reading and prayer.

There are, of course, some disadvantages to having someone in the home most of the day, under your feet, as it were. It isn't easy to be on show all day long, but it does pay off. Teaching a worker in the kitchen means starting from scratch, even showing how you want the dishes washed. Disciplining our children can be a sore point. God has said in his word, "Spare the rod and spoil the child," and so we need to discipline sometimes. I found it quite disconcerting if I would start to discipline one of our children and one of the girls would grab my arm (as they often do in their own homes to save the parents from losing their temper.) I would have to stop and try to explain why I was doing this, and in the meantime the child probably escaped the discipline.

It is not easy to be constantly with the same people day in and day out, whether nationals or missionaries. Our fellow workers might not be the kind of people we would ever choose as friends. But we are stuck with them, and they with us. I well remember when, as a young married woman, I was teaching one day and a senior missionary stormed into the classroom and told me off for some misdemeanour in front of the students. Couldn't he have taken me aside and done that? I thought. I tried to prevent the tears, but they came anyway. I don't know what my students thought that day. Bruce and I had the rule that when we felt there was any ill feeling or misunderstanding between us and our fellow missionaries, we would try to put it right "before the sun went down." This wasn't easy, but it paid off many a time.

The following poem helped me often too;

Acceptance
Acceptance is the answer to all my problems today.
When I am disturbed, it is because I find some
person, place, thing or situation,
some fact of life unacceptable to me and
I find no serenity until I accept that
person, place, thing or situation as being exactly
the way it is supposed to be at this moment.
Nothing, absolutely nothing, happens to
God's children by mistake.
Unless I accept life completely on God's terms,
I cannot be happy.
I need to concentrate not so much on what needs to
be changed in the ***world*** *as on what needs to*
be changed in ***me*** *and* ***my attitudes***
– Source unknown

133 Preparing For A Wedding

Bekelu was one of the girls who had been with us through most of her teenage years. While we were running the guest house at Babogaya she was working in the kitchen before or after school each day. Through our Bible studies she believed in Jesus and was baptised. When we moved to open the work in Kuriftu she said to us, "You are like my parents now. Can I please come and work with you at Kuriftu?" She had become a most competent cook and capable worker in the home, as well as having a tremendous gift for teaching children's Sunday School.

Later on she started praying that God would lead her to a Christian husband. She had known a young man, Alemaiehu Zewde, for many years and was fond of him as a friend. Alem, as he was known, had been a keen Christian in the earlier years and for a while had even been imprisoned for his faith. But on joining the air force he had sadly left his first love for the Lord. Being fond of Bekelu, he decided to write to her, and along with the letter he sent her a pair of beautiful shoes. She became confused, as she knew he did not have a spiritual desire as she did. Reluctantly she wrote to him, refusing his offer and returning the shoes. He was devastated.

Bekelu and Alem's wedding. 1994

Many of the local believers were praying Alem would return to his former faith, and some months later he did rededicate his life to the Lord. He wrote again to her, and this time she accepted his shoes.

We remember the first time he came to our home in Kuriftu to visit Bekelu and to meet us both. I guess we could say he was the typical "tall, dark and handsome" young man who could turn a girl's heart upside down. But more than that, we could sense he was now genuinely wanting to serve God and to be the kind of husband Bekelu was seeking. We felt honoured we could be involved right from the start of this love match.

Engagement in Ethiopia is as binding as marriage. Once the couple had secretly agreed together, Alem sent three elders to Bekelu's parents to ask for their daughter's hand in marriage. Protocol demanded that on entering the parents' compound, the visiting elders must wait until they have announced the purpose of their errand, before entering the house. In this case, after a protracted discussion, an agreement was reached and was followed by a celebratory meal. Someone must have spilled the beans in advance to Bekelu's mother, for she had prepared an appetising meal of the local food.

Then a wedding date was agreed upon. This needed to be after the grain harvest as only then would there be sufficient food available.

For a Christian wedding, regular pre-marriage classes were an important aspect of the preparations. We were most impressed by the commitment of the whole wedding party. For a year they met monthly for prayer and planning. Their desire was that the big day would be a blessing to all who attended and they were determined God should be glorified.

134 The "Dowry" and the Day

The exchange of gifts took place the night before the wedding and Norene and I were both invited to be present. There was no sign of the bride and groom, but the best man and his friends duly arrived with a large bulging suitcase. (We found out later that the bride was hiding behind a curtain, and so she heard everything without being seen.) I expect you could equate this to the dowry. Everyone crowded into the dimly-lit room, waiting to see what the bridegroom had sent for his bride and the bride's parents. On top of the suitcase was the gorgeous lacy wedding dress. (Only a few of us knew that the dress was a gift from a friend in New Zealand.) This was followed by clothing for the bride, including all her underwear. Every article was held aloft for all to see and comment on. Then, right at the end, the most expensive gifts – a gold chain and the two gold wedding bands.

Now the bride's parents received their gifts of new clothes for the wedding day. Having distributed all the gifts, the best man and his party waited for the parents' reaction. Yes, the wedding dress was beautiful and fit for their daughter. The dresses and the underwear were perfect, but how about shoes? Where was the perfume? After all, this was their daughter's special day. She must be dressed and treated like a queen. Half serious and half joking, the bride's father announced he could not permit the wedding to proceed the next day until all his requests had been met, that is, new shoes for the bride and her mother, and some perfume.

The best man and his entourage appeared devastated, as they said they had spent their last dollar on the dowry and yet more was required. The drums continued to beat and the singing grew louder, but money must be found to buy the remaining dowry items. (We found out later this was quite a normal and expected reaction from the girl's parents.)

How it all came together we don't know, but by 9:30pm the final dowry items had been bought and presented. And that's when the celebrations really took off. But after the meal Norene and I took our leave, knowing there would be no sleep that night as the whole village celebrated and worked towards the upcoming celebrations.

The men killed and dressed the fattened animal and the women prepared sufficient food for more than five hundred guests. Because no refrigeration was available, all food had to be prepared the night before the wedding.

The next morning the church was beautifully decorated with fresh flowers, while the bride dressed and waited with her bridesmaids in her parents' home for her groom and his friends to claim her. But this was no easy feat, for, as custom dictated, her friends playfully protected her for some time from these "strange" men. It was a tearful time for her mother as she was saying farewell to her daughter as a single girl. The noise was deafening, with singing, dancing and joy calls as the groom presented his bride with a bouquet of flowers before taking her back to his own parents' home. There they shared their pre-wedding meal with his family and friends.

The church service followed, with between seven hundred and eight hundred people present. I had been asked to give a message, which I centred around the story of Isaac and Rebekah. Ato Teshome, one of the elders, led the service and Ato Yohannes, the pastor, tied the knot. The singing, the clapping, the choir pieces, and the joy calls all made for a most enthralling service of praise to God. Several came to know the Lord in that service, including Bekelu's own mother. As mentioned earlier, the wedding party had prayed together before this important day and their one desire was that the guests would hear the gospel.

Following the two-hour service, photos were taken down by the lake where everyone was served light refreshments and a piece of wedding cake. The final wedding feast was held at the bride's parents' home in the evening, and all their neighbours and friends were invited. To make it possible for such a large gathering, a community tent had to be hired and erected in both homes. Tables, chairs and dishes were all borrowed from the neighbourhood to make this meal the most special day in their daughter's life.

135 Oyster Pearls

An angel paused in his downward flight
With a seed of love and truth and light
And said, "Oh where can this seed be sown
Where 'twill yield most fruit when fully grown?
To whom can this precious seed be given
That it will bear most fruit in earth and heaven?"
The Saviour heard and said, as He smiled
"Place it at once in the heart of a child."
– Lois Lebar

In my fascination with living by the sea as a child, I always imagined finding a real pearl every time I opened an oyster.

Living in Ethiopia, a thousand miles from the sea, we've continued to open "oysters" and have discovered some amazing "pearls" which have been cultivated by the Spirit of God. Let me tell you about some of them.

With another 'Pearl', a homeless boy

Many years ago a poor woman lived outside the boundaries of our mission compound. She had little money with which to feed herself and her daughter. We missionaries helped as best we could by giving the girl some work and she attended our mission school. She became a believer and proved to be an able student, eventually gaining an overseas scholarship which enabled her to graduate as a doctor. In later years she was appointed to a high government position in Ethiopia.

During our Kuriftu days we met many more "pearls."

First there were our two special boys. Indeed they were just boys when we first came to know them – **Mitiku** and **Paulos.** (See photo on page 221)

We first met Mitiku when we were surveying the property at Kuriftu. This skinny little seven- or eight-year-old attached himself to me and followed me around everywhere. He wore only a long shirt, which suitably covered everything. His joints, particularly his knee joints, were badly swollen and he was obviously in pain as he limped along behind me. Yet something about that little boy drew us to him.

Some months later as our container house was being shifted into the crater at Kuriftu, Mitiku was right there again. The first morning we woke up in our new home, he was waiting outside asking what he could do to help. His walking seemed to be deteriorating, and so what could we do? We figured he was half starving, and although we knew the danger of dependency, we gave him some breakfast. Was he hungry! From then on we became lifelong friends.

Dr Barry Hicks, a capable surgeon from Australia, called in to see us one day and willingly agreed to see if he could help Mitiku. Barry suggested fairly simple medication and a good diet, which of course he couldn't afford before, and the swelling seemed to go down in his joints. (Thank you, Barry, for your endless free consultations.)

Paulos, another skinny little boy, instantly won his way into our hearts also. He was downcast and malnourished and we were sad the day he told us his mother was taking him to the big city of Addis Ababa for schooling. Something just wasn't right. We knew he had a problem.

Weeks later the elders came to us with the disturbing news that Paulos and his mother were coming back to Debre Zeit because Paulos was sick. They told us what had happened. His mother worshipped evil spirits in her home at night. Before long these evil spirits entered Paulos and he was greatly disturbed. In fact he was so disturbed at night that although he was a good student, he had to give up his classes.

In desperation his mother took him many places to have these spirits exorcised, but to no avail. Finally she brought him to our church elders at Kuriftu, where after a tremendous struggle he was delivered, and he accepted Jesus as his Saviour. No wonder he looked so frail after those traumatic experiences. The elders asked if we could take an interest in him.

Now we had both boys most days and they proved to be good company for each other. Mitiku also understood what it was to love the Lord and both grew in their understanding of the Christian way.

With better food and care both started putting on weight and before long were able to attend the local elementary school. They came before and after school to help us with odd jobs, and in return had something to eat. Both became keen soccer players.

Since leaving Ethiopia we have kept in touch regularly, and we're so grateful for a Dutch SIM missionary who has "adopted" them as we did, and been a father figure to them. Both having graduated from a vocational trade school in Addis Ababa they now have full-time employment.

136 More Pearls

Then there was **Girima** and his wife **Ainalem** whom we have mentioned several times before. With their eight children we formed a special bond of friendship which we maintain today. Girima was always our encourager, as his favourite verse from the Bible was Romans 8: 28 – *In all things God works for the good of those who love him, who have been called according to his purpose.*

Often when we had disappointments in the work, Girima would arrive at our door and just say, "Romans 8:28." He even said this verse over and over as he was being cut out of the cab of his pick-up when he was almost killed in a serious traffic accident in Debre Zeit in 1990. (See photo on page 240)

Solomon and his wife **Terefech**, who had six children, worked closely with us and we learned much from this godly family. In fact Solomon was chosen as the chairman of the elders of the local church and ably fulfilled this position even after he developed bone cancer. It was in November 2003, during our final visit to Ethiopia, that we sat on his bed praying with him. We

Ato Solomon passed away shortly after this photograph was taken

reminded him with tears that he had knelt and prayed by Norene's bed back in 1988 when she was so sick. He was radiant and victorious even in suffering, and continued to have an outstanding testimony until God called him home a few months after we left.

Teshome and **Tirunesh** were the third couple we mentioned who were in leadership during the establishment of Kuriftu. They were family-oriented and later decided to leave Debre Zeit to live in Addis Ababa, where their six children pursued higher education in the capital. Their oldest daughter is now married to a fine Christian young man. (Teshome's photo is on page 225)

Our special friends **Belaye** and **Chaley** and their five children lived close by at Babogaya. (Belaye was mentioned in our story of Negussie, the communist youth leader who was exorcised of evil spirits. His photo is on page 197) As a young man Belaye became the first full-time evangelist in the local church and has spent his life reaching out to unbelievers. We developed a special relationship with him and stay in touch by letter. Recently, when we sent him a monetary gift which had been passed on to us by a friend in November 2004, we asked him what he had done with the money.

"First I bought a pair of shoes for my wife," he replied, "and then I bought new school uniforms for my two daughters, and then I bought a small tin of paint for our front door which had never been painted."

"And what did you buy for yourself?" I asked.

He just looked at me and smiled.

But that was Belaye, a selfless man of God.

We can't really stop here without mentioning some of our other special friends, all of whom have come to know the Lord. There is **Gaytu** and **Asagadech** and their five children. Gaytu holds a responsible position with the Compassion organisation, supporting children from poor families. They met at Kuriftu, as many couples did.

Then there is **Bekele** and **Tsehai**. He was often rebellious before he was converted, but what a transformation! This couple also met as they worked together in the Kuriftu project, and now have three children. Now he is, of necessity, self-employed and raises chickens and grows flowering plants to sell in the market. (All this just to keep 'body and soul' together.)

Abraham and **Sesaye** were also converted and met each other at Kuriftu. They have four children and struggle to make ends meet. He's a clever carpenter, but has difficulty finding enough work. In our Kuriftu days he had a miraculous escape. While on the roof of one of the children's homes he picked up an aluminium ladder touching the overhead electric wires and was thrown to the ground, narrowly escaping with his life. Through that experience he became a keen Christian.

Itaynesh, a girl who worked for us in the container at Kuriftu, has since married **Reta**, a church elder, and they have five children.

Ali, a Muslim, came to work for us at Kuriftu. He was assigned to help our son David, in the building of the dairy in 1990. Ali was converted and started evening Bible school. Later he had a growing burden for his own people and volunteered to return to the area of his birth, 600 kilometres to the north, to take the good news of the gospel. He suffered incredible persecution, was stoned several times, and barely escaped with his life. Despite the persecution, one hundred and five people have believed, as of 2004.

We must not forget to mention our deaf, dumb and one-eyed friend, **Zenu**. When she was thrown out of her country home, she came to the Kuriftu area to stay with her married sister. Soon after this she came down to our house in the crater to meet us. How difficult it was to interact with someone who could not hear and who could not even speak Amharic. Later she brought her young son to try to get her message across to us in a faltering way. By God's grace she understood enough to accept Jesus and be baptised.

Zenu, (deaf & dumb) holding Church key

The last time we visited Kuriftu she told us through her young son, "I was trying to think what I could do for God despite my limitations. I decided I would go to the church at dawn every Sunday and sweep, clean and dust God's house before returning home to dress in my better clothes to attend the service."

Lately we have been sending her flower seeds for her to propagate and sell. We're grateful, too, that the Compassion organisation has now begun to support her son. In a recent letter (December 2004) she sent the following message via an Ethiopian friend:

"To my holy father and mother… my words are not enough to express the kindness you have done to change my and my poor son's life… Even though my ears and one of my eyes doesn't work, you made me like any healthy people with bright life.....I am also praying in my language for you and your family..."

Weseney became a dear friend when she worked with us at Kuriftu. With four children to manage on her own, she did well to support them by continuing to work in the field and then in our home. At one stage her ex-husband returned to live with her and from then on she became sick for a few years and then died. We heard later he had died with the same symptoms. Since that time our own little church here in New Zealand and Compassion Ethiopia have been supporting these four orphans who are all going on in their Christian faith despite their sad circumstances.

A 'Pearl' Weseney died leaving four orphans

137 Unexpected Change of Direction

Our balmy evening was interrupted by a call on our newly-installed telephone. We were surprised to hear the voice of the SIM deputy General Director, John Cumbers, who was visiting Ethiopia. After the usual greetings he said he had something to ask us.

"Would you be willing to accept the position of acting director for SIM Ethiopia, until a new director is chosen?"

"No, I would not," I uttered with determination. For fifteen years I had been director for SIM New Zealand and we had both felt the time had come for us to return to Ethiopia and be out of administration duties.

When we left Ethiopia in 1970 because of our children's educational needs, we had made a vow that if ever the Lord opened the way we would return. We had been able to make a brief return from 1976 to 1977. But now, in 1989, we felt settled into our ministry at Kuriftu and planned to remain there at least until we reached retirement age, which was four years away. Furthermore, everything appeared to be going so well and there were signs of the Lord's blessing. It was a project we could adequately manage.

John must have wondered why we wouldn't even agree to consider his suggestion. Personally, I felt there were many more capable SIM personnel in Ethiopia who could adequately handle the task of the SIM directorship. But John didn't press us, and in the next few days returned to the USA.

Some months later we received another phone call from John, who had returned to Ethiopia to try to settle the matter of leadership once and for all. He had already visited most SIM missionaries at their various work locations. Strangely, he had not visited us nor asked our opinion for a nomination. When eventually he did come to visit us, however, our hearts sank. He told us he was still of the same mind, and having discussed the situation with the SIM General Director, Dr Ian Hay, and others in Ethiopia, we were being asked to reconsider our previous decision.

Like Jonah we felt like fleeing. As mentioned, we had never been so happy and fulfilled as we were at Kuriftu. Again we were at a crossroads in our missionary career. We simply did not want to move.

Were we willing to relinquish the control of the most cherished project in our missionary career to serve the mission in an administrative post? Our SIM General Director, along with his deputy, urged us to consider this challenge seriously.

Soon after that Dr Mulatu, the general secretary of the Word of Life churches to whom we were seconded, paid us a surprise visit. Instead of affirming our decision to remain at Kuriftu, as we expected, he said:

"I feel, Bruce and Norene, that you should accept Mr Cumbers' invitation to the SIM Ethiopia directorship as we would appreciate your input as SIM director. We must all trust the Lord to provide personnel to replace you here at Kuriftu."

This same sentiment was echoed by some of our missionary colleagues who came to visit us. For thirty-seven years we had been part of the SIM family and even although there had been times when we found it difficult to accept certain assignments, we had always proved God's enabling grace. The Lord seemed to be telling us to trust him. Again these words came to our minds:

My grace is sufficient for you for my power shows up best in weak people. (2 Cor 12:9, The Living Bible.)

We needed to unite in "weaving strong webs" (as our title suggests) to "tie up more lions," and so we accepted the challenge

Once we knew for sure we would not return to Kuriftu, there was much to accomplish before we left for a short break in New Zealand. Ato Girima was well able to carry on the administration with his team of workers. At least in Addis Ababa we would be only an hour away from Kuriftu and able to visit often. We were spoiled with many farewells, meals in homes and gifts.

Sad farewells and joyful reunions often seemed to follow in quick succession. With mixed emotions, we packed up to leave.

Bruce with the new administrator, Ato Girima Abebe

Chapter Ten

Addis Ababa

138 Mengistu Defeated

By the time we left Ethiopia on 1 February 1991 for our brief visit to New Zealand, President Mengistu Haile Mariam was in serious trouble. The Soviets, who had poured eleven billion dollars into supplying military hardware between 1977 and 1989, pulled the plug and Gorbachev told Mengistu that they would not renew their military treaty with Ethiopia after 1991. Cuba likewise terminated twelve years of military cooperation with Mengistu.

On 5 March Mengistu issued a proclamation introducing what he termed a "mixed economy," in which he envisaged the state, private investors and co-operatives participating. After seventeen years of brutal repression, it was doubtful there would have been many, either within Ethiopia or outside, who would have been willing to invest a dollar in the country.

By May 1991 things were becoming desperate for Mengistu and his vast army of more than 100,000 men. It was sickening to see convoys of buses, sometimes up to one hundred, loaded with young, untrained conscripts who were heading up north to the war zone. After minimal training they were sent to the front, but were no match for the well-trained and disciplined forces of the Ethiopian People's Revolutionary Democratic Front. The EPRDF was a coalition of two groups, TPLF (The Tigre People's Liberation Front) and the EPDM (Ethiopian People's Democratic Movement) which now controlled all of the Tigre Region to the north of Ethiopia. And its forces were making rapid advances on the capital, Addis Ababa.

On 21 May a light plane took off from Addis Ababa airport with President Mengistu Haile Mariam and his family fleeing from the country that he had successfully reduced to a basket case. Hundreds of thousands of people had been slaughtered, all in the name of Marxism. The vice-president called for a ceasefire, but the EPRDF did not reply. They were now savouring victory and were within a few kilometres of Addis Ababa.

Between Friday 24 May and Sunday 27 May an astonishing event, code-named "Solomon," took place. The remnant of the Falasha Jews were airlifted from Addis Ababa to Jerusalem. In total, 14,400 men, women and children, were transported in forty flights. The seats were removed from these planes in order to jam more people in, and in one flight alone a thousand passengers were transported in a Jumbo jet cargo plane all the way to Jerusalem.

At the same time the EPRDF forces were moving east towards Debre

Zeit, where the main air force base was located, and in so doing they passed by Kuriftu, the KHC children's centre where Norene and I had previously been living. The approaching forces, on seeing the new buildings (actually the new children's homes), fired a few mortar shells at them, no doubt thinking they must be connected to the air force base. Miraculously, twenty-foot shipping containers which had previously brought the pre-fab homes from the USA were still onsite. Being packed full of sacks of relief grain they acted as a protective barrier from those mortar shells. There was no damage to the houses, apart from a few small bullet holes caused by some of the trigger-happy soldiers.

Psalm 125:2 says, *As the mountains surround Jerusalem, so the Lord surrounds his people now and for evermore.*

The invading forces quickly realised their mistake and later gave protection from the looters who followed.

The previous evening, one of our fellow New Zealand missionaries, John Dakin, was travelling in the mission vehicle nearby when he was suddenly confronted with the advancing tanks. He was stopped, questioned, and detained overnight until the battle for the air force base was over. Then he was released to return to the SIM Babogaya rest and conference centre, where Margaret his wife had spent an agonising night, desperately seeking to learn what had happened to him.

139 We Are Farewelled

It was Sunday 27 May 1991 when the air force base fell. This was the very day Norene and I were being farewelled from Howick Baptist, our home church, for our return to Ethiopia. It seemed ironical that with many seeking to *leave* Ethiopia, we were preparing to *enter* it. (That morning, in fact, a report about John Dakin's detainment had been read from the pulpit, as John was also a member of our home church.)

The EPRDF forces were rapidly closing in on Addis Ababa, and many foreigners, fearing the city would be plunged into a terrible bloodbath, sought to leave via the few remaining flights. But our plans were to travel to the USA for consultation with the General Director regarding our new position of director, before proceeding to Ethiopia. We had to trust God that the situation would calm down again before we travelled our last leg of the journey.

The final battle for Addis Ababa started the next day, when the EPRDF forces entered the city. The airport closed, thus trapping those who wanted to leave and closing the door to those like ourselves who wanted to enter. The Ethiopian army capitulated with little resistance, thus sparing the city a terrible slaughter of both army personnel and civilians. Nevertheless, it was reported several hundred were killed that day.

Despite the EPRDF victory, it was a difficult time for both foreigners and Ethiopians, as retribution for past atrocities started taking place. Thousands and thousands of defeated Ethiopian soldiers were fleeing the EPRDF forces. Many had sold their guns for food and shelter, but others had looted the countryside. Many of the senior army officers who had transport available, fled to Kenya or the Sudan.

So in faith we left New Zealand on Thursday 31 May for the USA.

Finally, on 18 June, Alitalia announced it would be making its first flight back into Ethiopia. No difficulty in procuring a seat that day! The flight was almost empty. Few were game to enter Ethiopia at the time. We were happy to have the company of Claire Meckler, an SIM nurse who was also returning to Ethiopia. On the way we made an unscheduled stop in Luxor, Egypt, being informed it was too dangerous to fly into Addis Ababa after dark. The flight would be resumed in the morning, he said.

On the morning of 19 June we finally touched down at Addis Ababa airport. How grateful we were to hear how the Lord had protected the sixty-eight SIMers during the previous three turbulent weeks.

At the airport there was little indication that there had been a change in government, except that the EPRDF soldiers were guarding the airport building. They were tough, wiry and skilled freedom fighters from Tigre, having advanced with little equipment. In fact many of the soldiers guarding the airport were shoeless and wearing old army clothes. But they were disciplined and polite. There appeared to be little structural damage to buildings in the city, but the great battle that had taken place was evidenced by dozens of destroyed Ethiopian army tanks littering the streets.

140 The Dawn of a New Day

Barely had Norene and I arrived back in Ethiopia before we were swamped with urgent things to attend to. Our two-bedroom apartment was rather uninviting at that stage. Although beautifully cleaned, it was completely empty of furniture and curtains. The goods from our Kuriftu home had not arrived, and so it was difficult to settle in quickly. I was informed that the six-monthly council meeting had been delayed until our arrival, and would start in five days' time with me, the new director, as chairman. My task was to read through and try to digest all the matters which would be discussed at our council meeting. What a huge learning curve for me as I chaired the meetings, which continued throughout that week.

Unfortunately we learned, after our arrival in Ethiopia, that the deputy director and his wife were not able to return to Ethiopia, which left us with additional responsibilities. We then discovered we needed an office secretary.

Norene gallantly agreed to fill this crucial position until we could recruit a trained secretary for the position. Murray Dunn, our SIM New Zealand director, came to the rescue by recruiting New Zealander Sylvia Yandall to come out several months later. We were so grateful for Sylvia, who proved to be not only a capable secretary but also a special friend.

Even although some could not return, others filled the gaps. So we did have an effective administration team, including Lindsay Nicholls, Brian Clark, Bill Harding and Jean Sokvitne, with several others joining us later. Without their help I would have been completely snowed under. We had a weekly meeting together to catch up on the overall situation.

Dr Hay, the SIM General Director had given me a detailed job description, emphasising three important aspects of the ministry he wanted me to focus on. These were:

a) To prayerfully consider and present to him and the international council the name of a person whom the Ethiopia council would recommend as the next SIM director for Ethiopia.

b) To continue to seek to improve relationships with the Kale Heywet Church (KHC). This was the national church which had been formed as a result of the work of SIM missionaries throughout the past sixty years. I was to seek to prepare a memorandum of agreement between SIM and KHC.

c) To foster a genuine spirit of unity within the mission family as we prepared for future ministry under a post-Marxist government.

This mandate from Dr Hay was on my mind as I chaired my first Ethiopian council meeting, and in fact during my first two-year term. Because Norene and I had an apartment at the SIM guest house which was on the same compound as my office, I was able to be in my office by 7am, six days a week, and would often be there all evening as well. (I did come home to eat and sleep!) I seldom felt I had accomplished all I needed to in a day.

Many missionaries, Ethiopians and visitors wanted to come and discuss various matters too, and so the door of our home needed to be open also.

During this period we were thrilled to welcome Hudson and Rosemary Deane for several months as they offered to teach some courses at the Dilla KMTC (Kale Heywet Ministry Training Centre.) Hudson was also much appreciated as our speaker for the Spiritual Life Conference which we held regularly for our missionaries.

The SIM executive committee met regularly with the KHC leadership to begin the process of drawing up a memorandum of agreement, specifying the relationship between church and mission. We made good progress. After a special joint KHC/SIM meeting this minute was recorded:

"We acknowledge with gratitude the goodness of God in providing a beautiful spirit of mutual understanding during our two days together and a historic opportunity to consider our anticipated closer partnership for the glory of God."

One of the highlights for Norene and me was our regular prayer day, which was always held on the last Friday of the month. This had been a feature of SIM Ethiopia from its beginning and continues today. This was always a time of blessing for me personally and for our whole SIM family. Some were not able to come because of distance, but most missionaries made a special effort to leave their work to attend this time of prayer, sharing information, and fellowship.

SIM Administrative team, Addis Ababa

141 Famine Relief

Even before the airport reopened after the overthrow of the Mengistu government, the Relief and Rehabilitation Commission summoned all NGOs (Non-Government Agencies) to solicit their help.

"As you are certainly aware," they said, "the country has in the past been confronted by drought and war, which has resulted in famine and food shortages. In the past month the magnitude of these problems has increased."

As a mission we had always been active in helping in such situations. So Alex Fellows (one of our previous directors) and I made a trip into northern Wollo to see for ourselves the situation of the people there. (Norene remembers well the date of this trip, as we left Addis Ababa on a dull, drizzly day. It happened to be July 8, her sixtieth birthday. She said at the time it wasn't exactly the happiest birthday she ever celebrated, with no immediate family around her.)

Without doubt there was a food shortage. Some of the young children were undernourished, but they were not suffering to the extent they had in previous droughts. Nevertheless, a critical situation could develop within months if food were not found immediately.

What seemed so scandalous to us were the hundreds of burnt-out army tanks, rocket launchers and trucks littering the roads as we travelled north. In one place the locals told us to look down a steep ravine beside the road. There we were sickened to see a huge pile of bones and rotting corpses. To think that this waste of life had been due to the greed of a few wicked men!

We passed through the famous Mussolini tunnel built by Italian engineers. As a family we'd driven through this tunnel in 1968 when it was a two-lane highway. But this day it wasn't. It was full of Ethiopian army vehicles of all types which had been hidden inside for protection. When the EPRDF forces arrived they blew up the first and last vehicles in the tunnel, blocking escape for the others. Fortunately the road through the tunnel had been cleared enough to allow one-way traffic.

On completing our trip, Alex and I realised the urgent need was to use our SIM contacts and resources to avert this impending tragedy. We approached some of our past personnel with experience in relief programmes and asked them to consider coming back to Ethiopia to help us prepare a relief proposal to present to the government. The proposal was to care for 80,000 beneficiaries, by supplying them with fifteen kilograms of wheat, one and a half kilos of beans and five kilos of oil per month for at least three months. That meant we were looking for 3,600 metric tons of wheat, 360 metric tons of beans and 120 metric tons of edible oil.

Because there was no transport available to ship this large amount of food from the coast, which was hundreds of kilometres away over rough roads, we needed to purchase five smaller trucks and two eight-ton four-wheel drive Mercedes trucks and trailers. We expected the greater part of this grain and equipment to come from the Canadian government.

A few months later personnel had arrived from Canada, New Zealand and the USA to implement this famine relief project. Eight people had come at short notice to handle the logistics of getting the grain to the needy areas, and of hiring the Ethiopian staff needed to distribute the grain. Reporting to the donors and financially accounting for every dollar given for this massive programme was in itself a huge undertaking.

The number of beneficiaries we were asked to care for increased from 80,000 to 105,000. One of our logistics men informed me we needed 160 truck and trailer loads to meet our needs.

Fortunately only short-term relief was needed before the people's own crops would be harvested, and a disaster, as in 1974, was averted. We were grateful for the help of our short-term colleagues, two of whom were David and Annette Gander from Gore, New Zealand who worked hard to make this project successful.

Numerous opportunities were given to share the gospel, and through this programme a number became believers. Today, some twelve years later, several churches have been established in those areas where there had been no believers previously.

For I was hungry and you gave me something to eat, I was thirsty and you gave me something to drink, I was a stranger and you invited me in, I needed clothes and you clothed me, I was sick and you looked after me, I was in prison and you visited me. (Matt 25: 35)

142 Plastic House People

Gradually the disabled and burnt out tanks were taken off the streets of Addis and the city appeared to return to some form of normality. But hundreds and thousands of ex-soldiers were returning to the capital to try to eke out a living. Many of them had nowhere to sleep except under shop verandas or against stone walls. At nights they would pull sheets of old plastic over them for protection from the severe rains during certain months.

Before long some of the more enterprising started building little plastic shelters against the wall, completely blocking the footpath for pedestrians. My office was on the third floor of the building, overlooking one of the busy streets. The stone wall right opposite my window was one of their favourite sites. Before long forty crude shelters had been erected, housing a total of 115 people. Elsewhere in the city thousands more were living under the same conditions.

The new government suddenly faced a new crisis – what to do with all these homeless people? Truckloads of them were shipped out of the capital to the various towns and villages whence they had come, but the problem was too big to solve completely.

The family who lived on the footpath

Norene wrote:

"It was evening in Addis Ababa and we were just sitting down to our lighter meal of the day – fresh home-baked bread and a tasty casserole on the table. It was then that I thought of the families living in the plastic houses on the footpath across the road from our SIM apartment. Several times recently I had walked past the forty or so families, thinking to myself, I really must do something about these poor people, but they are so many.'

The Lord reminded me of what someone had said recently: "You can't help *all* of the people *all* of the time, but you can help *some* of the people *some* of the time." Someone else said, "If you see a great need, don't do nothing, do *something*."

That evening I asked our Ethiopian "daughter" to take some of the fresh bread and spiced tea to the couple with the cute little daughter. Later on as we came to know this couple, Tigist and Kebede, they remembered this first act of kindness we had offered them.

Tigist said one day:

"Do you remember a certain cold and wet night when you sent over some bread and tea to us? I was sitting on my sacks and blanket feeling sorry for myself. I had a bad toothache, I was almost due to have my baby, and I was hungrier than usual. Then Bekelu came over with this feast fit for a king, not for a beggar family. I had some belief in a God 'up there' but suddenly I sensed he had come down from heaven himself to comfort me.'"

This insignificant act of kindness started a friendship with that family that has continued. Shortly afterwards a little son was born right on the footpath, and we were asked to name him. What better name to give him than *Tarmirart*, meaning "miracle." Many times they came to our home for a meal or birthday party for the children and several times we were invited to their little plastic home for coffee or a meal. Shortly after this Tigist and Kebede came to the

Lord and tried to witness to others there on the street. Sadly Kebede died from suspected TB a few years later, possibly as a result of breathing in the fumes from the constant heavy traffic. We have remained in touch with this family and send help from time to time. In mid-2005 we received the heart-breaking news that Tigrist had also died, leaving her two teenagers as orphans.

During these years in Addis Ababa we welcomed even more family members and New Zealand friends to Ethiopia. My brother Ian, his wife Sylvia, and son Chris came for several weeks, as did Les and Joan Higham from Auckland. Both couples were interested to view the aftermath of war in Addis Ababa and then we took them on a short, guided tour to Kuriftu and Langano. Later on our oldest son Steve came with Gail his wife and three daughters, Erika (10), Megan (8), and Justine who celebrated her sixth birthday the day they arrived. They were fascinated to visit these plastic house people living on the footpath, and still remember sitting on a mattress right on the pavement while drinking Ethiopian black coffee and eating the local bread. Steve enjoyed showing his daughters the old haunts of his childhood such as Bingham Academy. (See their coloured photo.)

143 International Evangelical Church

Joe Harding, one of our close missionary colleagues, wrote the following report:

SIM missionaries have always had a burden to reach out to the internationals living in Ethiopia. They come from over a hundred countries of the world, serving as UN and embassy diplomats, business leaders, government officials and heads of non-government organisations (NGOs). In the early 1950s SIM established the Gospel Chapel as a place of worship in a rented facility in the heart of the commercial centre of Addis Ababa - the Piazza. In 1958 the chapel moved to the SIM headquarters, and services were held there until 1994.

In fact during the time of the Marxist revolution the SIM chapel played a crucial role in ministering to many expatriates and Ethiopian believers, as it was one of the few churches which the communists did not close down. Several ambassadors and other dignitaries attended the church. There were two packed morning services and one in the afternoon, with more than twelve hundred people in attendance. Finding a seat was nigh impossible at the first service unless one arrived thirty minutes early.

In 1978 the SIM chapel was officially renamed the International Evangelical Church (IEC), to be seen more favourably by the Marxist government. Bark Fahnestock, an SIM missionary and gifted preacher, was appointed pastor.

Since the chapel was crammed to bursting and the SIM facilities had no room to expand, the IEC began discussions with the leaders of the Evangelical

Theological College (ETC) to see if they could find a way forward. It was decided to draw up plans for a joint church and educational complex.

In early 1991 Joe Harding, the IEC/ETC project director, Pastor Bark Fahnestock, and elders Malcolm McGregor, Girma Demissie and Jim Goering, approached the Marxist government with a request for land. Astonishingly, the Marxist foreign minister and mayor of Addis Ababa favourably considered this request. Then, in the midst of the long bureaucratic process of obtaining the land and building permits, the Marxist regime fell.

With the change in government it was thought our hopes of getting the land might fail, but to our surprise and joy the new government granted our requests. So it was that on 22 November 1992 the IEC/ETC held a dedication service at which many expressed their gratitude to God for this miracle. The new property consisted of six acres (2.4 hectares) of prime real estate in the centre of Addis Ababa. And this for a church and college complex!

Architectural plans for the IEC/ETC were drafted by Malcolm McGregor and the newly formed company of Abba Architects. All these young Ethiopian architects had been helped spiritually through the IEC discipleship ministry.

Through sacrificial giving the IEC membership raised more than $US300,000 for the building project. At that stage Joe Harding and Girma Demissie were commissioned by the IEC to go to Europe and the USA to meet with potential donors, with the prayerful aim of raising an additional 1.2 million dollars. As churches and SIM supporters heard of the great vision of the IEC/ETC, God touched their hearts and they gave generously. God honoured the prayers of faith, and provided all the funds needed through his Church around the world.

Building materials were still in short supply in Ethiopia. Bruce Bond suggested the IEC elders inspect the new KHC church building at Kuriftu to see if that type of laminated beam construction interested them. They were duly impressed and awarded the contract to McIntosh Timber Laminates Ltd. of New Zealand. All the necessary building materials were later packed in twelve shipping containers.

Because of the intricacy of the building, experienced craftsmen from overseas were needed to give oversight. Wick Jackson, assisted by Mike Ring, Andrew Brown and Frank Carter all responded. They supervised the Ethiopian builders and trained many others in various skills to accomplish the huge task. This complex is now one of Addis Ababa's finest and most beautiful landmarks. The inclusion of Ethiopian architectural themes, especially that of the cross, the unique stonework and indigenous marble, all contribute to making it an outstanding attraction.

The grand dedication of the IEC/ETC took place on 4 March 1995. Thousands attended, with leaders from almost every denomination in Ethiopia, to celebrate the opening. A senior government official said at the time:

"This land was once an eroded landfill, but now it has been reclaimed for a beautiful church and college. May it be a place where hurting, poor and disenfranchised people can now be redeemed, and great leaders produced to build a strong Ethiopia."

The closing prayer was offered by Jim Goering of the World Bank. He prayed that the IEC and ETC would be "a light on a hill."

The IEC is continuing to impact thousands, and the ETC is training a host of leaders for the fast growing church in Ethiopia.

The building of the IEC/ETC complex in Addis Ababa 1995

144 A Bombshell

Just as my time as acting director was nearing completion, I received a bombshell. Dr Hay phoned.

"Bruce you'd better be sitting down when I tell you this news," he said. "The nominee you forwarded to me for the position of incoming director for SIM Ethiopia has not been accepted by the International Council of SIM."

I was shocked. All the members of the SIM Ethiopia council had prayerfully considered this matter and were sure we had suggested the right person. We had no other suggestions.

Dr Hay then said Gordon Stanley, one of SIM's deputy General Directors, would come over to Ethiopia to help us find a solution to our problem.

Norene and I were much concerned about some serious family needs at home and had promised to fill this acting position for a two-year period only. We felt the time had definitely come for us to return to New Zealand. So it was bitterly disappointing for us to be asked to allow my name to go forward for a further two-year term. Norene, especially, found this decision heart-rending. One of our dear missionary colleagues wrote the following to us:

"…We want to affirm you both in the Lord. We admire your dedication to Christ. You have our highest respect, especially during these last few days as you have sought the Lord regarding your future. We have agonised with you in this tough decision that has demanded devotion to your family as well as a continued dedication to service for the Lord and the church here in Ethiopia." Letters like that made it all worthwhile. Norene wrote to the family:

"…It is not that I don't love it out here, but we don't want you, our family, to feel neglected or even bitter that we always put the work first, before you, in your time of need."

At that time she wrote the following poem:

Discouraged
Lord, I can share this agony of soul
with so few others. Only you can understand
the crushing around my heart, the confusion of mind
which has overtaken me. Lord, let me hear you say,
"Lift up your eyes unto the hills,
from whence comes your help.
Your help comes from the Lord,
who made heaven and earth."
Over past years I have proved your grace sufficient
for many tragic times. Yet right now I cannot see
even the faintest light at the end of the tunnel.
It's like there's a fog before my eyes.
Lord, you must be there amidst the mist and cloud.
Please assure me you have not deserted me.
Now I hear you say, "A miracle is not a miracle
If you can see what I will do,
Neither is faith called faith, unless you cling to only me."
Lord, help me to hang in there in these dark days
and be like a willow strengthened by the winds of adversity
that now buffet my soul.
"Lift up your eyes to the hills, O my soul."

Gordon Stanley was understanding of our dilemma and suggested we go home for three months compassionate leave with travel expenses paid. How grateful we were for that offer! While in New Zealand we received the following fax message from Dr Hay:

"I am delighted to report to you that 100 percent of your peers have affirmed my nomination of you as Ethiopian Director. Congratulations! This unanimous vote confirms to all of us that this is the will of God. It also gives you a solid mandate in your position."

We felt humbled to receive such confirmation from the mission family, but were realistic. We and they were aware I had only a two-year term to serve before retirement.

The verse which spoke to us during these days was 2 Chronicles 15:7 – *Be strong and do not give up, for your work will be rewarded.*

145 Lake Langano (1964 -1975)

Langano for us is synonymous with holidays. For many years as a family we spent happy days on the shores of the lake, fishing, hiking, swimming and tramping. When we first started camping at Langano there were no roads or even tracks to the water's edge, but it wasn't hard to drive from the main road through the acacia trees down to the lake's edge, where we would pitch our tents.

But let us go right back to 1969, to the beginning of the SIM outreach there.

Albert Brant, one of our pioneer missionaries in Southern Ethiopia, had suggested to the SIM Council that we urgently search for a suitable site at Langano which could be used for a future camping ministry. So in May 1969 Bruce Hall, Herb Ediger and I had set off to find that site. Albert had brought to Ethiopia a twelve-foot aluminium dinghy to reach the island tribes on Lake Margureta. This we used to thoroughly explore all possible sites.

An area of tropical forest close to the beach, on the eastern shore, seemed to us to have great possibilities for a camping ministry. On enquiring we discovered that the absentee land owner, Ato Tadela Desta, was a friend of the mission and just might be willing to lease a small area to SIM.

Feeling satisfied the Lord had guided us, we set out in the dinghy for what we thought was a leisurely return trip across the lake to where our car was parked. But half way across, our fifteen horsepower motor spluttered to a stop and we discovered the water pump had given up. A good pair of oars enabled us to start rowing, but to our dismay we noticed a fierce storm brewing over the Arsi highlands. In a few minutes the violent wind reached us, and all we could do was keep our boat facing the storm and ask God for his protection. Our craft was blown across the lake and landed miles from our car.

Anyway, after protracted formalities with the landowner and government,

Norm and Betty Harrison, SIM missionaries from Canada, finally moved to the new site in October 1971. There was literally nothing there – no roads, no buildings, no water, no toilets and no vehicle for hauling material. For the first seven weeks they lived in a borrowed Volkswagen camper, while Norm organised the removal of enough bush for their first building. (Their two children, Cathy and Jeff, were in Bingham Academy, the SIM boarding school.)

They did, however, have a plentiful supply of pumice sand, and a fellow SIM missionary, Gordon Creighton from the nearby leprosarium, would often haul in building materials for them with his tractor and trailer. Because of this ready supply of sand, Norm set about making his own cement blocks – three hundred per day. In the meantime Betty was busy operating a bush clinic from a 12 foot by 12 foot tent.

After a brief furlough they returned in May 1974 with enough funds to buy a vehicle and to start some of the buildings. Betty was able to move into a new clinic, and the first ever youth camp was held with forty-nine young people from Shashamane. Norman wrote:

"During the afternoons at the camp the swimming and beach activities were a new experience for most of them. Betty and I had to run to keep up with them. They were happy days."

The Harrisons not only built the physical plant at Langano, including the various conference buildings and a new clinic, but with the help of some national believers, established a small Arsi church. Everything was going well, despite the fact that the Marxist revolution was progressing in most parts of the country.

In 1975, however, the government closed classes for senior high school and university students, and ordered the students into the countryside to teach the peasants the principles of Marxism.

Dark clouds were ahead for the Harrison family.

In December 1975 twelve of these students, sent by the government, arrived at Langano to start their indoctrination programme. Despite the fact that the Harrisons showed friendliness to these young people and invited them in for meals, one of them suddenly became mentally disturbed and tried to shoot Norm and Betty, who both fled out their back door to the shelter of the dense bush. They ran for three long hours to elude their would-be assassin. Poor Betty lost her shoes and even her water bottle early on in the flight. Finally they were able to find a suitable river crossing and sheltered in the hut of one of their Arsi friends. (Most of the people were friendly now because of all the medical help they had received.) Betty stayed there while Norm carefully made his way back to camp with a group of men.

Meanwhile the young man in question had managed to jumpstart the Harrisons' vehicle and had driven the fifteen kilometres to the main road, where the police seized and arrested him. Later on he was taken to Addis and admitted to a psychiatric hospital.

Shortly after that, in January, Betty became seriously ill and Norm was advised to drive her to the Soddu mission hospital. This took seven long hours, and because of her weak condition she became progressively worse, finally lapsing into a coma. The doctor warned:

"Norm, I don't think Betty will 'make it' until morning," he said.

Norm and the two children went through deep waters during the following days. But God gradually strengthened Betty and after a month she was well enough to fly home to Canada.

Sadly the Harrisons were not able to return to Ethiopia, but Dr Nathan and Doris Barlow were appointed to take their place and continued this strategic medical ministry.

146 Later Visit To Langano

During our '76–'77 stint my brother and sister-in-law, Grahame and Nola, came to Ethiopia to visit us and the Langano conference centre was on our itinerary. We had no problems reaching the SIM compound, even although crossing the nearby log bridge was scary. Nathan and Doris welcomed us warmly, and took delight in showing our visitors around the compound.

Before long, however, we were surrounded by a group of angry men. They demanded to know why we had come and why we hadn't waited for them to arrive and search our luggage before moving anything into the building. Of course we pleaded ignorance, but their presence and attitude was threatening. Finally they agreed to allow us to spend one night in the conference building.

Assuming our exit from the compound might be more of a problem than our entry, we decided on an early start the following morning. Perhaps our vigilante might not even be around, we theorised. Our worst fears were realised when we peeped out the door to find our vehicle surrounded by armed guards. What could we do? We all prayed together before taking out the suitcases one at a time.

Several threatening and abusive men met me.

"You must all be CIA spies," they accused, although it was doubtful any of them knew what that meant. "Open your suitcases!"

Somewhat sheepishly they began to pull out the contents. Although embarrassed by some of the ladies' garments on top, they still pulled everything out and then clumsily tried to repack them. I asked them rather aggressively:

"What have you found that is illegal for foreigners to possess?"

No answer.

The same routine followed with the next suitcases.

They had seen enough and I was told to pack the car. Norene and the visitors climbed in and amidst threats of what they would do next time, we proceeded across the dilapidated bridge and over to the western side of the lake. Our concern now was for Nathan and Doris Barlow who were virtually being held hostage.

Our suspicions were correct. Only a few months after our visit, the Kebele leaders demanded Nathan and Doris hand over all the clinic equipment, medication, the furniture from the conference centre and many of their personal belongings. Only then were they free to leave.

The compound was eventually taken over by the Ethiopian air force as an R&R centre for their officers. Having replaced all the stolen and looted equipment, they even erected a bailey bridge to replace the rotting structure across the stream.

Remarkably, for the next twelve years the facilities were used but not seriously abused. Near the end of the revolution, the air force packed up their equipment and left, even taking their bailey bridge with them!

147 Another Chance

Ten years later two Arsi farmers, Ato Hiripo Dubai and Ato Bedado Dedo made an appointment to see me in my office. I had never met them and wondered why they had come. Getting quickly to the point they said:

"We are from Langano and have been sent as the representatives of the local district. The elders have met and asked us to urge you as a mission to come back to Langano. Our women are suffering terribly in childbirth, many people are dying of malaria, and our children have nowhere to go to school."

I reminded them of the way the Harrisons and Barlows had been treated and how all the equipment had been looted and destroyed. They were quick to admit they had been led astray by the propaganda of the Marxist government and had suffered ever since SIM's departure in 1977..

"However," they said, "at the time when the Marxist government was finally overthrown on 28 May 1991, law and order completely broke down in the countryside. We heard that gangs were heading over to the SIM compound, and so we burned the old wooden bridge, hindering the looters from crossing the river. Then we took turns to guard the compound. Ever since we have protected the property with our own guards."

We ourselves had seen the utter destruction caused by these gangs of thugs on the far side of the lake. They had entered all the hotels and motels and stolen all the furniture, windows and window frames and even the doors and door frames. They had even begun to strip corrugated iron off the roofs.

Their story seemed almost too good to be true. In my mind I thought, God has obviously been weaving events together to make all this possible. This could mean we are being offered a further opportunity to work in the district.

I recognised that these people were ultimately seeking their own material benefits, but their confidence in us was remarkable. I reminded them that being Christians we would be teaching Christian principles. They said:

"We are happy for our children to be taught. They can make their own decision as to which religion they follow."

To me it was unbelievable. Here were two Muslim leaders sitting in my office, begging us as missionaries to return to their district. And this after a break of more than fourteen years! I assured the men I would talk with my colleagues and if they agreed we would come and visit them in Langano as soon as possible.

A few days later Norene and I made a memorable trip to Langano in order to give a first-hand report to our SIM Council members. The road was bad but the welcome remarkable. We had sent word that we were coming, and both men and women waited for us on the side of the stream, greeting us as though we were their long-lost parents.

Reaching the remains of the burnt-out bridge, we wondered how we would ford the river. No problem. We were led to where the stream emptied itself into the lake. A shallow delta had been formed at the mouth. How grateful we were the stream was not in flood!

Accompanied by a great number of local people we marched up to the old SIM compound, wondering what we would find inside. The grass had all been neatly cut with hand-sickles and the buildings seemed no worse for wear from the outside. A coat of paint would be the answer for all the communist slogans adorning the walls.

But the conference hall was empty. All movable furniture had gone and the kitchen had been left bare. Although there was a huge fireplace, one group had decided it was culturally more fitting to light a fire in the middle of the concrete floor where everyone could sit around and warm themselves. But what about the smoke? One look at the rafters told the story. Mosquito screens had long gone, and bats had taken up residence in the bedrooms, leaving their droppings inches thick. The whole building, in fact, smelt like a filthy toilet. But with some good shovels, brooms, disinfectant, paint and lots of elbow grease, the buildings could be repaired.

Beaming with pride, the guards showed us around the buildings they had so carefully guarded since the air force personnel had left.

The SIM council agreed this project had unique possibilities and should become a joint KHC / SIM project. This meant that in the future, if SIM were forced to leave the country, the national church would own the complex and carry on the ministry.

Later an important meeting was convened onsite at Langano, with representatives from the air force, the national church, SIM and hundreds of local people. What a sight, to see the Arsi men marching in with their two-meter spears! All parties signed a lengthy document giving KHC / SIM the land on which to build a clinic, school and conference centre. Following this significant ceremony a lavish feast, prepared by the Arsi women, was enjoyed by all. Also witnessing the ceremony were dozens of black and white colobus monkeys, who seemed to be watching with interest and excitement.

The area of land given for this project was about forty hectares or one hundred acres. It stretched from the eastern shore of Langano where the thorn trees grew, to where giant ficus trees thrived. These trees were home to colobus and vervet monkeys, and often a great troop of anubis baboons could be seen harvesting the ripe figs. Several families of bush pigs thrived on the property, together with various antelope. As far as birds were concerned, Langano was an ornithologist's paradise.

148 The Buheitel Story

Once our agreement was signed by all parties, it was important to find personnel who could head up the project. In 1993 a German couple, Hermann and Andrea Buheitel with their three young daughters, were appointed. Hermann went down on his own in February, and his family followed in the September. First Hermann faced the challenge of building some type of bridge to cross the boundary stream. Gaining permission to cut down enough hardwood trees, hauling them to the site and making a strong bridge was a huge accomplishment. Erecting a boundary fence through parts of the dense forest was also a major task, as was the re-roofing of several buildings where the corrugated iron had started to rust. Different people came to help for brief periods, and Andrea hospitably cared for all of them.

The Buheitels had been at Langano for almost a year when Andrea became ill. She told me on one of my visits that she was pregnant with their fourth child and had not been feeling well. Because of this they had recently made a trip to the Yirgalem Norwegian Hospital, further south, for a check-up. She did not improve, and on 4 February Hermann notified SIM via the two-way radio that they would need to travel to Addis Ababa (a three to four hour trip) for urgent medical attention.

On that day Norene and I had been invited to speak at the Arsi conference at Shashamane, about an hour further south of Langano. On our journey we met up with Hermann, Andrea and their daughters. How shocked we were to see how seriously ill Andrea appeared to be. We urged them to hurry on to Addis.

The next day, just as I was about to speak at the conference, a messenger came to tell me I must make an urgent call to Addis Ababa. What devastating news! Andrea had died that morning.

We assured Hermann we would return immediately. Excusing ourselves from the conference, we made the four-hour return journey to Addis. We found the family completely distraught, of course, and spent hours together as we made arrangements for the funeral, which involved notifying loved ones in Germany and trying to organise a burial plot in Addis Ababa.

After the burial service the relatives returned to Germany and it was agreed that a memorial service would be held at Langano, where the Arsi people could pay their respects and condolences to Hermann. In Ethiopia a *likso* (three-day period of mourning) is always held. Word quickly spread that this was to be held at Langano, and hundreds of men and women gathered to meet with Hermann. What a tribute to the Buheital family, as we realised hundreds of lives had been touched during their short period of service at Langano. Loud wailing greeted us as we drove onto the compound. Hermann was presented with a purple cape, indicating he was considered a mighty warrior. The men all contributed to buying an ox which was often slaughtered on such occasions. Most of the meat was eaten raw by the mourners.

As Hermann stood up to thank the large assembly of people for their sympathy and gifts of food, a hush fell over the crowd.

"Your respect and love shown to me and my girls is greatly appreciated," he said. "I want to tell you that I know for sure my dear wife, Andrea, is in heaven with Jesus her Saviour."

He went on to explain the simple gospel message of how Jesus, God's Son, had become our sin bearer and had promised us a home in heaven. No doubt this was the most poignant moment in the history of SIM's ministry at Langano. The people had seen this young family share their lives and message with them. Now, within a few short months, the mother had died.

Hermann felt the need to have a few weeks in Addis Ababa. but then insisted on returning to Langano to continue his ministry. Sister Lydia, a German nurse, agreed to go back with Hermann to care for his girls while he sorted out what his future should be. After three months he and the girls returned to Germany although he did return later for further service.

In 1994 SIM appointed Dan and Kim Scheel to Langano, where re-opening the clinic was a top priority. The Ministry of Health gave only temporary permission, until a standard-sized clinic had been erected, equipped and staffed. Kim reopened the clinic in 1997, while Dan was working on the huge task of building the new complex. Nancy Redman, a career SIM nurse, then joined the team, along with a capable national staff. In June 2003 the Scheels recorded in their newsletter that the medical staff had vaccinated 3,700 children against measles in one week, as well as dealing with a malaria epidemic and treating up to a hundred regular patients per day. What a heavy load our nurses and staff had to carry.

Meanwhile an agreement has been signed with the government to run a new elementary school at Langano. Dan and his building team have now completed this new complex. The school officially opened in October 2003 for the commencement of the Ethiopian year. The number of students fluctuates somewhat, because of the semi-nomadic habits of the Arsi people, but about three hundred students are being taught by four teachers, and two evangelists teach the Bible lessons.

In September 2004 Kim and Dan Scheel wrote in their news update:

"The five churches here in the Langano area got together for a baptism of the newest converts. More than seventy people were baptised last weekend. God is at work building his church here at Langano, and it's wonderful to have milestones, like a baptism, to mark the church's growth."

149 Lost In The Mud

Norene's story:

"You might as well be looking for a needle in a haystack, Norene."

So said one of my fellow missionaries.

We had arrived back for our eighth stint of missionary work and I was at the customs shed to clear our unaccompanied baggage. I was being led over an uneven cobbled pathway to find our boxes for inspection, and before I knew it, I was flat on my face. My weak ankle had done it again. Somehow I picked myself up and hobbled along on the arm of a customs official. Once back at the mission compound I soaked my ankle and bound it up well.

That afternoon, as Bruce was leaving for a weekend conference, I suddenly let out a cry of anguish.

"My diamond, oh, my precious diamond! It's gone!" I had been so concerned about my throbbing and swollen ankle that I hadn't even noticed my badly damaged engagement ring.

The scene of the morning's fall came back to me and I thought of all the muddy crevices between the cobbled stones. What's more, there had been a tropical downpour that afternoon.

I phoned a missionary friend, asking if she could take me back to the scene the following morning... just in case.

With crutches in hand I must have looked a sight, scratching around in the rocky ground. We both used a small hand broom to carefully brush the surface, and then resorted to little garden trowels to dig slightly deeper. It was then that Mike passed by and uttered his not-so-encouraging remark about the "needle in the haystack."

The crowd laughed and almost sneered when I told them I was asking God to help me find my diamond. At one stage I had shown them another stone about the same size.

"He must be some god if he finds that!" remarked a Muslim man.

After several hours we had to give up the search, but as I left I said to the bystanders, "If anyone finds the diamond, I'll give a reward of 100 birr (about $NZ25)."

During my lonely and depressing afternoon I listened to cassettes to lift my spirit. Of course I prayed too. One message on the tape brought tears to my eyes and even new hope that God might answer my prayer. It went like this:

When God comes to gather his jewels,
All his treasures of diamonds and gold,
I'll meet him up there in heaven so fair
When God comes and gathers his jewels.

Early the following morning there was a knock at our door. There stood an excited young Ethiopian man.

"A friend of mine has found your diamond!" he blurted out. He wants you to meet him at the customs shed at nine this morning."

With no husband at home, I had to ask a missionary doctor to accompany me. On our arrival at the sheds an older man came to the car window.

"I have your diamond, Ma'am, but first we have to talk. You are a *ferangie* (white person). I'm a poor family man. I want you to agree to educate all my five children before I return the diamond."

My heart sank. What an impossible demand! In his hand was a rather grubby ball of tissue. Could I even be sure my precious stone was inside it? It was tantalisingly close. After a little deliberation and a hasty prayer, I replied:

"I have offered 100 birr. Take the money or the diamond. You have the choice."

The seconds seemed like hours as he thought about this proposition.

Finally he answered, "I'll take the 100 birr."

That night Norene penned these words...

Some are like my lost diamond, I fear
In a much more serious plight,
Pressed down on all sides by worldly care,
Unable to reflect God's light.

Diamonds are meant to glitter and shine,
They reflect all the rays of the sun.
How sad if they're left in the dirt and the grime,
Joy and pleasure they give to noone.

"I seek you and never give up" says the Lord.
"When I find you I'll cleanse you anew,
As you pray and read from my precious Word,
I'll reflect my glory in you."

Postscript: Amazingly, Dr Ian Hay, our then General Director, in Charlotte, USA, was awakened from sleep that morning, being constrained to pray for us both. He even sent a fax asking if something was wrong. This turned out to be the time the diamond was found.

150 Ethiopia Stretches Out Her Hands To God

We will never forget 3 October 1993. Neither will 55,000 other people.

Just imagine how you would feel, having lived through seventeen years of a repressive communist regime, when almost all evangelical churches had been closed and the buildings either destroyed or used for other purposes, when believers were either imprisoned or killed – to experience the restoration of freedom! Was it any wonder that Christians in the capital, Addis Ababa, wanted to celebrate with a day of thanksgiving and praise?

It was two and a half years after the Marxist regime had been overthrown, that this great event was organised for Sunday 3 October. The largest venue in the city, the soccer stadium, was hired.

Nothing like this had been held before, and nobody knew how many would attend. But a choir of 1500 from all the evangelical churches in Addis Ababa had been trained, and 2,000 ushers were given the task of crowd control. Many of the believers arrived at six-thirty in the morning to procure a good seat.

Norene and I had been given a reserved seat and wondered what we would find on arrival at 8:30am. The place was jammed full already. Every one of the 45,000 seats was occupied and a vast crowd of 10,000 was standing in the middle of the playing field. It was a beautiful clear morning, being the end of the rainy season, but about mid-day the clouds gathered and down came the rain. We expected to see a rush for the exits, but not a soul moved. Instead, thousands of brightly coloured umbrellas popped open on the playing field, as everyone sheltered as best they could while revelling in the celebration.

Several church leaders took part in praying or giving praise. The first one gave praise to God for the overthrow of communism, the second for peace from war and bloodshed, and the third for freedom to worship. The choir led the crowds in enthusiastic singing, interspersed with the women ululating (a high pitched trill) to express their joy, while the men broke out with clapping. The noise was deafening.

What moved us most, however, was when one of the church leaders quoted from Psalm 68:31 – *Ethiopia shall stretch out her hands unto God in adoration.*

He asked those who loved God to respond by doing likewise. Everybody in that vast crowd lifted their hands in gratitude and praise to God.

They were acknowledging the miracles God had performed for them during those years of repression and suffering, and thousands openly wept. We were all deeply moved as we remembered how the Marxist regime had done everything possible to erase religious belief from the country. Yet the opposite had happened. From a fairly small number of evangelical believers in Addis Ababa prior to the Marxist regime from 1974, on this day in 1993 there were now many thousands of new believers with their arms outstretched.

Perhaps you will now understand why those of us privileged to attend that service will never forget it.

In fact ten years later, while attending a local soccer match in New Zealand where my grandson, Jordan, was playing, I spoke to the coach of the Ethiopian team, all of whom had come with their parents as refugees to New Zealand. He told me he was one of the vast crowd who had participated in that unforgettable service in 1993.

151 Lost On The Kitchen Table

We were concerned we had not heard for a day and a half from Jerry and Maija, working at Maaki, one of our more remote mission stations. Each morning and evening we had a radio link with all the missionaries living out of the capital, Addis Ababa. On the second day we decided if there was no response that morning, we would make an emergency trip by helicopter.

To our relief, Maija answered our call on Sunday morning. But her message was not good.

"Jerry has developed acute abdominal pain," she said. "He's not well enough to be driven out and needs urgent medical help."

Being a missionary nurse and being well experienced in diagnosing various problems, Maija continued:

"I believe he has acute appendicitis and needs immediate surgery."

Our medical staff in Addis carefully questioned Maija and reached the same conclusion.

Despite the unsettled conditions in Ethiopia at that time, a new organisation for Ethiopia, Helimission, had just managed to re-establish itself in the country. We were thrilled because our team of missionaries could now reach areas which were virtually inaccessible before. To add to this our own niece and her husband, Kaylene and Dean Yeoman, SIM New Zealand missionaries, were seconded to Helimission and appointed to direct their work in Ethiopia. The four Yeoman children, Dan, Rachel, Joshua and Sarah, were a delight to have in Ethiopia and we spent as much time together as our busy schedules permitted. Joshua and I were special mates.

The only way of reaching Maaki in an emergency was via a helicopter. Hence a quick Sunday morning call to Dean:

"Hi, Dean, it's Bruce here. We have an emergency. One of our missionaries down at Maaki needs immediate surgery. Do you think there's any possibility of flying a medical team down there this morning?"

"Sure, I think we could make it," said Dean. "We have a 'copter we could get ready in a couple of hours to fly your team down."

Preparing the helicopter and flight planning was only part of the job. Most of the time required was to obtain the necessary flight permit from the Security Service and the Relief and Rehabilitation Commission (RRC) under whom they operated.

"Thank you, Lord," I whispered. I knew if it were not for the help of Helimission that morning, we would have been in serious trouble.

Our Australian surgeon, longterm SIMer Barry Hicks, was always ready for a challenge, and together with Barb. Hartwig, our SIM medical supervisor, gathered together all the equipment they thought might be necessary. Then they set off on a two-hour flight to the sick man's bed.

Maaki was a remote area in southern Ethiopia, where SIM had established a clinic and agricultural ministry amongst the Mursi people. They were nomadic pastoralists who needed help with their animals and medical needs.

A Mursi woman wearing the traditional lip-plate

They were one hundred percent illiterate and the government had not established a presence among them because they lived in such a remote area. The men were usually stark naked and the women well known for the lip plates they wore. These Mursis were feared by the surrounding tribes because of their aggressiveness. They would go out and raid the neighbouring tribes, slaughtering the men and plundering cattle and women. On these raiding sorties the men travelled lightly. They would carry only a rifle, a small blanket to wrap around themselves at night, and a small wooden stool which could be used either to sit on or as a pillow.

It was among this war-like tribe that Jerry and Maija had chosen to live. Of course their language was strange and communication difficult, but gradually the Carlsons were being accepted. Jerry was continually introducing new varieties of fruit and vegetables into the area, while Maija held a daily clinic to care for their medical needs.

Now back to the medical emergency.

The medical team quickly examined Jerry and concurred with Maija's diagnosis. The kitchen table was moved to the window for maximum light, and a thin mattress was stretched out for the patient to lie on. The team paused to ask God to give them wisdom and skill to operate successfully. When Jerry heard he was to have an epidural he said, "I'm glad you brought our mail down with you. Now I have something to read during the surgery."

Everybody had their job to do. Even Dean, the helicopter pilot, held a flashlight to aid the surgeon. Surgery was successfully completed in an hour, and Jerry was carefully carried back to his bed. Everyone in the team was conscious of God's enabling through the whole procedure.

After a late lunch, the team left for their return trip to Addis Ababa. A few days later Maija sent the following message:

"Jerry still holding together. Thanks again for making the house call."

Jonathan Geddes of Australia was later appointed as a veterinary surgeon, and Barb his wife as an agriculturist. Cliff and Lynell Thomas of New Zealand also worked there until ill health brought them home.

152 Rebuilding Amharic Bible Schools

During the communist regime all sixteen Bible schools in Wollaita, in the southwest of Ethiopia, had been destroyed, as had many Bible schools in other areas.

As we discussed this need, we agreed with the KHC church leadership that we would put all our efforts and resources into an ambitious joint programme of building sixteen individual Bible schools in the Wollaita area over the next eighteen months. Sixteen more Bible schools were built later in other KHC areas. Each school offered training for students from forty-four individual churches. Many people were involved in this huge programme, but special thanks must be given to Dr Carlyle Dewey, our project manager, and Les Williams from SIM USA who helped us raise most of the necessary funds for this project.

We drew up a simple building plan. Each Bible school had two classrooms, with a storeroom and teacher's room in between. Each room had space for thirteen double desks, making it possible for a total of fifty-two students to be taught at one time in each school. This, multiplied by sixteen, gives an idea of the potential number of students who could be taught in these schools.

This was a joint project with the churches. As a mission we agreed to supply the roofing iron, nails, doors, windows, paint, blackboards and desks. All of these items were not available in Ethiopia at that time and needed to be imported from South Korea. The final cost was $US260,000, with the money coming mainly from Germany and North America. The churches in turn provided all the labour and the material for the walls, and sand, stone and cement for the floors. Many of the churches involved in this project opted to build the walls of their schools with cement blocks, but this was easier said than done since blocks were simply not available.

About that time, out of retirement came Hans and Brigitte Hagen, our German friends. Hans was able to teach the believers how to make their own blocks with home-made moulds, and to end up with walls plumb. The results were dramatic, and great was the rejoicing with the completion of each of the sixteen Bible schools in Wollaita.

153 The Cadre's Left Hand

It was after the KHC's annual church meetings, held in Soddu, Wollaitta, in September 1994, that Paul Balisky, the theological director, and I attended the dedication service of one of these new Bible school buildings at Sore, Wollaita. Some of the KHC executive and the local church leadership participated in the event.

As the dedication service was concluding, in walked a grey-bearded gentleman of beautiful countenance, Ato Fancho. With tears streaming down his face, he recounted for us the background to this historic moment.

"As a young man, even before the Italians invaded our country in 1935, I became a follower of Jesus Christ," he said. "After the Italians had gone, I gave some of my precious farm land to the local believers so they could build a small grass-roofed church. Many local people became Christians and we worshipped God with great joy. But it was a great disaster when the Marxist officials came to tell us we were not permitted to worship any longer in our church and that they needed our building for teaching their anti-God philosophy. Compulsory indoctrination classes were held each week and those who failed to attend were either fined or imprisoned. At these classes we were told that money previously given to the church would now be required as a tax to help with the re-education expenses. We were told to raise our left hand and chant, 'Ethiopia First! May the feudalists be wiped out!' Those of us who refused were beaten, imprisoned or fined."

Ato Fancho telling his story

He went on to say, "I was sad that God's house was desecrated, and although we were forbidden to worship together any more, many of us prayed in the safety of our own homes. I chose a 'sacred spot' in my corn field where I worshipped God each day.

"One Saturday, after our indoctrination classes and the collection of our 'tax' money, the two teachers (cadres) left, carrying our money into the local market where they bought and drank freely of the local brew. On the way home one of the men was so drunk that he lost his way and slept under a tree. Next morning, when his friends set out to find him, only his left hand, which he had raised to curse God, could be found. The hyenas had feasted on him during the night, but had not touched that cursed left hand. The other official experienced a mysterious illness which caused his body to swell up, and after much pain and suffering he too died. A great fear of God fell on all the people.

"After that frightening experience the communist officials refused to collect any more church money. Some years later, as tensions eased, the believers decided to collect money to buy enough corrugated iron to re-roof their building. The grass thatch needed renewing but was vulnerable to sabotage, hence the change to corrugated iron. The believers were warned that if they put a new roof on the building the government authorities would probably take it again for their own use, but they replied, 'The last time the government took our building away, two men died. They won't dare touch our building again!'"

The tears of the old man, Ato Fancho, were those of joy. God had answered his prayers, and those of many others, in that not only had freedom of religion been restored to his village, but also a new Bible school building had been erected on his previous property to train church leadership for the next generation.

154 English Theological Training

"Dynamic and effective leadership is the key to growth in any organisation," said Tom Eagstrom in his book, *The Making of a Christian Leader*.

The president of KHC, Ato Demise Madey, came to me in 1990.

"I am grateful to God," he said, "that he has kept some of our Bible Schools functioning during the revolution. However, there is still an urgent need to upgrade the KHC Bible school facilities."

I heartily agreed with Ato Demise that SIM needed a greater emphasis on theological training. The rebuilding of the thirty-two Amharic Bible schools was an important step, but at the same time SIM needed to develop a vigorous Bible teaching programme in English.

Before the revolution, only one English diploma course had been established at Dilla (Kale Heywet Ministry Training.)

But in 1984 SIM had helped the International Evangelical Church (IEC) to begin a diploma programme in Addis Ababa, known as the IEC evening classes. SIM assisted by providing instructors and classroom space at their headquarters. In 1992 the school changed its name to the Evangelical Theological College (ETC) and was accepted for accreditation with the Accrediting Council for Theological Education in Africa (ACTEA).

In 1994 Dr Paul and Lila Balisky moved to Addis Ababa, where Paul continued as SIM's theological director. Things began to happen. In 1995 the degree-granting Evangelical Theological College was relocated, together with the IEC, to a spacious new facility two kilometres south of SIM headquarters. The college owned by KHC was interdenominational, and jointly sponsored by SIM International, Kale Heywet Church and the International Evangelical Church. Today, in 2004, there are a total of 320 students enrolled and a total of 407 graduates from the three programmes presently offered: Bachelor of Theology, Assoc. Bachelor of Theology, and Diploma of Theology.

Besides the Dilla English diploma programme, KHC opened two more similar diploma colleges at Hosanna and Soddu.

155 Jonathan and David

We read in 1 Samuel 18:1 that "Jonathan became one in spirit with David and he loved him as himself." Little did I know in December 1954, when

I first met Mulatu Baffa, that fifty years later we would look back and realise God had indeed blessed us with a David and Jonathan relationship.

At the beginning of our friendship I had been his teacher, helping him prepare for an overseas scholarship, whereas he was my language tutor. Shortly after that, Norene became Alemai's "mid-wife." (See page 69)

After we had both retired and he was visiting some of his family in the USA, he wrote, "I am sorry to tell you that on 29 January 2004 I suffered a major heart attack and was taken by ambulance to the hospital."

Just ten days later, while painting our daughter's home in Auckland, I also suffered a heart attack and had been taken by ambulance to hospital. Mulu's comments were:

"It seems as though our journey towards our final destination, our eternal home, gets rougher and more painful, but with Paul we can say 'My grace is sufficient for you, for my power is made perfect in weakness.' 2 Cor 12:9."

What a privilege is ours, to think we are both children of the heavenly King and will spend eternity together. We have spent many happy times together throughout our working lives in Ethiopia, sometimes driving along rough bush tracks, sometimes flying in small aircraft to projects in remote places, and sometimes trudging through virgin forest, being awed by God's breathtaking creation.

Dr Mulu and his wife Alemai: 2003

We have spoken at church conferences together and we have visited community development projects together. We have visited Mulu's parents in a remote area and been graciously welcomed with a "fatted calf" and a bed for the night. We have welcomed Mulu to New Zealand and introduced him to family and friends. We have been in some dangerous gun battles together and experienced God's intervention and protection. We have admired Mulu's and Alemai's family of seven children, all now following the Lord.

It was in 1976 and 1977, during the Red Terror when Ethiopia was in great turmoil, that we shared so much of our lives together. Mulu at that time was the director of community development for all the Ethiopian KHC churches. Norene and I were seconded from SIM to work with the national church and were answerable to Dr Mulu. Together we initiated some projects in various parts of the country and today one can see the effects of some of those projects in the wider community.

In 1988 the Marxist government asked the church to be involved in caring for some of the war orphans, and so under the leadership of Dr Mulu (the KHC general secretary) the Kuriftu children's project was initiated. Norene and I were then seconded to establish the centre. So our close liaison continued, and we enjoyed frequent visits from Mulu and his wife, Alemai.

During one of their visits we experienced a particularly violent storm, with strong winds and torrential rain. Our home, which consisted of two twenty-foot containers side by side, with a six-metre gap between them to serve as our dining and entertainment area, was no match for the severe storm. We did have a tin roof over this area, but everything got soaked and even our refrigerator blew over with a strong gust. Alemai told us with tears in her eyes that she was touched by our willingness to live under such trying conditions, when she lived in a warm, waterproof house herself. Immediately the storm was over she went to the nearest village and bought us a little brazier and a sack of charcoal to keep us warm during those stormy nights of the rainy season.

After retirement from SIM and Ethiopia in 1994 we had three calls back to Ethiopia, but finally in 2003 we were invited to attend the 75th anniversary of the Kale Hiwot Church.

When our friends Mulu and Alemai heard of our coming they begged us to arrive early so we could spend time together at SIM's conference centre, the Kuriftu children's centre, and finally in their own home in Addis Ababa.

At that time I was far from well, and it seemed we all had the premonition that this would be our last visit together. A few short weeks after that reunion both Mulu and I experienced those severe heart attacks.

The biblical Jonathan and David became one in spirit. And we did too.

156 A "Macedonian Call"

During our last year in the directorship of SIM Ethiopia we received a delegation of Korean visitors from the Myung Sung Presbyterian Church. These men had heard of the outstanding growth of the national church in Ethiopia and had come to visit SIM and the KHC to see for themselves what marvellous things God was doing.

After returning home they sent a pressing invitation to me as director to bring to Korea a small delegation of missionaries and national church leaders.

So the morning of Sunday 27 March 1994, it was awesome to be led into this vast Korean auditorium in which every seat was occupied. Where would we sit?

Not a problem. The ushers had already worked this out. We were led to the front of the church where special seats had been reserved for the visitors. But this was no ordinary church service. In fact it was the early morning prayer meeting. We were told this was the second such prayer meeting of the morning, for the first one had started at 5am. We had to pinch ourselves to believe this was really happening – thousands and thousands of Christians rising so early to pray! The pastor gave a message, followed by the kind of prayer in which everyone prays out loud at once. At the appropriate time the organist started playing, and immediately there was silence. We were told these early morning prayer meetings took place every day of the week.

Where else would this take place, other than in the city of Seoul? No wonder fifty percent of the population are estimated to be evangelical Christians.

The Korean church was like a sleeping giant, just becoming aware of its responsibilities for the Great Commission, to share the gospel with those of other nations who had not yet heard.

We learn from Acts 16:9 that the apostle Paul had a vision in the night. He saw a man from Macedonia pleading with him, saying, "Come over to Macedonia and help us."

Our party consisted of Dr Mulatu Baffa, general secretary of KHC; Ato Worabo, KHC Board member; Ato Tilahune Haile; Bill Harding, SIM church growth co-ordinator; and Norene and myself. This megachurch had a membership of twenty-five thousand.

After our early morning prayer meeting we were ushered into another area of the church complex, where a sumptuous breakfast had been prepared for us. I'm sure the cooks had the idea we were all starved in Ethiopia, for our meals were more than abundant.

Sunday worship services started in earnest at 7am and continued through the morning, in order to allow everybody the opportunity to attend one service. The main auditorium seated only 3,000 people, but there were various overflow buildings where thousands of others could share via a remote TV linkup. Just imagine the parking nightmare, with hundreds of vehicles leaving after one service and hundreds more arriving for the next. Parking wardens were everywhere, organising the traffic. The driver left only when the car in front of him moved off.

I was privileged to be asked to speak at the evening service, and brought a challenge about the opportunity of taking the gospel to all the world. Again the auditorium was packed, and when I moved up to the pulpit to speak I was amazed to see two TV monitors, one on either side of the pulpit, giving me a distant but perfect view of the crowds in the two overflow rooms. Ear phones were attached to each seat for translation or amplification.

157 The DMZ

After such an encouraging day on Sunday, our Korean hosts made arrangements to take our party for a visit to the De-Militarised Zone. By minibus we were driven north until we reached a unique spot. None of us was aware that the South Korean government had built a memorial monument to remember the sacrifice of more than a hundred Ethiopian soldiers who had died fighting alongside the South Korean army in the early 1950s. As we stepped out of our vehicle in front of this monument, a lone bugler sounded the Last Post. As the last notes faded away a South Korean soldier appeared, carrying a huge wreath of flowers which our Ethiopian men placed on the war memorial.

After our coffee break we continued travelling north until we were met by an army escort vehicle. With siren sounding and red light flashing, we were escorted to the army base to be met by none other than the general himself. We were then led to the concrete steps of the army headquarters, where a group photograph was taken. I was amazed at the detailed preparation which had been made for that visit. As the general led us to the steps, we discovered our names written in chalk, indicating where we should stand. Because I was considered the leader of that delegation, I was placed next to the general, then the general's second in command next to him, and so on. They certainly had done their homework.

The general excused himself, but said he would be honoured if we would eat with him in the officers' dining room for the mid-day meal. In the meantime we were given a tour of the base. To our surprise the DMZ does not consist of a high, electrified barbed-wire fence, or an edifice similar to the old Berlin Wall, but in fact is quite a wide stretch of no-man's land which is carefully guarded twenty-four hours a day.

After our tour we were taken to the dining hall to share in one of the most luxurious meals we have ever enjoyed. Again our placement at the table had been carefully thought out, with our hosts sitting opposite us in order of rank. Our table utensils were gold and the food was a typical Korean meal. The general told me it was a great privilege for him to meet missionaries who had served in Ethiopia for so long. He said that he too was a Christian. I took the opportunity to ask him when and how he had become one, and he told me his amazing story.

"Periodically," he began, "the North Koreans tunnel under this strip of land called the DMZ and seek to infiltrate South Korea with their spies. One day our sensitive listening devices picked up the sound of tunnelling deep under the surface. Hardly even hoping for success, we drilled down looking for their tunnel. Miraculously, at one kilometre we drilled right through the middle of the North Korean tunnel. This was like finding a needle in a haystack and I knew it must truly be a miracle from God.

"After that I was determined to find out more about this miracle-working God. Once I had leave I went back to Seoul and sought out a pastor who showed me how I could have a personal relationship with Jesus Christ."

The following day we had various meetings with the church officials, encouraging them to become involved in sharing the Good News with those from other countries who had not yet heard. Today there are large numbers of Korean missionaries serving in many countries of the world including Ethiopia.

158 Time To Leave

From SIM *Contact* magazine, November 1994, by Kay Bascom:

"Sadness and nostalgia are inevitable accompaniments of the official retirement day (November 14) of Bruce and Norene Bond. Having served as director of the SIM work in Ethiopia from May 1991 to November 1994, Bruce Bond's leadership has been greatly appreciated, as has been his wife's supportive role. Theirs has been a long and fruitful service. It started in Ethiopia in 1954 and although it has been occasionally conducted from the New Zealand base, their mission career has spanned all of four decades. The Bonds are leaving behind the fruit of spiritual seeds scattered over Ethiopia, as well as Shashamane potatoes, Chencha fruit, Bishoftu beauty and Kuriftu products initiated by the 'man who talks to trees'..... Thanks be to God, and our thanks to you, Bruce and Norene. We pray God will richly bless this next New Zealand and family chapter of your lives."

The mission family were invited to a "top secret Bond bye-bye event" on Saturday November 5 from 3pm until 8pm. They were told not to breathe a word to the Bonds, with the order, "Ewe mutton tell Norene and Bruce."

A capable committee, headed up by Steve Jay, Sylvia Yandall and Jim Ardill, organised a games afternoon, a pig roast and an evening farewell programme. We were spoiled by all the attention of the (almost) full complement of SIM personnel and a great family day was enjoyed by all.

In the evening there was a large banner on the stage with the words, "Bless be the tie that Bonds" and great hilarity as Helen and Stan Tuck impersonated and roasted us as a couple. "Bald" Stan imitated me speaking at the prayer day sessions, and Helen ragged Norene to a tee with her video camera (a horizontal water pot) on prayer days and the ever present knitting needles clicking away. There were original songs and poems, and even a pig auctioning by MC Jim Ardill.

Some unusual gifts were presented, such as a huge potato as a reminder of one of the first potato crops ever introduced in the south of Ethiopia. We were both given special awards, such as the "Computer Whizkid Award" to Bruce for "stubbornness and bravery in the face of cranky hardware." Norene received the "Photographer's Award" for "the technology and the art of the video camcorder never being the same again."

The day was happy but sad as we anticipated leaving the work and the people we had come to love dearly. During our farewells in the different areas, we used the verses from Deuteronomy 2:7 and Joshua 23:14.

The Lord your God has blessed you in all the work of your hands. He has watched over your journey through this vast desert. These forty years the Lord your God has been with you, and you have not lacked anything... You know with all your heart and soul that not one of all the good promises

Our two Ethiopian 'Grandchildren' Josiah (L) and Jerusalem (R) "Julie" 2003

the Lord your God gave you has failed. Every promise has been fulfilled; not one has failed.

Before this day we had been farewelled by the Shashamane KHC in late October, and then by Kuriftu KHC a week later. On 13 November we went to Debre Zeit for our final weekend, staying with our Ethiopian "daughter" and her husband. We celebrated my 65th birthday there and I preached at the Kuriftu church that Sunday. Then on November 16 it was farewell to Ethiopia as we flew off into the sky towards Bombay.

"Another mission accomplished!" we said to each other. "Thank you, Lord!"

But it was not quite the end.

159 Lost Relationship

Following retirement we made several trips back to Ethiopia. The first was to do some research for Tear Fund New Zealand.

In a surprising turn of events one of our supporters in the south asked Norene, "If your ticket were provided, would you accompany Bruce?"

You can imagine Norene's response!

The second return trip was at the request of SIM to replace the host and hostess at the Babogaya rest and conference centre for a few months.

In the meantime we had been concerned about a situation that had developed in the Debre Zeit church with which we had worked closely from 1987 to 1991.

The church had been experiencing great blessing until a division arose over finance. Half the church wanted one thing and the other half wanted something completely different. All attempts to bring reconciliation had failed and the church was being torn in two. While back in the area we had the opportunity of ministering to these two divided groups. Unfortunately we had to hold two separate weekly Bible studies, for "never the twain would meet." We enjoyed fellowship with both groups and on our final night in Debre Zeit succeeded in organising a combined meeting. This was held in the home we previously lived in, at Kuriftu.

After fellowship over a tasty meal, I spoke from John 13:15 where Jesus said, "I have set you an example that you should do as I have done for you." And we started washing one another's feet.

Many tears were shed and forgiveness sought as the service continued, enabling us to conclude with the Lord's Supper. We were sure then that reconciliation would take place. Nevertheless, even after this step forward there remained some deep-seated problems and we all knew these could only be resolved by God's Holy Spirit continuing to work in their hearts through prayer.

A prominent believer said to us at the time:

"Satan sought to destroy the church through communism, but when that proved unsuccessful he changed his tactics to create discord and disunity between believers."

We believe this is true, for when the church is growing in leaps and bounds, Satan tries his best to destroy it.

Many people were concerned and prayed with us for unity to return. In fact it was not until a year or two later that we received a letter from one of our close Ethiopian friends. He wrote:

"I have good news for you. God has solved the problem we had here for a long time. He spoke to one of the elders, who decided to make peace with us all. After much discussion we met with the whole group. We poured out everything in our heart. It was God's time. There were tears and time to forgive each other. Thank you for your efforts and prayers to reconcile the lost relationship."

Since that time of reconciliation the Lord's power has been evident, in that many have believed and new fellowships have sprung up in several places.

160 75th Anniversary

A quite unexpected opportunity came our way in 2003. To celebrate the birth and the growth of the Kale Heywet Church (Word of Life) the executive of the KHC arranged to have a special celebration from 10 to 12 November 2003, marking their 75th anniversary. Past and present missionaries involved in working with the church were invited to attend. SIM New Zealand asked us both to attend, to represent New Zealand missionaries, past and present.

The motto for the celebration was "See I am doing a new thing. Now it springs up."

The chairman's welcoming speech is worth recording. Here are some excerpts from it:

"Dear Excellencies, Ladies and Gentlemen.

"Thank you so much for coming and joining us this morning as we start to celebrate the Diamond Jubilee of the Ethiopian Kale Heywet Church.

"The EKHC was founded by a group of a few highly-dedicated missionaries who came to Ethiopia seventy-five years back. The first group of missionaries, led by Dr Thomas Lambie, included three young men from America and one from Australia. These were Clarence Duff and Walter Ohman from the United States, and Glen Cain from Australia.

"At present the EKHC comprises 5,412 churches with 4.6 million members. The mission of the EKHC is to proclaim the good news of Jesus

Christ to the peoples of Ethiopia and beyond to the ends of the earth, so that people receive eternal life, become Christ's disciples, and are fulfilled spiritually, socially, mentally and physically to the glory of God.

"The EKHC was started in peripheral areas where there was no school, clinic or any other social services. In partnership with SIM the church had been running hundreds of primary schools, five high schools, six hospitals and sixty-three clinics before 1974 here in Ethiopia.

"The Kale Heywet Church development programme started as a national programme in 1974 during the famine in Wollo and Tigray, and the church has been able to save many hundreds of thousands of lives during the famine of 1974 and 1984.

"At present the church is providing child sponsorship to more than 10,000 children in partnership with various agencies. Two hundred Bible schools, four theological colleges, two women's skill development centres and a seminary continue to train leaders in theological studies and also to provide community training on development as well as HIV-AIDS prevention.

"We appreciate the efforts of the Ethiopian government to build peace, justice and freedom of religion. We also thank all our partners who have stood by our side both in good times and in bad. We praise the Lord for all our achievements over the last decades." (Ato Mamo Gebre/Meskel.)

Welcome Back to Norene in 2003

161 We Renew Acquaintances

For Norene and me it was a most memorable occasion to renew fellowship with hundreds of past friends and acquaintances. Although it had been ten years since our official retirement and several decades since we had seen some delegates, we were overjoyed to be remembered by so many people who knew us up to fifty years before. We must admit there were many who came up to us with the embarrassing question, "Don't you remember me? We met when you came to our area thirty-five years ago for a conference and you spoke on ..."

To be quite honest I could hardly remember going to that area, let alone what I spoke about. Ah, but these dear friends never forget! Fortunately they seemed to forget all the language faux pas we made and seemed to remember only the good things we were able to teach.

Another man said to us, "I remember one day when you were living at Shashamane. I had been a speaker at a conference. I was given food there, but they overlooked money for travel. As I was running down to the bus with a prayer in my heart but no money in my pocket, you ran out of your house and pressed ten dollars into my hand. I'll never forget that."

Of course we didn't remember that incident at all. How grateful we felt that we had listened to God's prompting that morning for this special servant of his.

Many times our eyes filled with tears as we shook the hands of some of those dear delegates whom we recognised as men who for many years had greatly suffered for their faith, being incarcerated and beaten in filthy prisons. Yet they had remained faithful and were rejoicing with us that they had been counted worthy to suffer for Christ's sake. What a privilege it was for us to even be associated with such men.

We were both interested to meet again the president of the KHC church, Dr Tesfaye Yacob.

"I must be the only one here today," Norene told him, "who can say I held you in my arms when you were a two-day-old infant."

Tesfaye's father was an evangelist at the Shashamane leprosarium in our early days and we visited the home when Tesfaye was born. His father, an old man now, was also at the meetings and his first question was, "How is your firstborn, Istepharnos (Stephen)?"

Heaven will be like this as we meet around God's throne.

At one of the celebration dinners, Norene was seated next to one of the leading lights in the women's ministry of the Kale Heywet Church. She said to this lady, "I don't think we have met, have we?"

"Oh yes we have," she replied. "As a young girl I was present at your wedding celebration at Shashamane, as I was the daughter of one of the evangelists there. I admired you so much and used to creep near your house to have a glimpse of you as you were caring for your young children."

We were privileged to have Dr John Stott as the main speaker. His messages on the church from the book of Acts were masterful, as one would expect. The points of his first message will remain with us for a long time:

(a) A living church is a learning church.
(b) A living church is a caring church
(c) A living church is a worshipping church
(d) A living church is an evangelising church.

He also presented a powerful message on the "Strategy of Satan" and how the church must be aware of all his strategies and tactics which don't seem to change over the years. His first three points were:

(a) Physical persecution
(b) Moral compromise
(c) Social distraction.

He warned us to be aware of the attacks of Satan first of all from without. Then, if he is not successful that way, he will attack our relationships within the church. How true that is!

Near the end of the celebrations Norene and I were asked to give our greetings to the thousand or so delegates. With joy we were able to say to them, "You know, we are really Ethiopians even although our skin is white. We were married in Ethiopia, our children were born in Ethiopia, and the best years of our working lives were spent in Ethiopia. Now we have a life full of wonderful memories and 'tomorrow' we will spend eternity with you in our heavenly home."

The text we left with them was 1 Thessalonians 2:19 – *For what is our hope, our joy, or the crown in which we will glory in the presence of our Lord Jesus when he comes? Is it not* **you**? *Indeed* **you** *are our glory and joy.*

With eyes brimming with tears, we left the podium to a tremendous ovation. It was as though the people were saying to us, "Thank you for coming and sharing your lives with ours. Because you and others like you came here, we will share eternity together."

When Spider Webs Unite, They Can Tie up a Lion.

---

[1] To read of how God undertook during those turbulent days, read *Living With The Red Terror* and *Count It All Joy* by John Cumbers, and *Hidden Triumph In Ethiopia* by Kay Bascom.